Sir Gawain and
the Classical Tradition

Sir Gawain and the Classical Tradition

Essays on the Ancient Antecedents

Edited by E. L. RISDEN

McFarland & Company, Inc., Publishers
Jefferson, North Carolina, and London

LIBRARY OF CONGRESS CATALOGUING-IN-PUBLICATION DATA

Sir Gawain and the classical tradition : essays on the ancient
antecedents / edited by E. L. Risden.
    p.   cm.
Includes bibliographical references and index.

ISBN 978-0-7864-2073-5
softcover

1. Gawain and the Grene Knight.   2. Gawain (Legendary character)—Romances—
History and criticism.   3. Classicism—England—History—To 1500.   4. Arthurian
romances—History and criticism.   5. Romances, English—History and criticism.
6. English poetry—Classical influences.   7. Knights and knighthood in literature.
8. Mythology, Classical, in literature.   I. Risden, Edward L., 1957–
PR2065.G31S567 2006
821'.1—dc22   2005012768

British Library cataloguing data are available

©2006 E. L. Risden. All rights reserved

*No part of this book may be reproduced or transmitted in any form
or by any means, electronic or mechanical, including photocopying
or recording, or by any information storage and retrieval system,
without permission in writing from the publisher.*

Cover art: Knights in combat, 1500 (Pictures Now)

McFarland & Company, Inc., Publishers
   Box 611, Jefferson, North Carolina 28640
     www.mcfarlandpub.com

Contents

Preface 1
Introduction (Stefan Thomas Hall) 3

Geoffrey of Monmouth and the *Gawain* Poet: Remembering Troy
 (William F. Hodapp) 17
The Treason of Aeneas and the Mythographers of Vergil:
 The Classical Tradition in *Sir Gawain and the Green Knight*
 (Russell Rutter) 30
Mortal Hopes: The Trojan Framework of *Sir Gawain and the
 Green Knight* in a Doctrinal Context (Randi Eldevik) 49
Ritual Sacrifice and the Pre-Christian Subtext of Gawain's
 Green Girdle (Peter H. Goodrich) 65
Treasonous Founders and Pious Seducers: Aeneas, Gawain, and
 Aporetic Romance (Nicholas Haydock) 82
The "Tresounous Tulk" in *Sir Gawain and the Green Knight*
 (E. L. Risden) 112
The Fierce Achilles in Chaucer, Gower, and the *Gawain* Poet
 (Rosanne Gasse) 121
Classical Analogues—Eastern and Western—of *Sir Gawain*
 (Zacharias P. Thundy) 135
Sir Gawain and the Green Knight: Classical Magic and Its Function
 in Medieval Romance (Mickey Sweeney) 182

About the Contributors 211
Index 213

Preface

This project began several years ago as a dinner conversation at a convention of the Midwest Modern Language Association in St. Louis. We moved quickly from "Just who is that tulk in line three of *Sir Gawain and the Green Knight?*" to "Why does the poem begin and end with substantial allusions to Troy?" to "What did the poet know about the classical world and how heavily did he rely on it thematically?" More than a pleasant aperitif, the discussion continued loosely but periodically for some time until we decided to try to organize a session or two at subsequent conferences to generate papers exploring our questions. We began in a session with the same title as this volume held at the joint meeting of the Medieval Association of the Midwest and the Committee for the Advancement of Early Studies at Ball State University in 1999, and we continued with a followup at the 2002 MAM conference at St. Norbert College. Papers from those sessions seeded this volume. It aims, through a collection of essays by diverse interested scholars, to address one of the puzzling and fascinating questions of the great medieval poem: what classical antecedents affected or directed the poem, not only in its opening and closing allusions, but in its themes, concerns, and composition? Editor and contributors sought to explore that problem each according to our own lights and by different methods, but particularly with the hope that we might add small increments to the rich critical heritage of the poem in such a way that students and scholars may benefit from our work. Professor Hall's introduction provides an expansive background for our efforts, and each subsequent essay explores some detail of the classical influence—*classical* construed in fairly broad terms, so that we might move in realms from the Greek and Roman to the Arabic, Christian, and Celtic, contemporaries of the Roman world. Often scholars have omitted such considerations as Professor Thundy's study of Arabic influences or Professor Eldevik's on pre–Christian influences, not out of disrespect, but because we lack the knowledge necessary to reach and plumb those sources. We see these chapters as *essays* in the old sense of *attempts*, efforts to grapple with the issues and stimulate conversation and research. We have aimed not at an exhaustive analysis of the poem, but illuminating one of its many enticing mysteries through careful scholarship and creative thinking.

To attempt a general review of the scholarship on *Sir Gawain and the Green Knight* would daunt the hardiest of scholars, so I have left the act of scholarly backgrounding to the authors in their individual chapters. While each essay ties the poem in some way to the classical world, each also aims in some way to contribute to a satisfying reading of the poem. Often the essays will treat the same allusion or metaphor or even the same lines in quite different ways: we see that fact as a strength, as evidence of creative collaboration rather than contradiction—few great poems bear only monolithic reading, and *Gawain* is certainly a great poem worthy of our continuing efforts. Though we may differ in our interpretations, we wish also to express our respect for the willingness to differ: from well-defended argument comes deepening appreciation if not always agreement. The pleasure of the ambiguities of the poem and of critical activity outweigh any desire for definitive conclusions, though we have tried to draw those, too, where we felt comfortable doing so. We hope through this lens to draw readers into our debates and through them back again into the most finely wrought of the medieval English romances.

An earlier version of Professor Thundy's essay appeared in *Classical and Modern Literature* 12 (1992): 169–78, as "More on Classical Influences in *SGGK*"; I wish to thank Professor Dan Hooley, editor, for permission to reprint. The other essays here appear in print for the first time.

Introduction

Stefan Thomas Hall

UNIVERSITY OF WISCONSIN–GREEN BAY

The fourteenth-century English alliterative poem *Sir Gawain and the Green Knight* has long been admired by scholars for its morally complex plot and brilliant poetics. Copied together in one manuscript (MS. Cotton Nero A.x) with three other alliterative poems, *Pearl*, *Patience*, and *Cleanness*, its survival is not just fortunate but miraculous. For Chaucer and Langland, for instance, we have a great number of manuscripts which circulated in the Middle Ages and which have survived to this day, a testament to their popularity in their own day. By comparison, the poems penned by the *Gawain* poet most likely did not enjoy the same widespread popularity in Fourteenth- and Fifteenth-Century England which those of his contemporaries so clearly did, and yet, to many, the poems of the Pearl manuscript, especially *Sir Gawain and the Green Knight* and *Pearl*, shine as crown jewels of fourteenth-century English poetry.

Scholars have for a long time labeled the flourish of English alliterative poetry in the Fourteenth Century as a "revival," and, indeed, there is little evidence that much serious alliterative poetry was being composed in English from the Twelfth through early Fourteenth Centuries. The large number of alliterative poems that we find in the manuscripts of the Fourteenth and Fifteenth centuries would suggest such a renewed interest in this "archaic" and "English" verse form. Yet why were poets of the north and west of England in the Fourteenth Century so willing to embrace the alliterative style when continental models of verse form from the Italian and French seemed adequate enough media for Chaucer and Gower (among others) for subject matter ranging from allegory to romance to fabliaux to exemplum to socio-political satire? Borrowings and verbal echoes among alliterative poets seem to indicate a kind of "school" of poets who not only understood the rules of the meter which they were composing but often shared common vocabulary words and sometimes even thematic concerns. It is safe to assume that we can dismiss the notion of an overnight relearning of alliterative verse in the Fourteenth Century by such a large number of poets. Yet the manuscript evidence for alliterative verse (apart from Layaman's verse chronicle *Brut*) before the collection of lyrics in Harley MS 2253 (copied sometime in the years 1314–49) would suggest that nobody was composing alliterative verse except for short one- or two-line snippets here and there as marginalia, etc. Among others, Elizabeth Salter, James R. Hulbert, and Angus McIntosh all have argued for a re-evaluation of the term "alliterative revival," pointing to an unbroken tradition of alliterative prose, metrically sometimes quite reminiscent of the Middle English alliterative long-line, which existed from the time of Ælfric and Wulfstan through numerous sermons and homiletic writings. This poetic tradition along with its culminating revival we may in fact call more accurately an "alliterative survival," suppressed though it may have been and influenced by continental materials as it apparently was—the Old English practice hadn't died.

Indeed, with the often archaic vocabulary of Fourteenth-Century English alliterative poetry, we often find remnants of Old English and Old Norse, which calls to mind the prestige that poets of Anglo-Saxon and Scandinavian cultures enjoyed at court. Indeed, Fourteenth-Century English alliterative poets, assuming the role of society's proverbious and wise counselors, seemingly felt the need to preach more than poets like Chaucer or Gower, and, to use Fourteenth-Century vocabulary, the title we might adopt for the alliterative poet is "soth-segger," or one who says the truth. This facet could be just one of the reasons why alliterative verse enjoyed such a renewed popularity in Fourteenth-Century England. Alliterative poets addressed important socio-political concerns such as plague and famine, over-taxation to pay for the king's wars,[1] and oppression of poor illiterate farmers and peasants.[2] We need only look to Langland's A-text of *Piers Plowman*, composed in 1369 shortly after a particularly bad harvest affected by crop disease. Relief was nowhere to be found, farmers starved, social classes remained outrageously unequal, and the young King Richard, still a boy, was the hope of the country, though later despised as an adult by many.[3] And these alliterative poets were not just grumbling in the outlying regions of the north and west: Langland, for instance, likely wrote *Piers Plowman* while living in London: "And so y leue yn London and opelond bothe" (C-text, 5.44). "Piers the Plowman" also became one of the buzzwords amongst the peasants who revolted in 1381.[4] Langland's cries for social reformstruck home with men of the lower class, both literate and illiterate, both in the capital and in the "uplands."⁵ Similarly, though the *Gawain* poet has often been exiled by critics to a baronial court in Cheshire, other scholars have argued that he too spent some time in London or abroad, possibly, like Chaucer, with the Black Prince in France.⁶ Alliterative poets, like their patrons, were part of an increasingly mobile English society full of political maneuvering and social unrest.

Political issues comingled with religious ones in the Fourteenth Century, so it is no surprise that religious matters also figure highly in the subject matter of alliterative poetry: the cardinals of Avignon and Rome electing two opposing popes, which eventually led to war; growing anti-fraternal sentiment due to abuses of power and moneygrubbing amongst the friars; growing literacy of the educated laymen; Wycliffe's call for a Bible in the English which everyone could read. Langland and the school of poets he inspired attacked all of these subjects. Truth must be sought, reform was in order, and alliterative poets took it upon themselves to show the way. Poems like *Mum and the Soth-segger* and *Pierce the Plowman's Crede* both attack friars, and while *Pierce the Plowman's Crede* is the more overtly Lollard of the two, both stress, as Langland had in *Piers Plowman*, that there was a need for people to seek out truth in both the political and religious worlds— a truth which is best found in alliterative poetry and in the devout Christian hearts of poor, pious plowmen who know the way to salvation and truth better than any friar. Perhaps the most important truth to pursue concerned salvation and how to live one's life. Like Langland and the poet of the alliterative saint's life *St. Erkenwald* (once believed to have been written by the *Pearl* poet), the poet of *Sir Gawain and the Green Knight* and *Pearl* tackled these topics. By God's grace, or *cortesye*, as she calls it, the Pearl maiden, though she died before she was barely old enough to say her Paternoster, becomes a queen in heaven, and grace and courtesy figure highly in the thematic fabric of *Sir Gawain and the Green Knight* as well.

In their search for truth, alliterative poets often became extreme perfectionists. Langland's *Piers Plowman*, a work in constant revision, clearly reveals this, as do the *Gawain* poet's obsession with details, multiple significations, symmetry, and the mathematically precise structure of his poems.⁷ Alliterative poetry was not limited to political and religious harangues: it embraced a wide variety of genres from the romance (*William of Palerne* or *Sir Gawain and the Green Knight* or *Rauf Coilyear* or *Golagros and Gawane*) to dream vision (*Winner and Waster, Piers Plowman, Pearl, The Parlement of Thre Ages*), from exemplum (*Cleanness, Patience, The Pistel of Susan*) to saint's life (*St. Erkenwald*). Common to all poems in the alliterative tradition was the attention to detail, sometimes digressing into catalogues, lists, processions, or extended rants.⁸ We see this, for instance, in Langland's list of folks in the prologue or the portraits of the seven deadly sins, the *Gawain* poet's encyclopedic knowledge of armor or how to properly field dress a deer, the Pearl maiden's educating/lecturing of her father, or the poet of *Cleanness* who gives his audience three lengthy Biblical paraphrases (and several interludes) to stress the importance of being pure in mind and manners. In Fourteenth-Century alliterative poetry, genre distinctions sometimes get blurred. Langland's poetry is diffcult to pin down: he employs the dream vision (sometimes even a dream within a dream), medieval sermon and commentary, and a variety of topological, typological, anagogical and allegorical interpretational levels. And while *Sir Gawain and the Green Knight* has been labeled a romance, it is not a typical romance in many ways, which is perhaps one of its many appeals.[9]

The genre of many alliterative poems could be summed up as "sothsaying," to use the alliterative poets' own vocabulary. These poets were not country bumpkins, and they were not merely provincials complaining at length. They were at times more "courtly" than London court poets. The *Gawain* poet, for one, clearly seems to have been well connected to a noble court, perhaps in Cheshire (where his dialect places him), or perhaps in north Stafford, where his geographical knowledge is strongest. There is only the River Dane separating the two shires, though the political allegiances of the Cheshiremen lay with Richard II, while the Earl of Stafford along with Lancaster supported Henry Bolingbroke.[10] Cheshire was caught in the middle and on the wrong side in the Battle of Shrewesbury in 1403— perhaps a quarter of a century after the poems of the *Pearl* manuscript were copied, but, nevertheless, the political alliances had been developing along similar lines for some time. The connection of *Sir Gawain and the Green Knight* with the Order of the Knights of the Garter has long intrigued scholars, sparking numerous theories about who the poet's patron might have been.[11] Maybe a Garter Knight, but which one? There were several Garter Knights to choose from who lived on either side of the River Dane. The connection to the Garter Knights fits with his Arthurian theme, at any rate, as King Edward III, the founder of the Order, seems to have fantasized that he was King Arthur reincarnated, throwing Arthurian-themed parties and establishing a "Round Table" of sorts with his Garter Knights. Which side of the River Dane our poet was from or whom he wound up serving may never be determined, but all of this clearly points to the fact that though there was a lot of real estate between London and the baronial courts in the northwest, political matters of the royal court would have still influenced the *Gawain* poet.

Alliterative poets were wise men, seeking the truth and willing to proclaim it, even if, like Langland or the *Gawain* poet, they had not quite found it in their own society and felt the need to remind their society of the values which mattered most. As Geoffrey Shepherd reminds us, the alliterative poet usually presents himself as a wise man who speaks from experience and knowledge, just as the Anglo-Saxon *scop* in *Beowulf* is one wise in the old lore and poetic vocabulary. Truth was not to be found in the new ways of the world, but in a return to and re-evaluation of old lore and the teachings of the Bible. The poet of *Winner and Waster* laments that at one time there were lords who "loued in thaire hertis / To here makers of myrthes pat matirs couthe fynde" (19–20), but apparently this is no longer the case. It is a call to alliterative poets to assume the role of the soth-sayer, the wise man tending his beehive as in *Mum and the Sothsegger*, keeping the wasters at bay. He must be the keeper and adviser of his society, reminding them of the necessity of living honestly and looking toward their reward in heaven. The *Gawain* poet, for instance, brilliantly assimilates his own society's chivalric code of honor with a heavenly code, the earthly lord's contemporary court with its knights and ladies with the Lord's heavenly court and its angels. If there is any theme running through all of the poems in the Pearl manuscript, it seems to be that bad manners—impatience, uncleanness, dishonesty, discourtesy—are bad, but bad manners toward God are worse.

Clearly, the poet of *Sir Gawain and the Green Knight* was no uneducated rustic living in the wilds of northwest England. He was a "court" poet and a thinker of great sophistication, a soth-sayer, combining English alliterative meter with romance, the matter of Britain, and a wide-ranging knowledge of Celtic lore, continental materials and Latin classics (as this volume illustrates). In what many believe is his most complex poem, our poet chose for his soth-saying a romance set in the world of King Arthur, but *Sir Gawain and the Green Knight* is a rather curious Arthurian poem. To begin with, Arthur's court is "young," and there is no real evidence of a "Round Table" in use at Camelot, though one is mentioned in a couple of spots.[12] There is no Merlin, bare mention of Lancelot, no Galahad. Arthur's court is an English/British one, as much like a Fourteenth-Century English court as it might be at any rate. Likewise, as a romance *Sir Gawain and the Green Knight* is also curious.[13] It rises above practically all other Middle English romances, with its attention to knightly values, courtesy, and even courtly love, if only in a perverted sense with Gawain as the hunted one instead of the hunter.[14] True to the romance genre, however, the poem includes magic and the supernatural, which numerous critics have explored in connection to Celtic lore of the beheading game and the Green Man.[15] So we may safely argue that the poet of *Sir Gawain and the Green Knight* clearly chose to write in his own inventive manner in a genre and about subject matter which were both popular and "courtly" in Fourteenth-Century English society.

Few scholars, however, have earnestly explored the *Gawain* poet's apparent knowledge of and use of classical materials. The *Gawain* poet begins his poem by situating his own story within the greater history not just of the Arthurian world but also of Britain itself, rehearsing what would have been common knowledge to his contemporary audience concerning Britain's founding by Aeneas's descendent Brutus. Likewise, the poet of *Winner and Waster* begins his poem with a reference to the fall of Troy:

> Sythen that Bretayne was biggede and Bruyttus it aughte
> Thurgh the takynge of Troye with tresone withinn,
> There hathe selcouthes bene sene in seere kynges tymes,
> Bot neuer so many as nowe by the nynedele [1–4].[16]

But unlike *The Destruction of Troy* or Chaucer's *Troilus*, *Sir Gawain and the Green Knight* and *Winner and Waster* only allude to the fall of Troy without making the matter of Troy the main subject of their works. So the references by these two alliterative poets have often been given little treatment by scholars. Nevertheless, the matter of Troy was widely popular in Middle English literature and linked Britain's history to the fall of Troy, but how did medieval English audiences view the fall of Troy? As a *felix casus* which led to the founding of their great nation, as a tragedy turned to triumph, as history, or as a sobering reminder that all great nations (even England perhaps) have the potential of falling? The scholars who have contributed to this collection of essays study the *Gawain* poet's knowledge and use of the classical tradition. They have not only comprehensively surveyed what previous scholars have written about *Sir Gawain and the Green Knight* and the classical tradition, but have also produced a wide range of insightful interpretations of what at first might seem to be a rather limiting topic, a fact which illustrates just how versatile and complex the poet of *Sir Gawain and the Green Knight* and his poem actually are.

William F. Hodapp's essay, "Geoffrey of Monmouth and the *Gawain* Poet: Remembering Troy," is a good starting point for a discussion of the essays in the present collection. Hodapp provides a nice, brief survey of the Latin sources which dealt with the matter of Troy which would have been available to medieval writers such as Geoffrey of Monmouth and the *Gawain* poet. Geoffrey's expansion of Nennius's ninth-century chronicle romanticized and retextualized the history of Troy and of Britain. The *Gawain* poet, Hodapp argues, engages in much the same retextualizing of the history of Britain as Geoffrey had by drawing on both the Latin chronicle tradition of Geoffrey and his predecessors Dares and Dictys and also on the poetic tradition established by Vergil and Homer before him. Hodapp sees a blurring of the distinction between medieval historian and poet, both of whom recast the past at the same time as they remember it. Texts about the matter of Troy and the matter of Britain become the accepted versions of events, but each author has his own reason for referring to and using history in the way he does. Homer's *Odyssey* is in a sense about the art of storytelling, while Vergil's *Aeneid* recasts the story once again, and so on throughout the classical period and Middle Ages. Storytellers like Odysseus, Aeneas, Geoffrey, and the *Gawain* poet are quite capable of omission, embellishment, and invention, as the various transformations of the Troy story clearly show. Hodapp sees Arthur's reinterpretation of Gawain's mark of shame as a badge of honor at the end of the poem as a kind of model for authorial re-interpretation in general, and the Gawain poet's closing reference to Troy immediately after this scene reminds his audience that the *felix casus* of Troy mirrors the *casus* (*felix* or otherwise) of Camelot and perhaps even warns his Fourteenth-Century English audience to be wary of a similar fate for their own society.

So the *Gawain* poet was clearly capable of using the historical reference to the matter of Troy and Britain in his poem in order to complement the broader historical and moral concerns he wished his audience to understand. In "The Treason of Aeneas and the Mythographers of Vergil: The Classical Tradition in *Sir Gawain and the Green Knight*," Russell Rutter looks closely at the medieval tradition of Aeneas as a traitor of Troy and as a founder of a new nation, a tradition developed largely by Dares, Dictys, and Guido, well-known authors to students of Chaucer's *Troilus*. But Aeneas was also seen by allegorizing commentators like Servius, Fulgentius, and Bernardus Silvestris as a model for mankind, a model of human development from childhood to maturity. It is in this respect, as a model of mankind, Rutter argues, that Sir Gawain resembles Aeneas. Sir Gawain's story, like Aeneas's, represents a development from childhood to maturity, with all of the errors and faults which we find in the hero of the *Aeneid*. Both men, Aeneas and Gawain, are driven by their sense of duty, but unlike Aeneas, who departs the burning Troy never to return and goes on to found a new nation, Gawain must return to where he started, Arthur's young court, New Troy as it were, fully aware of his fault and the "slipperiness of earthly things."

The seriousness amidst all of the laughter and games in the poem is also detected by Randi Eldevik. In "Mortal Hopes: The Trojan Framework of *Sir Gawain and the Green Knight* in a Doctrinal Context," she argues that Gawain is not the typical romance hero who is rewarded for his accomplishments at the end of his quest. His failure is what the poet wishes us to see, and his prominent self-reproachment and sense of guilt serve as clues to what is important to the author and the lesson he is trying to impart. But do Arthur and the rest of his court apart from Gawain get it? Arthur's young court is meant to learn a lesson, as is the *Gawain* poet's own audience, and it is the references to the fall of Troy which begin and end the poem to which Eldevik believes attention must be paid in order to determine what that lesson is. Eldevik sees these as "dark" references, hinting not so much at a *felix casus*, such as the fall of Troy, which enabled the great nations of Rome and Britain to be founded by Aeneas and Brutus, nor some sort of *felix culpa*, like Adam's eating of the apple which eventually led to Christ's redeeming mankind, but to the sad and serious reality that nations do fall and men do sin. The opening lines of *Winner and Waster*, cited above, also refer to the fall of Troy and the founding of Britain by Brutus in a rather apocalyptic tone. Eldevik draws an insightful parallel between Gawain and Boethius as well, two men doomed to death, but while Boethius has the logic of philosophy and the certain knowledge of God's order and mankind's free will as consolation, what does Gawain have? He trusts in the magic of the girdle instead of the eternal rewards of heaven. Could we read *Sir Gawain and the Green Knight* as a *contemptus mundi* piece, the moral of which Arthur and his young court do not understand?

The next essay in this collection (as does the last) reexamines the supernatural and magic in *Sir Gawain and the Green Knight* in light of classical sources. In "Ritual Sacrifice and the Pre-Christian Subtext of Gawain's Green Girdle," Peter H. Goodrich approaches the poem in the light of the portrait of pre–Christian Celtic/Germanic cultures which classical Latin authors such as Strabo, Tacitus, Caesar and Dio Cassius painted, a somewhat dark and barbaric portrait of pagan cultures like the early Britons who practiced ritual human sacrifices. Archaeology backs up this view, and Goodrich draws our attention to the Lindow Man found in a peat bog near Manchester who seems to have been ritually sacrificed or executed. The Celtic elements in the poem have long interested scholars, but Goodrich goes a step further and detects a pagan "subtext" in *Sir Gawain and the Green Knight*, a sort of cultural memory of ritual human sacrifice which, though blurred by the passage of time, and though purposefully suppressed by the demands of Christian religion, seems nevertheless to have lingered in the *Gawain* poet's own northwestern English culture. Britain, our poet tells us in lines 23–24, is famous for the number of ferlies, or marvels, which have happened there:

> Mo ferlyes on þis folde han fallen here oft
> Þen in any oþer þat I wot, syn þat ilk tyme.[17]

The poet's allusions to the Celtic/Germanic past, Goodrich argues, serve to create tension between Christian and pagan paradigms and present to his audience a portrait of Britain's past which is inclusive of magical, pagan elements.

Part of the success of *Sir Gawain and the Green Knight* as a poem, as the essays in this volume demonstrate, lies in its inherent suggestiveness of the poet's intellect and learning. Nicholas Haydock's "Treasonous Founders and Pious Seducers: Aeneas, Gawain, and Aporetic Romance," for instance, further investigates the *Gawain* poet's indebtedness to Vergil's *Aeneid*. Haydock argues that the attempts by students of the poem to pin down direct verbal borrowings from classical authors like Vergil have tended to be relatively unsuccessful because scholars have not fully explored the *Gawain* poet's figural imitations of Vergil. The *Gawain* poet, he argues, has thoroughly internalized the influence from Vergil. Haydock provides figural readings of the Green Knight's holly branch, Gawain's shield, the magic girdle, and the hunt scenes juxtaposed with the bedroom scenes in fitt 3, all of which the *Gawain* poet seems to have modeled after material from Vergil but translated into his own fourteenth-century, Christian, English, court culture. The poet tells us in stanza 1 that in the history of Britain there have been "boþe blysse and blunder" (18), and Gawain's accomplishments, according to Haydock, are aporetic: Gawain's achievements are symbolic of both bliss and blunder, like the *felix casus* of Troy and like Aeneas's defeat and triumph, his treason of one and establishment of another nation.

E. L. Risden's "The 'Tresounous Tulk' in *Sir Gawain and the Green Knight*" offers another classical model which the *Gawain* poet may have had in mind for his hero, that of Odysseus. Like the other contributors to this collection of essays, Risden sees the references to Troy at the beginning and end of *Sir Gawain and the Green Knight* not just as isolated allusions in the frame of the poem but as a "guiding metaphor for the whole poem." Who is the traitor, the "tresounous tulk" mentioned in line 3? The usual interpretation is Aeneas, the ancestor of Brutus and Arthur and the kings of Britain and England, but other famous traitors (or tricksters perhaps) who took part in the Trojan War included Antenor (as he is portrayed in Chaucer's *Troilus*) and Odysseus, famous for his "tricherie" in bringing Troy to its end. And while there are some discernible parallels between Aeneas and Gawain, as Rutter points out, Risden finds as many convincing parallels between Odysseus and Gawain, both of whom in their circular journeys pursue the ultimate goal of returning home alive, enduring the temptations and tribulations, gaining experience, and developing as characters. Although the *Gawain* poet would not have known Homer directly from the Greek, there were numerous Latin materials which dealt with Odysseus as a traitor, and the essays by both Risden and Thundy make it pretty clear that the *Gawain* poet was familiar with this great hero of the Greeks. The last two lines of *Sir Gawain and the Green Knight*, along with the references to Troy and the parallels between Gawain and Odysseus, Risden suggests, are the poet's way of reminding his audience that though all earthly cities fall, we must look to the New Jerusalem for stability.

Rosanne Gasse's "The Fierce Achilles in Chaucer, Gower, and the *Gawain* Poet" answers Haydock's call for a more figural reading of the poem and situates the *Gawain* poet's knowledge and use of classical materials within a broader fourteenth-century English cultural awareness of the matter of Troy alongside authors such as Chaucer and Gower who dealt directly with Trojan materials. She focuses her attention not on Aeneas or Odysseus as a heroic model for Sir Gawain but on the complex figure of Achilles, whom Chaucer mentions twice in the *Troilus* as the fierce slayer of both Hector and his brother Troilus and whom Gower mentions some ten times in his *Confessio Amantis*. In Gower's story of "Achilles and Deidamia," Achilles shows both his feminine and his fierce manly sides, and Gasse sees a figural typecasting of the masculine and the feminine aspects of Sir Gawain, hunted by Lady Bertilak who herself is both fierce and feminine. Gawain is ultimately more closely parallel to Aeneas, to whom, as we know, Achilles was an archenemy and a major cause of the downfall of Troy. According to Gasse, the *Gawain* poet, like Chaucer and Gower, was thoroughly capable of this kind of figural use of types, employing the Achilles-type with all of his facets.

The *Gawain* poet's figural uses of classical sources are explored even further by Zacharias P. Thundy in "Classical Analogues—Eastern and Western—of *Sir Gawain*." Apart from the poet's knowledge of Celtic lore, which other critics have been alert to point out, Thundy sees clear indications that the *Gawain* poet knew Vergil and Ovid and knew about Homer, especially in his creation of the Green Knight, who resembles Charon the ferryman. Gawain's scar from the Green Knight's axe blow, furthermore, resembles Odysseus's scar, and the green girdle resembles the veil of Ino which Odysseus uses as a belt in Book 5 of *The Odyssey* to avoid drowning. Like Haydock and Rutter, Thundy provides a nice survey of the Troy materials which the *Gawain* poet may have known, yet Thundy sees other possible materials the *Gawain* poet may have known and used in Arabic sources such as the *1001 Nights*. This should come as no surprise since Chaucer was apparently also familiar with the *1001 Nights*, as the tales of his Squire and Merchant make clear. Gawain, like Odysseus, Aeneas, and Shaharazad, is a masterful talker and uses his verbal prowess to escape certain death, and all of these stories to some degree are about the art of storytelling. Thundy also sees parallels between the Green Knight and al-Khadir, the green man from Persian lore, and Thundy suggests that the *Gawain* poet's mathematical structure of 101 stanzas, year-and-a-day quest, and obsession with the mathematics of the pentangle may have been influenced by his knowledge of Arabic materials.

While scholars such Goodrich see the magical elements in *Sir Gawain and the Green Knight* as a reflection of the poet's knowledge or use of British cultural lore, Mickey Sweeney's "*Sir Gawain and the Green Knight*: Classical Magic and Its Function in Medieval Romance" makes a strong argument for situating the poet's attitude toward magic, both spiritual and secular, in the Classical tradition. The medieval Christian church branded some magic as evil or pagan, and yet at the same time the church insisted upon the miracles of its saints and the healing powers of its relics. Sweeney traces this ambivalent attitude toward magic to the classical world and writers such as Apuleius, Ovid, Tacitus, even Jerome and Pliny the Elder, all of whom were widely read and revered in the Middle Ages. From ancient times human beings have believed in magic, and it is with magic that human beings attempt to exert control over their world, assert their free will, and come to grips with the gods whom they also believe have some control over their universe. The *Gawain* poet, Sweeney argues, uses magic in his romance in order to explore Sir Gawain's faith in and relationship with God, to explore Gawain's assertion of free will, and to explore what power Gawain, St. Mary, and Morgan le Fay actually exert in the world of the poem.

As this introduction has shown, the essays in this volume address not just those classical materials and traditions the Gawain poet likely knew but also how he used them in the creation of *Sir Gawain and the Green Knight*. The hero Sir Gawain emerges as an Aeneas or Odysseus figure (Rutter and Haydock, Risden and Thundy), perhaps even as an Achilles (Gasse), while the matter of Troy flows seamlessly into the matter of Britain (Hodapp, Sweeney, and Eldevik). Yet the *Gawain* poet's knowledge of and use of classical materials is not restricted to simple translation or allusion; instead, he employs "figural echoes" of classical materials (Haydock), cultural memories and traditions of Britain's past (Goodrich), and romantic retextualizations of Trojan and British materials (Hodapp), all of which were within his and his audience's "medieval horizon" (Gasse). This collection of essays should inspire an appreciation of the poet's soth-saying and sophisticated poetic knack for bringing together not only the traditions of his native England but also its British past and his nation's epic origins after the fall of Troy. Without a doubt, this collection of essays will inspire future scholars to continue to explore in even greater detail the beautiful complexities of *Sir Gawain and the Green Knight* and to explore the possibility of his use of the classical tradition in its companion poems, *Pearl, Patience,* and *Cleanness.*

Notes

1. See *Winner and Waster* (edited in Turville-Petre), which complains of Edward III's over-taxing and spending on his French campaign.
2. See the *Song of the Husbandman* in the Harley MS 2253 (edited under the title "The Evils of Taxation" in Turville-Petre) in which the speaker complains he has had to pay his taxes twice because the beadles keep coming round with documents—which he presumably cannot read—saying he has not paid up.
3. See *Richard the Redeless*, edited by Barr, in which the poet complains about Richard not listening to good advice—especially the advice an alliterative poet might give him—and then proceeds to tell him how best to rule the kingdom.
4. See John Ball's letters edited in Dean.
5. See Middleton.
6. Most recently suggested by Revard.
7. See Thundy's essay in this collection.
8. See Shepherd.
9. See the essays by Hodapp and Eldevik in this collection.
10. See McKisack, esp. 491–96.
11. For a recent investigation of the connection between the *Gawain* poet and the Garter Knights, see Carruthers.
12. Remember the seating arrangement at the Camelot Christmas feast with Arthur at the high table.
13. See Eldevik's article in this collection.
14. See the essays by Hodapp and Gasse in this collection.
15. But see the essays by Thundy, Goodrich and Sweeney in this collection, which explore this topic in light of the *Gawain* poet's knowledge of classical sources.
16. Cited from Turville-Petre's edition.
17. The opening lines of *Winner and Waster* (cited above) reflect a similar but more apocalyptic view of the marvels which have occurred and, according to that poet, are increasingly occurring during his own lifetime in Britain

Works Cited

Barr, Helen, ed. *The Piers Plowman Tradition.* London: Everyman, 1993.
Carruthers, Leo. "The Duke of Clarence and the Earls of March: Garter Knights and *Sir Gawain and the Green Knight.*" *Medium Ævum* 70 (2001): 66–79.
Dean, James M. *Medieval Political Writings.* Kalamazoo, MI: Medieval Institute, 1996.
Hulbert, James R. "A Hypothesis Concerning the Alliterative Revival." *Modern Philology* 28 (1930–31): 405–22.
Langland, William. *Piers Plowman: An Edition of the C-Text.* Ed. Derek Pearsall. Berkeley: U of California P, 1978.
McIntosh, Angus. "Early English Alliterative Verse." *Middle English Alliterative Poetry and Its Literary Background.* Ed. David Lawton. Cambridge: Brewer, 1982. 20–33.
McKisack, May. *The Fourteenth Century: 1307–99.* Oxford: Oxford UP, 1959.
Middleton, Anne. "The Audience and Public of *Piers Plowman.*" *Middle English Allitera-*

tive Poetry and Its Literary Background. Ed. David Lawton. Cambridge: Brewer, 1982. 103–23.

Revard, Carter. "Was the Pearl Poet in Aquitaine with Chaucer?" Paper read 23 February 2002 at the 26th Annual Conference of the Medieval Association of Mid-America in Manhattan, KS.

Salter, Elizabeth. "The Alliterative Revival I." *Modern Philology* 64 (1966–67): 146–50.

———. "The Alliterative Revival II." *Modern Philology* 64 (1966–67): 233–37.

Shepherd, Geoffrey. "The Nature of Alliterative Poetry in Late Medieval England." *Proceedings of the British Academy* 56 (1970): 57–76.

Sir Gawain and the Green Knight. Eds. J. R. R. Tolkien and E. V. Gordon. 2nd ed. rev. Norman Davis. Oxford: Clarendon, 1967.

Turville-Petre, Thorlac, ed. *Alliterative Poetry of the Later Middle Ages: An Anthology*. Washington, D.C.: Catholic U of America P, 1989.

Geoffrey of Monmouth and the *Gawain* Poet: Remembering Troy

William F. Hodapp

COLLEGE OF ST. SCHOLASTICA

> Si þen þe sege and þe assaut watz sesed at Troye,
> Þe borȝ brittened and brent to brondez and askez,
> Þe tulk þat þe trammes of tresoun þer wroȝt
> Watz tried for his tricherie, þe trewest on erthe.[1]

So opens the late-fourteenth-century poem *Sir Gawain and the Green Knight*. Written in a northwest Midlands dialect of Middle English and surviving in a unique manuscript copy that includes three other narratives, arguably by the same poet (MS. Cotton Nero A.x, Art. 3), *Sir Gawain and the Green Knight* consists of 2,530 lines, most of which alliterate. The poet organized the poem into 101 stanzas of varying length, the longest of which is 38 lines, and punctuated each stanza with a bob and wheel (i.e., a two-syllable line, the bob, followed by four rhyming lines, the wheel).

Most scholars and critics consider this poem the best Middle English romance; some might even name it the best medieval romance in any vernacular. However, many of the poem's strengths—its interlaced plot, its tight focus on the main action, its exploration of the hero's psyche, its delight in concise descriptive detail—mark *Sir Gawain and the Green Knight* as atypical of the genre: ironically, it is not necessarily a representative example of medieval romance. Still, these strengths continue to draw readers to the poem: readers who delight in the poet's ability to tell a story and are intrigued by the poem's many interpretive possibilities. *Sir Gawain and the Green Knight* clearly fits Umberto Eco's notion of an "open text," one that invites and supports various readings and interpretations.[2]

For all the poem's freshness and delightful artistry, scholars and critics also have long recognized that the poet drew on rich traditions for many of the poem's elements. Indeed, one particularly intriguing area of work for scholars has been the poem's relationship to other texts: namely, the poet's presumed sources on the one hand and the poem's analogues to various narrative and descriptive details on the other, what we might now call the poem's "intertexts." Elisabeth Brewer, for instance, building on years of investigative work by numerous scholars, published in 1973 an anthology of English and French sources and analogues to the poem. Now in its second edition (1992), Brewer's anthology continues to be useful to scholars and readers interested in comparative analyses of various elements and conventions in the poem, including the beheading game, the arming of the warrior scenes, and the temptation theme, among others.[3] In addition to the kinds of texts Brewer anthologizes, other works similarly serve as intertexts to the poem. The Latin chronicle tradition, for example, and subsequent literary works based on it, also provide context for understanding aspects of the poem, particularly the references to Troy. In this chapter, I shall explore the intertextual relationship between the Latin chronicle tradition, in particular Geoffrey of Monmouth's *Historia regum Britanniae*, and *Sir Gawain and the Green Knight*. I wish to suggest in each case that the authors remember the Trojan story in an effort to articulate their own understanding of the past and the lessons to be drawn from it.

From the time of Homer until well into the modern period of Western culture, the story of Troy exercised a powerful influence on the imaginations of numerous authors and their audiences, and there seems to be at least a kernel of historical veracity to the tale. Modern scholars and archeologists generally agree that the city Frank Calvert and Heinrich Schliemann identified in the nineteenth century as Troy was sacked after a siege sometime between 1250 and 1240 B.C.E.[4] Presumably, this sacking or one like it provided the basic impetus for the story, which apparently most classical Greeks considered as history, not legend or myth.[5] Written down around the eighth century B.C.E., the Homeric corpus, representing a much larger though no longer extant body of epic literature, provides insights into the story of Troy as a literary subject; in a sense, we might even say that the ancient traditional poetry which Homer's *Iliad* and *Odyssey* represent created the story of Troy, thereby textualizing an event in an effort to remember and understand it, as well as to entertain.[6] As with all narrative, historical or otherwise, telling the Trojan story allowed the Greeks, in a sense, to revisit Troy and the Trojan War via the texts attributed to

Homer and others. For instance, in *The Odyssey* we hear of the final battle for Troy from three different pro-Greek perspectives: first, Menelaos recounts to Helen and Telemachos his experience inside the wooden horse and gently chides Helen for nearly betraying the Greeks (4.271–89); second, in an ancient literary scene somewhat analogous to modern war films, Demodokos the blind poet sings of the Trojan Horse at the Phaiakian court, causing Odysseus to weep (8.499–520); and finally, Odysseus himself recounts the story when telling the Phaiakians of his experiences in the land of the dead (11.523–37). Within the dramatic context of the poem, these three storytellers recall Troy for their audiences and, by telling their stories, revisit the scene of destruction, if only through the images and details they express in words.

In the Latin Middle Ages, the Homeric corpus was known only by reputation. Though Dante, for instance, places Homer as "poeta sovrano" among the virtuous non-Christians in the first circle of hell, he never read the Greek poet.[7] Rather, Dante and other medieval authors primarily knew Troy as filtered through Rome, that is, classical Latin literature. Briefly turning to Roman culture, then, we similarly find an effort to recall and revisit Troy through storytelling, but largely from the Trojan perspective rather than the Greek. In his *Aeneid*, for example, Vergil offers two versions of the fall of Troy.[8] Shortly after landfall at Carthage, Aeneas, hidden by a cloud his mother Venus provides, enters a newly constructed temple to Juno. There carved in relief on a wall he sees a series of portraits ("pictura") depicting the Trojan War (1.464–94), the poem's first telling of the story. As with Demodokos's song in *The Odyssey*, this ekphrasis offers a secondhand report of sorts, the reading of which causes Aeneas, like Odysseus at the Phaiakian court, to weep. Immediately following this moment of grief, Dido and her entourage enter the temple to worship Juno and, in response to his grief, she welcomes Aeneas to her court. In the second version of the story—all of Book 2—Aeneas tells a wrenching tale of Troy's fall to an eager audience of Carthaginians. Like Odysseus and Menelaos in *The Odyssey*, Aeneas offers an eyewitness account of Troy's destruction. Here, we find the details of Sinon's treachery and Laocoon's death, the slaughter of Trojans and the murder of Priam at his household altar, the confusion of a night battle and the flight of survivors. By telling his tale, Aeneas revisits Troy and the brutal chaos of the final battle, in which he escapes the burning city carrying his father, Anchises, and leading his son, Ascanius, but losing his wife Cruesa in the mayhem. Holding Dido and her court's rapt attention, Aeneas offers the story from the perspective of the conquered. And, like his literary counterpart Odysseus at the hands of the Phaiakians, he receives a sympathetic hearing for his tale, the telling of which, though filtered through Aeneas, allows all to remember Troy in its last hours, at least within the dramatic context of Vergil's poem.

Though perhaps the most widely known, Vergil's *Aeneid*, of course, is not the only classical Latin version of the Troy story. Ovid, for instance, in *Heroides 1*, retells aspects of the story from Penelope's perspective in her letter to Ulysses, and he recounts the story more fully in *Metamorphoses* (Books 11–14), from building the city's walls to its destruction and Aeneas's subsequent journey to Italy.[9] We also find treatments of the story in three late-antique Latin works, two of which are purported to be translations of chronicles by Dares the Phrygian and Dictys of Crete who, like Aeneas and Odysseus, offer eyewitness accounts of the war. In the *Ephemeridos belli Troiani libri*, the narrator Dictys—a companion of the Cretan leader Idomeneus—claims to have observed the war from the Greek side; in contrast, Dares—a priest of Hephaestus in Troy (mentioned in *The Iliad* 5.9–10)—claims in *De excidio Troiae historia* to have fought for the Trojans.[10] The third text, the anonymous *Excidium Troie*, differs from Dares and Dictys in its emphasis on the mythological background to the war and its retelling of Aeneas's wanderings and the foundation of Rome.[11] Dating, respectively, from the fourth, fifth, and early sixth centuries C.E., these texts were received in the Middle Ages as historically accurate and formed the basis of several medieval retellings of the story. The *Excidium Troie*, for instance, used as a school text on the continent, was a source for among others the Spanish *El libre de Alexandre* (13th c.), the Italian *Istorietta Trojana* (14th c.), the German *Gottweiger Trojanerkrieg* (14th c.), and the French *Eneas*.[12] Similarly, with its pro–Trojan stance, Dares' text especially appealed to medieval authors temperamentally attuned to the Latin tradition, and it inspired a range of texts, including the earliest known adaptation of the story in a vernacular, the tenth-century Irish *Togail Troi*, as well as among others Benoit de Sainte-Maure's widely known *Roman de Troie* (ca. 1165), a long (over 30,000 lines) Old French poem dedicated to Eleanor of Aquitaine, Joseph of Exeter's *De bello trojano* (ca. 1190), an erudite Latin rhetorical poem, and the Icelandic *Trűjumanna Saga* (ca. 1260).[13]

Also inspired in part by the Latin versions of Troy, Geoffrey of Monmouth extended the story in his account of the origin and history of Britain. Completed around 1136 and dedicated to Robert, Earl of Gloucester, the illegitimate son of Henry I, and to Waleran, Count of Mellant, the son of Robert de Beaumont,[14] Geoffrey's *Historia regum Britanniae* purports to be a historical chronicle much like Bede's *Ecclesiastical History*, though he is clearly romanticizing historical detail—a charge of which even his near contemporary William of Newburgh accused him (ca. 1190).[15] Using both a chronicle form and genealogical lists, Geoffrey traces approximately 1,900 years of the history of the Britons, from Brutus, who arrives in England around 1100 B.C.E., to the final king, Cadwallader, who dies in 689 C.E. Three personalities dominate the *Historia*: again Brutus, the legendary founder of Britain; Belinus, who, according to Geoffrey, conquers Gaul and sacks Rome with his brother Brennius in 390 B.C.E.; and, of course, Arthur of Britain. Surviving in some 215 manuscript copies, of which 58 complete texts date from the twelfth century, Geoffrey's *Historia* was quite popular throughout the High to Late Middle Ages and it, in turn, inspired other texts, ranging from Wace's Old French translation, *Roman de Brut* (ca. 1155), also dedicated to Eleanor of Aquitaine, by the way, to the Middle English alliterative *Morte Arthure*, which in depicting Arthur as warlord follows the king's conquest of Gaul, his subsequent betrayal by Modred, and the final battle as first presented in Geoffrey's text.

While Geoffrey's treatment of the Arthur story is important for understanding the twelfth-century interest in the so-called matter of Britain, we shall leave it for the present and focus our attention on the first section of his *Historia*. Taking his cue from Vergil, and expanding a brief story found in Nennius's ninth-century *Historia Brittonum*,[16] Geoffrey presents an eponymous myth about the founding of Britain, thereby establishing a claim for the Trojan origin of the British people. Following a discussion of the geography and ethnography of Britain, much like Bede's opening of his *Ecclesiastical History*, Geoffrey briefly summarizes Aeneas's struggles to establish a Trojan presence in Italy after Troy's fall, offering really just a bare outline of the second half of *The Aeneid*. He then moves quickly through the history of Ascanius, son of Aeneas, father of Silvius, and grandfather of Brutus. This Brutus, as Geoffrey tells the story, fled Italy after killing his father in a hunting accident, freed a group of Trojans from slavery in Greece, then led them on a raid in Aquitaine before establishing them on the island of Albion. Unlike his great-grandfather Aeneas, who met fierce resistance from Turnus in Italy, Brutus and his band of Trojans settled a land largely unoccupied, except for a few giants. Upon defeating the giants, ultimately killing all of them, the Trojans, as Geoffrey observes, "Agros incipient colere, domos aedificare, ita ut in breui tempore terram ab euo inhabitatem censeres" [began to cultivate the fields and build houses so that in a short time you might have supposed the land inhabited from an early age][17]—in other words, the Trojans brought civilization to the island. (Presumably, the giants did not count as inhabitants; in the *Historia*, of course, the giants represent the wild and untamed that must be conquered to establish civilization and order.) Brutus then promptly renamed Albion Britain after himself and, at the same time, he also renamed his companions Britons. Adding a significant touch of originality to Nennius's story, Geoffrey next recounts how Brutus built a capital city on a carefully selected site on the Thames, stating, "Condidit itaque ciuitatem ibidem eamque Troiam Nouam vocauit" [and so he founded a city there and called it New Troy] (14). Now settled in a new land, with a new name for themselves and a new city of Troy in which to live, Brutus and company were no longer defeated and enslaved Trojans but conquering and free Britons.

As Julia Crick rightly notes, "Geoffrey's intentions remain buried in his work and its relationship to his sources," yet we can tease out a number of possibilities.[18] Indeed, Geoffrey's intentions in writing the *Historia* seem at least fourfold. First, he wishes to forge a solid link between the Britons and the Trojans through the Brutus story. Second, from this foundation myth, which takes the Trojan/Roman ancestral myth Vergil tells in *The Aeneid* as its model, he wishes to draw parallels between his own British history and Norman histories such as Dudo of Saint-Quentin's *Gesta Normannorum* and William of Jumieges' *Gesta Normannorum ducem*.[19] In this move, Geoffrey's *Historia* demonstrates what became a somewhat common phenomenon in other areas of medieval Europe, namely, as Jean Seznec observes, "a whole people claiming a mythological hero as ancestor, choosing him, as it were, for their progenitor and patron."[20] Third, Geoffrey strives to valorize the history of the Britons by recounting a long, continuous line of rulers between Brutus and Cadwallader: a line that reaches its pinnacle under Arthur's reign before finally breaking up under Anglo-Saxon pressure. Curiously, he ignores the fact of the Roman conquest of Britain, choosing instead to treat Britain as a tributary state of the Empire rather than conquered province. Finally, in writing primarily for a Norman audience, a people who had in turn recently conquered the Anglo-Saxons, he tries to show, in part, the Briton precedent of rule, that is, like the Normans the British kings also ruled on both sides of the Channel. Geoffrey's text probably could not have been written at a more receptive time or in a more receptive culture, for twelfth-century Anglo-Norman courtly society seems to have been primed for the story. Although the Arthur story apparently held no appeal for the Anglo-Saxons, we find renewed attention to Arthur within a generation of Geoffrey's writing the *Historia*. In recalling the Trojan story, then, Geoffrey quickly tempers any grief over the loss of Troy by extending the story, even revising its ending, into the foundation story of a new nation—the fall of Troy becomes a *felix casus*, if you will, for it led to the New Troy of Britain.

This "fortunate fall" seems to be the idea to which the *Gawain* poet alludes when mentioning Troy in the opening lines of his poem, though, at first reading, why he does so is not as clear. In fact, many first-time readers of the poem in translation often miss the Trojan reference altogether, and simply push on to the main story. Once the poet "gets down to the business at hand," so to speak, and begins to present the main story—the gathering of the Round Table in Camelot at Christmastime—Troy quickly fades into the background and readers focus on Gawain's adventures until line 2525 reminds them again of the destroyed city. With the story of Troy receding so far into the background of Gawain's story, we may fairly ask why the reference is even present at all. What if, for instance, the two-stanza, 36-line prologue was missing? Would the story be at all different? Considering the precarious nature of medieval texts, we may with no difficulty speculate on this scenario, for it seems these lines could be erased without much apparent change to the story. A modern editor, then, perceiving scribal corruption in a few spots, might emend a line or two for clarity or transition; to illustrate, line 37, which would now be line 1, could be edited to something like "Arthur the kyng lay at Camylot vpon Krystmasse," for subsequent context reveals clearly to whom the noun phrase "ðis king" refers. Our editor could next add a note explaining what appears to be an obscure reference to Troy in line 2525 and, voilà, the Troy story almost entirely fades into a murky background. By the way, some modern retellings of the poem—for example, one version written for children and another, a film version released in the early 1980s, starring Sean Connery as the Green Knight—do treat the story as though the prologue was indeed erased; they simply ignore Troy. Fortunately, however, we have the complete poem: a poem so carefully and efficiently wrought that were we to ignore the details, we would risk misreading it. So what do we do with a detail such as Troy?

As with other elements in the poem, the poet, of course, is quite deliberate about his Trojan references. These references, as several scholars have noted, place the poem squarely within the historical context of the founding of Britain: the context just reviewed based on Geoffrey of Monmouth's *Historia*.[21] The poet uses this historical context as one way to indicate time in the poem. Arnold Soucy, for example, notes that the poet structures the poem as a linear pattern (i.e., Gawain's movement from pride to self-knowledge) within four cyclical patterns that mark time. First, we find the simple chronology of the narrative cycle, that is, the major and minor events that constitute the plot. Covering the space of a little over a year, the narrative cycle begins and ends at Camelot and includes, among several other events, Gawain's journey through the bitter wilderness, the Christmas celebration and subsequent temptation at Hautdesert, and the fulfillment of the challenge at the Green Chapel. The second cycle we find, compressed primarily in lines 491–535, is seasonal. The poet, beginning in one winter and ending in the next, marks the year's passage with descriptions of spring conquering winter before surrendering to summer, which in turn is defeated by fall. As Marietta Patrick points out, the passage of the seasons traditionally suggests mutability[22]; the violence of the imagery suggests that this change is a struggle. The third cycle marking time in the poem is the liturgical year. Gawain's story begins at Yuletide, specifically New Year or the Feast of the Circumcision (January 1), progresses through "crabbed lentoun" (502), and passes Michaelmas (September 29); he then prepares to leave Camelot on All Saints' Day (November 1), arrives at Hautdesert on Christmas Eve (December 24), and spends Yuletide with the garrulous host and his charming wife until the New Year. The fourth cycle, then, is historical, as the references to Troy draw the poem into the larger context of the history of Britain as understood in light of the Latin chronicle tradition.[23]

Sir Gawain and the Green Knight, however, is not itself a historical chronicle; it is a romance. Unlike the historian who, as Aristotle notes, is primarily concerned with the past as it actually was, the poet can be concerned with the past as it might have been.[24] In this sense, the poet is more likely to shape the material to explore a specific artistic purpose, which the historian, concerned principally with fact, strives to avoid. Yet, concerning medieval histories, we would not want to draw too sharp a line between historian and poet. In discussing medieval historical writing and the historian's use of rhetorical *inventio*, Ruth Morse has demonstrated that while the historian is indeed interested in fact, he is also interested in telling a good story and drawing moral lessons from history.[25] Though, from a modern view, Geoffrey's *Historia* does not stand as sound historical writing, he casts it as historical chronicle, and it clearly was read so in the Middle Ages. As the manuscripts reveal, texts associated with the *Historia* tend to be ones taken as legitimate histories in the Middle Ages; these associations indicate in part the context in which Geoffrey was read. Appearing most frequently, for instance, is Dares' *Historia de excidio Troie*, found in 27 *Historia* manuscripts; interestingly, Nennius's *Historia Brittonum* appears in seven manuscripts, Dudo of Saint-Quentin's *Gesta Normannorum* appears in two, and the *Gesta Normannorum ducem* in various redactions appears in six.[26] As Crick concludes, "the reception of the *Historia* suggests that, despite the work's potential as an entertaining narrative, it circulated, both inside and outside Britain, by virtue of its functional value.... Its great popularity apparently depended on its informational rather than a recreational or even edifying value."[27] Concerning the relationship between medieval historical and imaginative writing, we would do well to remember Nancy

Partner's observation that "during the whole of the Middle Ages, history enjoyed many freedoms of fiction; and fiction, in turn, masqueraded as fact—no serious deception was intended by either."[28] Again, through his Trojan references, the *Gawain* poet draws on, or at least alludes to, historical writing like Geoffrey's *Historia* to help set the context for his story but, like all poets who write about the distant or legendary past, he is somewhat anachronistic as he shapes his material to meet his own and his audience's needs.[29]

In addition to marking time, then, the Troy story seems to serve a larger purpose for the poet, as the final stanza of the poem suggests. In the stanza's first eight lines (2505–12), Gawain offers a public confession and explains why he wears the green girdle, saying: "Þis is þe token of vntrawþe þat I am tan inne, / And I mot nedez hit were wyle I may last" (2509–10). Gawain claims the girdle for himself and defines its significance as his own special public reminder of his fault. The poet then writes:

> Þe kyng comfortez þe knyȝt, and alle þe courts als
> Laȝen loude þerat, and luflyly acorden
> Þat lordes and ladis þat longed to þe Table,
> Vche burne of þe broþerhede, a bauderyk schulde haue,
> A bende abelef hum aboute of a bryȝt grene,
> And þat, for sake of þat segge, in swete to were [2513–18].

As all the fellowship laugh and revise the significance of the green girdle from a mark of shame to one of honor, Gawain remains curiously silent. The poet, then, quickly concludes the poem:

> Þus in Arthurus day þis aunter bitidde,
> Þe Brutus bokez þerof beres wyttenesse;
> Syþen Brutus, þe bolde burne, boȝed hiderfyrst,
> After þe segge and þe asaute watz sesed at Troye, iwysse,
> Mony aunterez here-biforne
> Haf fallen suche er þis.
> Now þat bere þe croun of þorne,
> He bring vus to his blysse! Amen [2522–30].

Rounding out the historical references (this adventure happened in "Arthurus day") and referring his audience to sources for verification ("Brutus bokez"), the poet repeats nearly verbatim the poem's opening line, reminding his audience of Troy's demise. Gawain's silence in the preceding final scene resonates in this reference and encourages readers to reconsider his response, or lack of it, to the court. Perhaps in his silence he is overreacting to the entire affair; perhaps in wishing to claim the green girdle solely for himself he remains trapped in foolish pride; or perhaps he perceives something the others do not. His silence is suggestive and, while he has returned to Camelot a changed man, it is difficult to see if the court has learned anything from his experiences. The court's laughter at the end remains ambiguous, but, in light of the reference to Troy's fall, it is also a bit foreboding.

The destruction of Troy for Geoffrey of Monmouth is largely a *felix casus* as it ultimately ushers in the foundation of Britain at Brutus's hands. The *Gawain* poet echoes this view in the poem's first two stanzas: from the fall of Troy a great line of rulers arose in Britain, the noblest of whom was Arthur. His final reference, however, works quite differently. As he closes the poem's historical context by repeating the opening line, the poet remembers Troy's fall more than its rejuvenation, and he encourages his audience to do so as well. Troy, then, becomes a lens or frame through which the audience can view Gawain's adventures and the court's reaction to them. And, just as Troy fell through "tricherie, ȝe trewest on erthe" (4), so too does Camelot, as readers of Geoffrey would know. But of course, in the world of *Sir Gawain and the Green Knight*, Camelot's fall remains in the future; so, in a sense, this final reference to Troy, quickly following an image of a laughing, apparently joyful court, seems abrupt. Unable to respond to Gawain except through laughter, the court understandably remains unaware of its future demise; the poet's audience, however, most likely knows the whole story. Thus, while Geoffrey of Monmouth remembers Troy's destruction in part to celebrate its rebirth in Britain and possibly its subsequent renewal at Norman hands, the *Gawain* poet remembers Troy in the poem's closing lines to suggest the similar end Camelot faces and, perhaps more importantly, to remind his own audience of the mutability of life.

Notes

1. *Sir Gawain and the Green Knight*, eds. J. R. R. Tolkien and E. V. Gordon, 2nd ed. rev. Norman Davis (Oxford: Clarendon, 1967), 1–4. All line references to *Sir Gawain and the Green Knight* are to this edition and hereafter will be cited parenthetically in text.

2. *The Role of the Reader: Explorations in the Semiotics of Texts* (Bloomington: Indiana UP, 1979).

3. Elisabeth Brewer, ed. *Sir Gawain and the Green Knight: Sources and Analogues*, Arthurian Studies 27 (Woodbridge: D. S. Brewer, 1992). See also Larry D. Benson's general discussion of sources in *Art and Tradition in "Sir Gawain and the Green Knight"* (New Brunswick, NJ: Rutgers UP, 1965), 3–55.

4. Peter Green, *Ancient Greece: An Illustrated History* (London: Thames and Hudson, 1973), 44; for the story of the "discovery of Troy," see Susan Heuck Allen, *Finding*

the Walls of Troy: Frank Calvert and Heinrich Schliemann at Hisarlik (Berkeley: U of California P, 1999).

5. Richmond Lattimore, Introduction, The Iliad of Homer (Chicago: U of Chicago P, 1951), 12. Hereafter, book and line references to The Iliad will be cited parenthetically in text. Similar references to The Odyssey are also to Lattimore's The Odyssey of Homer (New York: Harper, 1965, 1967).

6. Other epics also entail retelling an historical event as springboard for its action: the anonymous Old French Chanson de Roland, for instance, or Torquato Tasso's Gerusalemme Liberata.

7. The Divine Comedy: Inferno, trans. Charles S. Singleton, vol. 1, Bollingen Series 80 (Princeton: Princeton UP, 1970), 4.88.40.

8. In-text parenthetical references of The Aeneid are to Vergil, Ecologues, Georgics, Aeneid I-VI, ed. and trans. H. Rushton Fairclough, rev. ed. G. P. Goold (Cambridge, Mass.: Harvard UP, 1999).

9. Heroides and Amores, 2nd ed., trans. Grant Showerman, rev. G. P. Goold (Cambridge: Harvard UP, 1977); Metamorphoses, 2 vols., 2nd ed., trans. Frank Justus Miller, rev. G. P. Goold (Cambridge: Harvard UP, 1984).

10. Dictys Cretensis, Ephemeridos belli Troiani libri a Lucio Septimio ex Graeco in Latinum sermonem translati, ed. Werner Eisenhut (Leipzig: B. G. Teubner, 1973); Daretis Phrygii, De excidio Troiae historia, ed. Ferdinand Meister (Leipzig: B. G. Teubner, 1873); see also Margaret J. Ehrhart, The Judgment of the Trojan Prince Paris in Medieval Literature (Philadelphia: U of Pennsylvania P, 1987), 31–32.

11. Excidium Troie, ed. Keith Alan Bate, Lateinische Sprache und Literatur des Mittelalters 23 (Frankfurt: Peter Lang, 1986).

12. Ibid., 8.

13. Leslie Diane Myrick, From the De Exidio Troiae Historia to the Togail Troi: Literary-Cultural Synthesis in a Medieval Irish Adaptation of Dares, Troy Tale, Anglistische Forschungen 223 (Heidelberg: Universitätsverlag C. Winter, 1993); Benoit de Sainte-Maure, Le roman de Troie, ed. Leopold Constans, 6 vols. (Paris: Librairie de Firmin Didot, 1904–12); Joseph of Exeter, Trojan War I-III, ed. and trans. A. K. Bate (Warminster: Aris & Phillips, 1986); Trüjumanna Saga, ed. Jonna Louis-Jensen, Editiones Arnamagnaeanae ser. 8, vol. 9 (Copenhagen: C. A. Reitzels Boghandel, 1981); see also Ehrhart, The Judgment, 37; Renate Blumenfeld-Kosinski, "Troy Story," in Dictionary of the Middle Ages, ed. Joseph R. Strayer, vol. 12 (New York: Charles Scribner's Sons, 1989), 219–21.

14. The issue of the text's dedication is actually more complex than I suggest here. Of the 215 manuscripts, 162 are dedicated to Robert alone, nine to Robert and Waleran together, and one to Robert and King Stephen; 43 have no dedication (Julia Crick, The Historia Regum Britanniae of Geoffrey of Monmouth IV: Dissemination and Reception in the Later Middle Ages [Cambridge: D. S. Brewer, 1991], 113–20).

15. In the preface to his Historia, William stated: "in libro suo, quem Britonum historiam vocat, quam petulanter et quam impudenter fere per omnia mentiatur nemo nisi veterum historiarum ignarus, cum in librum illum inciderit, ambigere sinitur" [practically no one unless one is ignorant of ancient histories can doubt, when happening on that book, how much he impudently and shamelessly lies throughout in his book, which he calls a History of the Britons] (The History of English Affairs: Book 1, ed. P. G. Walsh and M.J. Kennedy [Warminster, Wiltshire: P. G. Walsh and M. J. Kennedy, 1988], 30). Similarly, the earliest known witness of Geoffrey's book hints that its initial reception among historians was questionable. Geoffrey's contemporary Henry of Huntingdon, author of Historia Anglorum, read the text in 1139 and, after describing in Epistola ad Warinum his own futile attempt to discover oral or written evidence of the reigns

between Brutus and Caesar, writes: "Hoc tamen anno, cum Romam proficiscor, apud Beccensam abbaciam scripta rerum predictarum stupens inueni. Quorum excerpta, ut in epistola decet, breuissime scilicet, tibi dilectissime, mitto" [nevertheless, this year, when traveling to Rome, I was amazed to find texts about the above-mentioned reigns at Bec Abbey. I send you, dearest friend, very brief extracts of them, of course, as it befits in a letter] (Neil Wright, "The Place of Henry of Huntingdon's *Epistola ad Warinum* in the Text-History of Geoffrey of Monmouth's *Historia regum Britanniae*: A Preliminary Investigation'" in *France and the British Isles in the Middle Ages and Renaissance*, ed. Gillian Jondorf and D. N. Dumville [Woodbridge: Boydell P., 1991], 93). Henry—"stupens"—offers, according to Wright, "a first, faint adumbration of the misgivings with which some mediaeval historians ... received Geoffrey's *Historia*" (91).

16. Nennius briefly describes Britto's (i.e., Brutus's) lineage and accidental killing of his father while hunting (*Nennius: British History and the Welsh Annals*, ed. and trans. John Morris [London: Phillimore, 1980], 10–11.60–61).

17. *The Historia Regum Britanniae of Geoffrey of Monmouth I: Bern, Burgerbibliothek, MS. 568*. Ed. Neil Wright. Cambridge: D. S. Brewer, 1984, 13. Hereafter, I shall cite page references to the *Historia* parenthetically in text.

18. *Op. cit.*, 2.

19. Writing ca. 996–1015, Dudo of Saint-Quentin traced the history of the first three Norman dukes. William of Jumieges, drawing on Dudo, continued the story through William the Conqueror. First writing the text ca. 1060, William revised it ca. 1070 to include the conquest of England. Orderic Vitalis and Robert of Torigni updated the text again in the early twelfth century. The *Gesta Normannorum ducem* exists in several redactions. For both Dudo and William, the Danes—ancestors of the Normans—descended from Antenor, who became their king after the fall of Troy (see *The Gesta Normannorum Ducem of William of Jumieges, Orderic Vitalis, and Robert of Torigni*, ed. and trans. Elisabeth M. C. Van Houts [Oxford: Clarendon, 1992], 14–17).

20. *The Survival of the Pagan Gods: The Mythological Tradition and Its Place in Renaissance Humanism and Art*, trans. Barbara F. Sessions, Bollingen Series 38 (Princeton: Princeton UP, 1953), 24.

21. See, for example, Tolkien, Gordon, and Davis, *Sir Gawain*, n1, p. 70; Theodore Silverstein, "Sir Gawain, Dear Brutus, and Britain's Fortunate Founding: A Study in Comedy and Convention'" *Modern Philology* 62 (1965): 189–206; Laila Gross, "Telescoping in Time in *Sir Gawain and the Green Knight*'" *Orbis Litterarum* 24 (1969): 130–32, 137; Arnold Francis Soucy, "Linear Pattern within the Cyclical Pattern of *Sir Gawain and the Green Knight*" (Diss.: U of Minnesota, 1972), 1–21; J. M. Leighton, "Christian and Pagan Symbolism and Ritual in *Sir Gawain and the Green Knight*'" *Theoria* 43 (1974): 50.

22. "A Reading of *Sir Gawain and the Green Knight*'" *Ball State University Forum* 24 (1983): 29.

23. The *Gawain* poet is not alone among Middle English poets to allude to Troy, particularly Brutus, in a narrative not otherwise connected to Troy. We find similar references, for instance, at the beginning of *Wynnere and Wastoure* (ed. Stephanie Trigg, EETS 297 [Oxford: Oxford UP, 1990], lines 1–4) and near the middle and at the end of the alliterative *Morte Arthure* (ed. Mary Hamel [New York: Garland, 1984], lines 1692–99, 4342–46).

24. *Poetics*, in *The Rhetoric and the Poetics of Aristotle*, trans. Ingram Bywater (New York: Modern Library, 1954, 1984), 1459a 21.256.

25. *Truth and Convention in the Middle Ages: Rhetoric, Representation, and Reality* (Cambridge: Cambridge UP, 1991), 85–124.

26. Crick, *op. cit.*, 37–9, 44–45.

27. *Ibid.*, 224.

28. *Serious Entertainments: The Writing of History in Twelfth-Century England* (Chicago: U of Chicago P, 1977), 3.

29. Cinthio, the Italian humanist, defends this type of anachronism, saying "though the poets write of ancient affairs, they nonetheless seek to harmonize these with their own customs and their own age" ("On the Composition of Romances'" in *Literary Criticism from Plato to Dryden*, ed. Allan H. Gilbert [Detroit: Wayne State UP, 1962], 270).

The Treason of Aeneas and the Mythographers of Vergil: The Classical Tradition in Sir Gawain and the Green Knight

Russell Rutter

ILLINOIS STATE UNIVERSITY

The traditions received from the breakup of the classical world and transmitted to the fourteenth century associated Aeneas with the betrayal of Troy, which was tottering on the brink of defeat, besieged by a superior Greek force and in danger of being starved into capitulation. The story of this betrayal is not Homeric; indeed, Homer was known in the fourteenth century only in a fragmentary Latin translation. Medieval authors in search of information about Aeneas relied not on Homer, or even on the *Aeneid*, but rather, often first, upon the narratives supposedly produced by Dares the Phrygian and Dictys the Cretan. Mere Latin forgeries, these narratives nonetheless gained credibility with medieval readers because they omitted Homeric battles of the gods, emphasized various love interests and purported to be eyewitness accounts. Though "a short work in bad, flat Latin prose of extreme simplicity, verging on stupidity, obviously written very late in the decline of Latin literature" (Highet 51), Dares' *Fall of Troy* describes Aeneas and Antenor's conspiracy to betray Troy in return for the safety of their families and goods, and their active part in first admitting the Greeks, then guiding them to the royal palace so they could murder Priam, Hecuba and their followers. Together, Dares and Dictys emphasize the "murderous, lustful, lying, and deeply treacherous" nature of the Trojan nobility (Baswell 18).

In the fourteenth century, Aeneas was considered not only a traitor but also, especially in allegorizing commentaries on the *Aeneid*, the figure of *humanum genus*. Vergil's work, allegorizers argued, figured the development of humanity on its journey from childhood through concupiscible youth to enlightened maturity. That such an interpretation might arise from the *Aeneid* attested to Vergil's reputation among scholars as a deeply learned author whose works would repay the efforts of even the most painstaking commentators. Servius's comment on Book 6 of the *Aeneid* typifies this attitude:

> Truly, all of Vergil is filled with learning, in which this book holds preeminence.... And some things in it are put straightforwardly, many are from history, and many concern the profound learning of the Egyptian philosophers and theologians, so much so that a great many [commentators] have written separate treatises on each of the book's topics [quoted in Baswell 92].

Allegorical interpretation proceeded from just such respect for Vergil's learning. Fulgentius's *Exposition of the Content of Vergil according to Moral Philosophy* (late fifth or early sixth century) was "fundamental to all later Vergilian allegory," providing "the general model for the major statement of twelfth-century allegoresis," the commentary attributed to Bernardus Silvestris (Baswell 96–97). Central to Bernardus' commentary, as to that of his master Fulgentius, is "an attention divided between the microcosmic progress of the individual soul through the ages of man, and an exploration of the scientific microcosm through which that symbolic everyman moves" (Baswell 115).

The Vergilian tradition, then, coexisted with "the troubling penumbra of the counter-tradition" embodied in Dares and Dictys and, for purposes most material to the present essay, led to the notoriously ambiguous opening lines of *Sir Gawain and the Green Knight*" (Baswell 20) that introduce Vergil's hero:

> þe tulk þat þe trammes of tresoun þer wroȝt
> Watz tried for his tricherie, þe tewest on erthe.
> Hit watz Enneas þe athel ... [3–5].[1]

In these lines, Aeneas is both the treacherous "tulk" and the "athel" who began the conquest of the west. Both the charge of treason (which, because legitimate, is "þe trewest on erthe") and the good that followed upon the settlement of the western isles, including England, could be referred back ultimately to Aeneas.[2] Aeneas, then, was an ambivalent figure. In this interpretation, the "blysse and blunder" (18) that mark Brutus's conquest of

Britain also mark the deeds of his famous progenitor: the "blunder" of Troy's betrayal and the "blysse" of western conquest are alike attributable to Aeneas.

Sir Gawain and the Green Knight begins and ends with references to the siege of Troy and to Aeneas and his descendants. More than two centuries before the writing of Sir Gawain, Geoffrey of Monmouth had popularized the story that King Arthur and his relations were descended from survivors of the fall of Troy. In the Galfridian story, copied so frequently that it became commonplace, the Arthurian court becomes an analogue to the court of Priam at Troy. The Gawain poet extends this analogy by casting Sir Gawain as a type of Aeneas. Gawain possesses in his way the sort of inner flaws that made Aeneas a traitor and a wanderer but also a possessor of the capacity to mature through error, both traits lovingly dwelled on by allegorizers of the Aeneid.

The parallel between the ambivalent, questing Aeneas and the ambivalent, questing Gawain illuminates episodes that have continued to prompt debate among interpreters of Sir Gawain: Gawain's acceptance of the Green Knight's challenge, the dalliance with Lady Bertilak that eventuates in his concealment of the green sash, his profound disgust at having betrayed the ideals of chivalry and courtesy, and the lighthearted response of Arthur's courtiers to Gawain's tale of his adventure at the Green Chapel.[3] As Arthur's court is a figure of Troy, so also is Gawain a figure of Aeneas.

The Medieval Tradition of Aeneas the Traitor

The tales concocted in the names of Dares and Dictys might have lain in quiet obscurity had they not been translated and enormously expanded by Guido delle Colonne into his *History of the Destruction of Troy* (ca. 1287). Like their Continental counterparts, medieval English authors were captivated by Guido's narrative, which became the source of the alliterative *Gest Hystoriale of the Destruction of Troy*, the *Laud Troy Book*, Lydgate's *Troy Book*, and William Caxton's *Recuyell of the Histories of Troy*. In the prologue to the *Gest Hystoriale* was expressed in English, perhaps before the completion of *Sir Gawain*, the widespread conviction that Homer's stories of the Trojan War were contaminated by lies:

> He [Homer] feynet myche fals was neuer before wroght,
> How goddes foght in the filde, folke as þai were,
> And other errours vnable þat after were knowen,
> That poyetis of prise have preuyt vntrew[.] [41, 45–47].

The *Gest* insists on Guido's veracity precisely because he followed not Homer but rather the accounts of the Trojan War produced by Dares and Dictys:

> Dites full dere was dew to the Grekys,
> A lede of þat lond & loged hom with:
> The tothyr was a Tulke out of Troy selfe,
> Dares, þat duly the dedys be-helde [61–64].

The motive for Aeneas and Antenor's actions in Dares is mixed: they consider the fall of Troy inevitable and they wish to protect their families and their goods in the face of what they consider Priam's fatuous and suicidal commitment to the cause of honor. For Dares, the conduct of Aeneas and Antenor seems at once treasonable and to some extent justified by exigency. Guido does not totally neglect this ambivalence, but he gives to Book 29 of his *History of the Destruction of Troy* the stark rubric of "de proditione Troie per Eneam et Anthenorem" (217: "concerning the betrayal of Troy by Aeneas and Antenor"), a rubric echoed in the *Gest*, where the parallel book is called "The xxviij Boke: of the Counsell of Eneas and Antenor. Of the treason of the Cite" (364). All nuances of motive are eliminated in the flat assertion that Aeneas and Antenor betrayed their city to its enemies in order to preserve their own lives, families, and goods. According to the *Gest*,

> Antenor & Eneas, with þaire avne sons,
> Serchid by hom-seluyn in sauyng hor lyues,
> ffor deiryng with dethe of the derfe grekes:
> And yf þo weghes on no wise might of wo pas,
> The toune to be-tray, truly, þai thoght [11192–96].[4]

That Aeneas and Antenor were actuated primarily by desire to save themselves is reiterated in passages such as this:

> Therfore cast is hit cointly by thies kene traytours,
> Vnder proffer of pes, pryam to lose;
> Hor Cité to dissaiue in sauyng hor lyuis,
> And all Troy to be-tray, and the triet londis [11228–31].[5]

Most arresting of all is the description of Aeneas and Antenor leading Greeks to Priam's palace so they can slay him, Hecuba, and everyone else unfortunate enough to be there:

> When the derke was done, & the day sprange,
> The grekes by þere gydes of the great traytouris,
> Entrid into ylion egerly fast:
> No defence þai þere found in the faire place,
> And dyden all to the dethe with-outen dyn more [11956–60].[6]

Small wonder that the *Gawain* poet refers to the treachery of Aeneas and Antenor as he opens his poem about Gawain and the court of King Arthur, descended as they were from the dispossessed Trojans who, it was believed, had settled much of the Western world, England included. As a pattern of Aeneas, labeled a betrayer by Guido and his popularizers, Gawain carries within him instincts he cannot trust. Carrying with him the weight of Aeneas the blackguard, Gawain cannot expect to do other than choose mistakenly and fail signally. Carrying with him at the same time the potential of Aeneas the hero, Gawain cannot do other than try to achieve the quest he undertakes and, in the end, to lament that he has fallen short.

The Mythographic Tradition of Aeneas as Everyman

In his discussion of allegory and literary exegesis, Boccaccio posits four kinds of fiction: (1) fables, such as those of Aesop, that lack all semblance of truth, (2) narrative "which at times superficially mingles fiction with truth," (3) narrative which "is more like history than fiction," and (4) narrative that, though it contains a semblance of truth, actually contains none. Under the third category, Boccaccio observes, "For however much the heroic poets seem to be writing history—as Vergil in his description of Aeneas tossed by the storm, or Homer in his account of Ulysses bound to the mast to escape the lure of the Sirens' song—yet their hidden meaning is far other than appears on the surface" (*Boccaccio on Poetry* 14.9, 48–49).[7]

Allegorizers of the *Aeneid* focus their attention mainly on the first six books of the poem. For them, Aeneas reached maturity after his meeting with Anchises in the Elysian Fields. The rest of the *Aeneid* chronicled the result of Aeneas's newly acquired maturity and understanding: his subjugation of Latium.

For the allegorizers Books 1, 2, and 3 of the *Aeneid* represent the childhood and adolescence of Aeneas as *humanum genus*. The counterpart of these books in *Sir Gawain* is Gawain's initial meeting with the Green Knight at the court of the "childgered" (86) Arthur and his acceptance of the Green Knight's challenge. Book 4 of the *Aeneid* represents allegorically "the spirit of adolescence, on holiday from paternal control" (Fulgentius 127). The counterpart of this book in *Sir Gawain* is Gawain's experience at Bertilak's castle, especially his wager with Sir Bertilak and his dalliance with Lady Bertilak. The wily chatelaine permits him to win the game of bedroom badinage while she plays a more serious game, inducing Gawain first to accept the green sash and then to conceal from Sir Bertilak the fact that he has done so. Books 5 and 6 of the *Aeneid* represent allegorically Aeneas's progress from immaturity to mature understanding. Their counterpart in *Sir Gawain* is Gawain's enlightenment at the Green Chapel. But herein resides a dissonance. We know—because Vergil spends six books telling us—that Aeneas goes on to found Rome. However, we can only imagine what Gawain does after he returns to Camelot. The closing stanzas of *Sir Gawain* show us that Gawain believes he has failed, and that the courtiers who stayed warm and dry at Camelot offer Gawain only laughter, perhaps tempered with sympathetic good intention. On this problematic ending I shall offer thoughts at the end of the present essay.

Gawain's Acceptance of the Green Knight's Challenge and the Vergilian Allegoresis of Youth in the Aeneid, Books 1–3

Fulgentius argues that the shipwreck that Aeneas and his followers experience in Book 1 represents the hazards of being born. Aeneas's initial inability to recognize his mother and later to address her, then, represents the state of infancy (125). That the infant Aeneas cannot recognize Venus reflects merely the biological fact that infants in general cannot recognize their mothers (126). Fulgentius continues, "In books 2 and 3, Aeneas is diverted by such tales as those by which a garrulous child is usually diverted" (126). Fulgentius emphasizes the significance of Aeneas's journey in Book 3, dwelling especially on his burial of his father, Anchises. For Fulgentius, this reflects the fact that "youth as it grows up casts off the burden of parental control" because "boyish zest rejects paternal discipline" (127).

Bernardus Silvestris deepens the psychological and emotional dimensions of Fulgentius's commentary. Whereas Fulgentius argues that Aeneas cannot recognize Venus because small children cannot recognize their mothers, Bernardus introduces the concept of the "two Venuses, one lawful and the other the goddess of lust." The lawful Venus is the goddess of harmony, or justice, i.e., Astraea, but "[t]he shameless Venus ... is carnal concupiscence which is the mother of all fornications" (10–11). Amplifying Fulgentius's statement about youth and parental control (noted in the previous paragraph), Bernardus dwells on the constancy of maturity and the inconstancy that forms so prominent a feature of adolescence. Bernardus deduces that Aeneas's journey from Troy to Antandros allegorically represents the passage "from the natural heat of the first age which burns the body" to "the inconstancy of adolescence" (18). Aeneas's ships are the desires that lead to inconstancy (19). The burial of Anchises is the last stop on the way to young manhood, the nature of which is described in Book 4 (24).

In our allegorizing paradigm, the womb from which Gawain is born is the court of King Arthur at Camelot. In the first section of *Sir Gawain*, Christmas and the New Year occasion celebration and renewal. The *Gawain* poet's totalizing and superlative description captures neatly the tone of youthful exuberance that characterizes Arthur and his court. One can note the strategically placed superlatives (I have added the italics):

> Ay watz Arthur fle *hendest* ... [26]
> þe *most kyd* knyȝtez vnder Krystes Seluen
> And þe *louelokkest* ladies þat euer lif haden,
> And he þe *comlokest* kyng, þat þe court haldes; [51–53]
> þe *hapnest* vnder heuen,
> Kyng *hyȝest* mon of wylle—[56–57]

Equally revealing is the *Gawain* poet's use of the totalizing adjective "all" (I have added the italics):

> Rekenly of þe Rounde Table *alle* þo rich breþer [39]
> With *alle* þe mete and þe mirþe þat men couþe avyse [45]
> *Al* watz hap vpon heȝe in hallez and chambrez [48]
> With *all* þe wele of þe worlde þay woned þer samen [50]
> For *al* watz þis fayre folk in her first age [54]

The style mirrors the outlook of youth "in her first age," a time never to be recovered. Repeated emphasis falls on the ludic nature of the activities in which this group of nonpareils engages. In this context is presented Arthur's well-known custom of refusing to eat until he has witnessed an extraordinary thing—a strange story, a joust, or "sum mayn meruayle" (94), though marvels in this setting are related primarily to the digestion of sumptuous food, augmented by kissing games, carols, and sports.

In terms of the analogy that opens the poem, this is the world of Troy before the Trojans even dreamed of their vulnerability, much less experienced nine years of war followed by destruction. Arthur, after all, though a grown man, partakes of the youth of *humanum genus* as portrayed in the first three books of the *Aeneid*:

> Bot Arthure wolde not ete til al were serued;
> He watz so joly of his joyfnes, and sumquat childgered.
> His lif liked hym lyȝt; he louied þe lasse
> Auþer to longe lye or to longe sitte,
> So bisied him his ȝonge blod and his brayn wylde [85–89].

Whatever the virtues of energy and the avoidance of long-lying and long-sitting, it may be doubted that being "childgered" or possessed of a "brayn wilde" equips either Arthur or his caroling courtiers to cope with the surprise that abruptly gallops into the palace in the form of a giant green man wearing green garments studded with green gems, wielding green weapons, and astride a green charger. The intrusive stranger disrupts the festive Christmas world of Arthur's court, request "a Crystemas gomen" (283). Gawain accepts his challenge and plays with the Green Knight the first part of the beheading game, the result of which we know.[8]

By introducing the contest between Gawain and the green visitor, the *Gawain* poet broadens the scope of play to include the agonistic contest, the life-and-death challenge that Gawain accepts and, later, the more subtle but nonetheless life-and-death Exchange of Winnings bargain that Gawain makes at Bertilak's castle. When the Green Knight asks for a game, he speaks not of the caroling, kissing idiom of the youthful, "sumquat childgered" (86) Arthur, but rather recalls the idiom of the Anglo-Saxon *Battle of Maldon*, in which Byrhtwold, surrounded by enemies, his leader dead, resolves not to run away from what he calls the "wigplegan" or "battle play," that special blend of gamesmanship and fatalism that so often defines the outlook of the Anglo-Saxon warrior hero. Bertilak introduces a dimension to play that Huizinga describes this way in *Homo Ludens*:

> Though play as such is outside the range of good and bad, the element of tension imparts to it a certain ethical value in so far as it means a testing of the player's prowess: his courage, tenacity, resources, and, last but not least, his spiritual powers—his "fairness" ... [11].

After the Green Knight departs, Arthur attempts to gloss over what has happened, as if it were customary, a sort of Handy Dandy with edged tools:

> Wel bycommes such craft vpon Cristmasse—
> Laykyng of enterludez, to la3e and to syng—
> Among þise kynde caroles of kny3tes and ladyez [471–73].

The similarity between interludes that prompt courtiers to laugh and sing and a beheading game that reduces them to stunned silence is, to adapt Gavin Douglas's comparison between Caxton's *Eneydos* and Vergil's *Aeneid*, like the similarity between the devil and St. Augustine: it doesn't exist.[9] If Arthur's court represents the world of security, simplicity, and warmth, the Green Knight brings to it a dimension it lacks: ambiguity, struggle, and, because his form of play tests what Huizinga calls the "spiritual powers," an opportunity for growth. In taking up the Green Knight's challenge, Gawain leaves the world of Christmas games to enter a world in which he must play a game governed by rules he does not understand. Gawain is born in a way that no other member of Arthur's court has been or, apparently, dreams of being.

In this birth, Gawain, like Aeneas, inherits a destiny, which is foreshadowed in King Arthur's avuncular assurance that Gawain will meet successfully the challenge he has taken upon himself. "Kepe þe, cosyn," Arthur tells Gawain,

> þat þou on kyrf sette,
> And if þou redez hym ry3t, redly I trowe
> þat þou schal byden þe bur þat he schal bede after [372–74].

As we have seen, Arthur is quite dismissive of the Green Knight's ability to survive beheading, implying that it is "craft" (471), some sort of illusion. Arthur's words to Gawain could be construed as similarly dismissive. Gawain will survive because the threatened beheading is no more real than the illusory one the court supposedly witnessed. Again, Arthur may suggest that Gawain will survive "þe bur þat he schal bede after" because he believes that Gawain will not encounter the Green Knight at all. Whatever Arthur may intend, though, his words resonate in the world of maturity that Gawain—but never Arthur—later enters. In that world, Arthur's words will prove prophetic. Gawain will indeed have the capacity to endure the coming blow, and without such meretricious aids as the infamous green lace supposedly affords. Gawain's capacity to endure, based upon his unimpeached fidelity to his word, is precisely what Morgan le Fay, through her proxy seductress, will attempt for three days to undermine. The poem gently reminds us that Gawain is always free to fall but certainly sufficient to have stood.

The words of the Green Knight himself reinforce this sense of Gawain's indwelling strength. Readers and hearers of the poem need to know at this point that Gawain will actually reach the Green Chapel, yet Gawain has no idea where the Green Chapel is. The Green Knight addresses both concerns in a single line: "Forþi me for to fynde, if þou fraystez, faylez þou neuer" (455). If Gawain searches for the Chapel, he will surely find it, a statement that suffices for him and doubtless satisfied everyone who heard the poem. Of course, assertions that a knight can endure hardship and assurances that he will find what he seeks if he sets out in search of it are the very stuff of medieval romance, scarcely unique to *Sir Gawain and the Green Knight*. However, these features and others to be noted later, read in light of Vergilian allegoresis, reinforce the analogy between Gawain's journey and its attendant wandering, error, and self-discovery that for allegorizers of the *Aeneid* constituted the progress of Aeneas—of *humanum genus*—from childhood to maturity.

Gawain's Acceptance of the Green Lace and the Vergilian Allegoresis of Young Manhood in the Aeneid, Book 4

Between the account of the youthful court in the first section and the account of Gawain's journey of the last three sections lie the celebrated, meditative stanzas on the passage of time and the irretrievable loss of days (491–535). These stanzas constitute a textually instantiated barrier between the youthful court where Gawain was also young and the same court to which, having matured, Gawain returns only to discover that the courtiers cannot understand his experience and conviction that he has failed. Gawain will find that he cannot reverse time, cannot go home again, once he has met the challenge at the Green Chapel.[10]

For Fulgentius Book 4 represents "the spirit of adolescence, on holiday from paternal control," that "goes off hunting, is inflamed by passion and, driven on by storm and cloud, that is, by confusion of mind, commits adultery" (127).[11] At the urging of Mercury, "introduced as the god of the intellect," Aeneas quits his passionate involvement with Dido: "So passion perishes and dies of neglect; burnt to ashes, it disintegrates. When it is driven from the heart of youth by the power of the mind, it burns out, buried in the ashes of oblivion" (127). For Bernardus Book 4 "describes the nature of young manhood." Even the public disgrace he experiences after he has taken refuge with Dido in a cave does not deter Aeneas because he is young and dominated by passion (26). Aeneas leaves Dido and puts passion aside only after Mercury chides him for truancy from his mission. Dido's death on a funeral pyre signifies that "abandoned passion ceases and, consumed by the heat of manliness, goes to ashes, that is, solitary thoughts" (27).

A counterpart to Aeneas as he is allegorized by such commentators as Fulgentius and Bernardus, Gawain leaves a world of security, simplicity, warmth, and childhood to enter a larger world of ambiguity and struggle, but also growth. For Gawain this world includes hunting and that form of incipient venery that the *Gawain* poet terms "luf-talkyng" (927), and it leaves him considerably less certain of his identity than when he entered it. The Exchange of Winnings bargain involves Bertilak and Gawain in separate forms of venery, and subtle comic effect derives from wondering whether, in his brush with venery in its amatory sense, Gawain is more like the hunter, Bertilak, or like creatures for which Bertilak hunts.

After the essential first step—what Fulgentius and Bernardus call birth—both Gawain and Aeneas experience passions that may deflect them from their quests. Aeneas's liaison with Dido challenges him in two ways. First, he is led to indulge his passion when one form of venery—the hunt, dampened by a sudden shower—leads to the other form of venery—sexual license in a handy, nearby cave. Second, Aeneas loses sight of the mission upon which he has embarked. Gawain is similarly menaced. No challenges to his physical prowess can impede his search for the Green Chapel. Indeed, the *Gawain* poet needs only a few lines in which to mention Gawain's encounters with bulls, bears, boars, wolves, and dragons," not to mention "wodwos" and (720–23), as he forges northward. Other poets would have spent dozens of lines on this type of material.

The essential challenge, like the one Dido presents to Aeneas, is mental. It uses Gawain's vaunted reputation for courtesy against him. Bernardus allegorizes Aeneas's eagerness to enter the cave with Dido as the state of the young man "led to impurity of the flesh and of desire by excitement of the flesh and by the abundance of humors coming from a superfluity of meat and drink" (25). Indeed, Gawain awakes after his hearty meal of the previous night to discover a temptress sneaking into his chamber, where she lays siege to his chastity and his courtesy, virtues by which he was identified in the arming scene. She tries to undermine his "clannes" (653) by playing upon the "fela3schyp" (652) that prompted him to make the Exchange of Winnings bargain with his host, then manipulates his "fraunchyse" (652), "cortaysye" (653) and "pité" (654) until Gawain's reputation for courtesy appears to be in question. How can he be so reticent, she asks, and still be Gawain (1292–93, 1481–86)? Because he is so sensitive to suggestions that he has failed to live up to his reputation, Gawain can be led to accept the green lace and, despite their bargain, to conceal this crucial fact from his host. To the temptress, of course, passion is passion, so, having failed to arouse Gawain's concupiscible passion, she smoothly shifts gears and arouses his passion for life—and thus his fear of death. Courageous enough to undertake his quest and capable of resisting overt evil, Gawain is yet sufficiently immature to accept the lace he thinks will protect him from the fury of the blow that Arthur earlier told him he could withstand without such assistance.[12] Finally, at the Green Chapel Gawain acquires knowledge, as Aeneas did when he plucked the golden bough and entered Avernus. Whereas Aeneas passes through an initiation so he can go on to found a new empire, Gawain returns to his friends only to endure their laughter.

Gawain's Epiphany at the Green Chapel and the Vergilian Allegoresis of Maturity in the Aeneid, Books 5–6

Both Fulgentius and Bernardus considered Book 5 pivotal, a description of Aeneas's gradual turning from "wandering sight" (the significance given to the death of Palinurus) and his liberation from youth into maturation. Bernardus urges that in this book, Aeneas's ability to control his ships allegorizes temperance (28). At this point Aeneas is told "to descend to earthly things through thought, and there he will see his father ..." (29). Though Bernardus does not say so explicitly, the allegorical sense of this search in the underworld seems to be (1) that one can know the Creator only by knowing things of this world and their transient frailty and (2) that the movement from youth to maturity recapitulates the journey of *humanum genus* from the Earthly City to the Heavenly City (30).[13]

In Book 6, the now-liberated Aeneas reaches the temple of Apollo, which for Fulgentius represents "studious learning" (128). Aeneas's quest for the way to the underworld represents allegorically the principle that "when anyone considers the future he must penetrate obscure and secret mysteries of knowledge" (128). Once Aeneas has plucked the golden bough, he recalls tearfully his liaison with Dido because at this point he has achieved wisdom (131). Later Aeneas attaches the golden bough to the gateposts and thus enters Elysium, "where, the labor of learning now over, he celebrates the perfecting of memory ..." (132).[14]

Bernardus allegorizes Achates as study and the Sybil as divine counsel, so Achates' return with the Sybil represents that "study exercised in the arts brings forth understanding" (34). This situation is not possible until the loss of Palinurus, "wandering vision," who dies when Aeneas is ordered to see his father. The death of Palinurus signifies that Aeneas's "wandering sight passes away" (30). The fact that when Aeneas goes to the underworld, Achates is restored as a companion shows "that as long as Aeneas is detained in lechery, study is abandoned; indeed, when he exerts himself in meditation, he regains study" (39). When Aeneas descends to the underworld, he sees dead companions and past experiences. As Bernardus puts the matter, "[T]he mortified vices of the first ages return through imaginary representations ... whenever the imagination reflects on past errors... ." Aeneas's meeting with Dido signifies the "remembrance of past pleasure... ." (79). Like Fulgentius, Bernardus says that Aeneas's placing the golden bough "across the threshold" of the Temple of Apollo represents allegorically the fact that he commits to memory what he has discovered by experience and instruction.

Gawain's experience at the Green Chapel, like Aeneas's descent into Avernus, leads him to knowledge. First tempted by his guide to abandon the quest, then left alone to face the horrific nature of the place, complete with the sound of someone somewhere grinding an axe, he presses on. Bertilak knows that Gawain has not been totally faithful to the Exchange of Winnings bargain, so he inflicts upon Gawain a small nick, the emblem of his failure to maintain absolutely the reputation that he had earlier claimed. As when he trekked through the frozen Wirral, Gawain has resisted overt temptation, this time in the form of the guide's promise to "lelly you layne and lauce neuer tale" (2124) if Gawain chooses to flee. However, he finds that he has capitulated to covert temptation by retaining what Bernardus termed the "remembrance of past pleasure ..." (79), the green lace accepted ostensibly out of courtesy but really in the frightened hope that he might cheat death yet keep his bargain.

Death might have been easier to accept than the combination of hearty fellowship and galling consolation the Green Knight offers Gawain:

> As perle bi þe quite pese is of prys more,
> So is Gawayn, in god fayth, bi oþer gay kny3tez [2364–65].

The Green Knight then adverts briefly to what is, he urges, Gawain's understandable desire to preserve his life:

> Bot here yow lakked a lyttel, sir, and lewté yow wonted;
> Bot þat watz for no wylyde werke, ne wowyng nauþer,
> Bot for 3e lufed your lyf—þe lasse I yow blame [2366–68].

This nettlesome and consolatory understatement (note the delicate use of "Bot ... Bot ... Bot") only confirms what Gawain is already prepared to believe—that he was heroic except for the fact that he was not heroic. How impossible it is to achieve the perfection embodied in the chivalric ideal. How fragile is human life, but how well concealed is this fragility when it takes its truth claims for granted. Before the assembled court, Gawain displays the hated green lace and confesses ruefully,

> þis is þe bende of þis blame I bere in my nek.
> þis is þe laþe and þe losse þat I la3t haue
> Of couardise and couetyse ... [2506–8].

But Gawain is isolated, his sense of shame outside the ken of the court. Arthur tries to comfort him, but "alle þe court als / La3en loude þerat ..." (2513–14). Perhaps the court's attempt to transform the green lace from a badge of shame into a commemorative insignia is a "brilliantly imaginative and tactful reaction" to Gawain's plight (Mann 200). It seems to me, though, that Gawain is in no state of mind to appreciate it or to be consoled.

After portraying his progress from youth through young manhood to maturity, Vergil recounts Aeneas's fulfillment of his destiny to found Rome out of the ashes of Troy. The mature and perfected Aeneas, leaving behind him the vagaries of youth, arrives at a maturity in which, as a man governed by *pietas*, he establishes a new nation. By contrast, Gawain, now filled with a mature man's awareness of the slipperiness of earthly things, can only return to what he left—a court that remains youthful, excitable, and unaware of the transient frailty of such things as reputation and even life. The *Gawain* poet modifies the allegorizing tradition to emphasize an event that would have a Vergilian counterpart only if Aeneas had returned to Troy and been laughed at for regretting his liaison with Dido. Like Aeneas, Gawain progresses from spiritual youth through young manhood to maturity, but Gawain's maturity brings in its train only frustration and a sense of having failed, each compounded by laughter but not ameliorated by the court's attempt to turn the lace into a decoration. Whatever sense one attributes to it, this laughter distinguishes the ending of *Sir Gawain and the Green Knight* from the ending of the *Aeneid*. In this distinction resides, I think, a political implication.[15]

Gawain carries from his encounter at Bertilak's castle and at the Green Chapel the kind of knowledge that Aeneas carries from his liaison with Dido and his subsequent visit to the underworld: prophetic knowledge. Stated in its simplest terms, this prophecy tells the audience of *Sir Gawain* that it is descended from the Trojans, and that it derives its glory from the Trojans. If you are Trojans in strength, remember the fate of Troy and avoid becoming Trojans in weakness. Given the dissonance between Gawain's lonely sorrow and the circumambient mirth of the courtiers to whom he tells it, one need not wonder that Gawain, the man who has lived on the boundary between infinite, idealized aspiration and the wasting finitude of human capabilities, should be unheeded in his own place.

In "A Toccata of Galuppi's," Robert Browning meditates upon the fate of Venice, once the jewel of the Mediterranean but now a husk of its former greatness:

As for Venice and her people, merely born to bloom and drop,
Here on earth they bore their fruitage, mirth and folly were their crop;
What of soul was left, I wonder, when the kissing had to stop?
Dust and ashes [40–43].

One might speculate that in Gawain's expression of the fragility of human ideals and the court's lack of comprehension, the *Gawain* poet was pointing to forces that would one day transform the glittering world of games, carols, and heedless lords and ladies, into the image of ancestral Troy—which descended from splendid power into "dust and ashes." The celebration of Troy and the court of King Arthur as emblems of England—

Troynovant—coexisted with the disquieting knowledge that Troy had burned to the ground and Arthur's court, fallen prey to lust and faction, had long since self-destructed. Meanwhile, the glories of Edward III faded into military defeat, prolonged royal senility, domination by Dame Alice Perrers, and social unrest that one day would lead to Richard II's forced abdication. Perhaps the *Gawain* poet believed that the English nobility, figured in Arthur's heedless court, was frittering away its inheritance, just as its Trojan and Arthurian predecessors had done so long ago[16]

Notes

1. All quotations from *Sir Gawain and the Green Knight* follow the edition of Malcolm Andrew and Ronald Waldron, *The Poems of the Pearl Manuscript*, 207–300 and are documented parenthetically by line number.

2. Davis (*Sir Gawain* 70n3–5) analyzes the grammar of this passage to show that the *Gawain* poet apparently displaced onto Aeneas the role of traitor, which in other sources he shares with Antenor. Aeneas is thus both traitor and man of destiny. Hence Antenor's minuscule role in *Sir Gawain*.

3. Gawain's dalliance and his subsequent conviction that he has failed have been attributed to riddling oaths or to Gawain's motives for taking them (Blanch and Wasserman; Strite; Thomas), to his realization that he tried to neutralize the Green Knight's magical powers by accepting a supposedly magical lace (Mann), to the possibility that so "festive" a poem closes off definitive interpretation (Benson 207), and even to the *Gawain* poet's alleged male bias (De Roo 252–53). Derek Brewer and Jonathan Gibson's excellent *A Companion to the Gawain Poet* neglects the possible influence of classicism on *Sir Gawain and the Green Knight*. I hope the present essay goes some way to compensate for this omission.

4. What in Dares had been a plan involving Antenor and a host of other Trojans, including Aeneas, in Guido became a plot almost exclusively fomented by "Anchises cum eius filio Henea, Anthenor etiam cum eius filio Pollidamas" (222; "Anchises with his son Aeneas, also Antenor with his son Polydamas").

5. The *Laud Troy Book* likewise stresses the theme of selfishness over anything resembling interest in the welfare of Troy:

> Anchises, that waried wyght,
> That Ancien schrewe, that olde knyght,—
> And his sone, fals E[n]eas,—
> And Antenor—thes thre, alas!—
> And his sone Palidamas—
> These foure be-gan the compas:
> How thei myght best saue her lyues
> And alle her godis & here wyues: [17237–44]

For a comparable passage, complete with the rhetorical denunciations one might expect from the master of aureate diction, see Lydgate's *Troy Book* 4.5128–41.

6. See the *Laud Troy Book* 18273–78 and Lydgate's *Troy Book* 4.6389–91 (where Guido is named as the source). Probably every reader of *Sir Gawain and the Green Knight* would have accepted Caxton's later assertion that "Eneas and of Anthenor... were open traytours vnto theyr Cyte and also to theyr Kynge and lord" (667).

7. Boccaccio invokes a tradition that extended back to Roman times and was still

vigorous in the sixteenth century. St. Augustine was "compelled to remember I know not what errors of Aeneas ... and to weep for a dead Dido, because she killed herself for love" but later did so almost automatically (*Confessions* 1.13, 17). Fulgentius embraced the *Aeneid* as an allegory of the cycle of human life and Aeneas as a kind of Everyman (Latin: *unusquivus*). Fulgentius causes Vergil to say, "In all my writings I have introduced themes of natural order, whereby in the twelve books of the *Aeneid* I have shown the full range of human life" (*Content* 122). Closer to the *Gawain* poet's time, Bernardus Silvestris attributes to Vergil didactic motives similar to those ascribed to him by Fulgentius, e.g., "We are recalled from appetite for unlawful things by [Aeneas's] immoderate love for Dido" (*Commentary* 4). Vergil becomes "a philosopher" who teaches "self-knowledge" by means of the "exposition which wraps the apprehension of truth in fictional narrative..." (*Commentary* 5).

8. Such scholars as Strite and Thomas urge that the Green Knight's challenge is ambiguous enough to allow for the possibility that Gawain inferred a beheading game even though the Green Knight did not imply one. I find this argument somewhat unconvincing. The Green Knight seeks someone "þat dar stifly strike a strok for an oþr" (287; cf. 294: "I schal stonde hym a strok"). Though a "strok" need not be the blow of an axe, the size and prominence of the Green Knight's axe, as well as its status as a prize, call attention to it and implicitly define the game as an exchange of axe blows. That the renowned warriors of Arthur's court remain silent in the face of the challenge suggests fear of beheading, not mere pusillanimity in the face of the Green Knight's large size and exotic demeanor. If the Green Knight actually does not intend a violent "gomen'" he is a master ironist who manipulates the appearance of an axe-wielding contest to mask the reality of a friendly bout of fisticuffs. Moreover, his irony, if it be that, escapes the court, Gawain, and Arthur, not to mention readers over the course of five centuries. However one interprets it, though, the challenge constitutes an irruption of serious complexity that Arthur and his gamesome court never fully comprehend, any more than they comprehend Gawain's decision to seek the Green Chapel or, later, his reasons for believing that he has failed.

9. Equally significant is the courtiers, regret that Gawain must depart in search of the Green Knight:

> Bi Kryst, hit is scaþe
> óat òou, leude, schal be lost, òat art of lyf noble!
> ...
> Who knew euer any kyng such counsel to take
> As kny3tes in cauelaciounz in Crystmasse gomnez? [674–75, 682–83].

Arthur's courtiers, grumbling about "gomnez'" appear to suppress the memory of the beheading that so amazed them a year before and to ignore the world of "wigplegan" in which, as Huizinga shows, games are serious business. Consistent with this behavior is their *blasé*, though apparently covert, ridicule of Arthur for having allowed Gawain to keep his word by embarking in search of the Green Chapel. The courtiers are still in a state ascribed by Bernardus to the infant, who, "though willing to be pleased, does not know what he wants or whether it is reasonable" (14). Neither the mythographers nor, in my view, the *Gawain* poet attaches blame to infancy: it is merely a stage of life through which one must pass to reach maturity. The crux of *Sir Gawain* is that Gawain matures and the court does not. Douglas's comment comes from the prologue (137–43) to Book 1 of his translation of the *Aeneid* (Douglas 4).

10. The narrator of Sir Gawain remarks, "þa3 men ben mery in mynde quen þay han mayn drynk, / A 3ere 3ernes ful 3erne and 3eldez neuer lyke" (496–97). With these lines, Andrew and Waldron (226) compare lines from "Sometime Think on Yesterday'" from the Vernon manuscript:

> Whon Men beoþ muriest at heor Mele'
> Wiþ mete & drink to maken hem glade'
> Wiþ worschip & wiþ worldlich wele
> þei ben so set, þey conne not sade;...
> But in heor hertes I wolde þei hade'
> Whon þei gon ricchest men on array'
> Hou sone þat god hem may degrade'
> And sumtyme þenk on ȝusterday.

The *ubi sunt* motif heard in *Sir Gawain* is also heard in school texts such as Catullus, "[A]t vobis male sit, malae tenebrae / Orci quae omnia bella devoratis" (4: "But curse upon you, cursed shades of Orcus, which devour all pretty things!"); in such laments as *Deor*, with its refrain, "þæs ofereode, þisses swa mæg" (Bolton 93–94); in elegies like the one for Edward IV, with its variations on, "Art thowe agoo, and was here yesterday?" (Robbins 111–13); and even in the sententious wanderings of Chaucer's Egeus: "This world nys but a thurghfare ful of wo' / And we been pilgrymes passynge to and fro" (*CT* I 2847–48). The stanzas on the passage of time and the irrecoverability of yesterday emphasize departure from childhood, figured as Arthur's court. Whereas Aeneas cannot return to Troy, Gawain will try to return to Camelot. But no one will understand his sense of failure any more than they understood why he insisted on searching for the Green Chapel in the first place. In *Sir Gawain* as in the allegorized *Aeneid*, youth cannot comprehend age and age cannot recover youth.

11. Chaucerians will recall the Wife of Bath's "Certes I am al Venerian / In felyng" (*CT* III 609–10). Fulgentius, editor, quoting Spenser's *Faerie Queene* 1.6.22, "And follows other game and venery'" discerns "a likely play of words on hunting (venatus) and sexual activity (Venus)" (*Content* 148, sect. 16n1). In the eighteenth century, Benjamin Franklin's *Autobiography* advised, "Rarely use venery but for health or offspring" (79). The context does not imply reference to sylvan exercises involving gun and gamebag.

12. Placing *Sir Gawain and the Green Knight* in the tradition of Vergilian allegoresis implicates it in the debate about the relationship between maturity and moral failing. Moral failings in the young can be chalked up to lack of experience, but in mature persons, such failings signify self-indulgence that, if protracted, renders wrongdoing habitual. This line of thinking seems to inform Bernardus's assertion that passion is a problem inherent in youth (26) and Boccaccio's insistence that Vergil sought "to show with what passions human frailty is infected, and the strength with which a steady man subdues them" (*Boccaccio on Poetry* 68). Chaucer's Theseus regards Palamon and Arcite with indulgence because he recalls the folly of his own youth (*CT* I 1799, 1813–14). When Troilus and Paris oppose the return of Helen to the Greeks, Hector dismisses them as "young men, whom Aristotle thought / Unfit to hear moral philosophy" (*Troilus and Cressida* 2.2.166–67). Castiglione's Cardinal Bembo concedes "that since the nature of man in youthfull age is so much enclined to sense, it may be graunted the Courtier, while he is yong, to love sensually" as long as "in his ripe yeares" he becomes "good and circumspect and heedfull" (312). For Sir Thomas Browne, "The same vice committed at sixteene, though it agree in all other circumstances, at forty[,] swells and doubles from the circumstance of our ages" (*Religio Medici*, sect. 42). By the time he returns to Camelot, Gawain thinks more like Browne than like Theseus.

13. "For Bernard, then, the implicit story of the *Aeneid* is not just that of the ages of man. Far more, it is the soul's journey through the city of this world to the city, never quite explicitly stated, of God" (Baswell 116). Gawain recapitulates this journey.

14. Fulgentius clearly associates the golden bough with learning, and the meeting with Dido as a sign of penance that learning enables. Perhaps Gawain's antifeminist remarks have their basis in Fulgentian comments on Dido as "a shade now void

of passion and its former lust" (131). Such remarks would be all the more bitter if Gawain, like Bernardus's Aeneas, "is not yet of such perfection that he is not moved by the departure of what pleased him" (91). Gawain's insistent memory of his breach of courtesy may adapt the mythographer's formula that wisdom is acquired through recollection of youthful experience—its wandering and its failures. For Gawain, such reflection leads to isolation from a court, which has little experience to recollect.

15. I agree with Benson's conclusion that *Sir Gawain* "is a tragic romance with the sad moral that perfection is beyond our grasp," but I'm not so sure that the poem is also "an unromantic comedy with the happy point" that people can approach perfection (243). In a narrow sense, of course, "we have no way of knowing whether or not (or for what reason) Gawain may have joined the court in its laughter" (Longsworth 147n6), but Gawain's conviction that he has failed militates against the notion that he might have shared in the general merriment, whatever the courtiers' precise intentions might have been.

16. I am currently studying *Sir Gawain*, interpreted in light of classical tradition and Vergilian allegoresis, as a political commentary on Richard II's reliance, in his decline, upon the men and resources of the Northwest Midlands, where *Sir Gawain* was probably written. I wish to thank my long-time colleague and old friend Professor John C. Shields, for reading a draft of this essay and sharing with me his knowledge of Vergil and the classical tradition.

Works Cited

Andrew, Malcolm, and Ronald Waldron, eds. *Poems of the Pearl Manuscript: Pearl, Cleanness, Patience and* Sir Gawain and the Green Knight. York Medieval Texts. 2nd ser. Berkeley: U of California P, 1978.

Augustine. *Confessions*. Trans. Vernon J. Bourke. *The Fathers of the Church*. Vol. 21. Washington: Catholic U of America P, 1953.

Baswell, Christopher. *Vergil in Medieval England: Figuring the* Aeneid *from the Twelfth Century to Chaucer*. Cambridge Studies in Medieval Literature 24. Cambridge: Cambridge UP, 1995.

Benson, Larry D. *Art and Tradition in* Sir Gawain and the Green Knight. New Brunswick: Rutgers UP, 1965.

Bernardus Silvestris. *Commentary on the First Six Books of Vergil's* Aeneid. Trans. and intro. Earl G. Schreiber and Thomas E. Maresca. Lincoln: U of Nebraska P, 1979.

Blanch, Robert, and Julian N. Wasserman. "Medieval Contracts and Covenants: The Legal Coloring of *Sir Gawain and the Green Knight*." *Neophilologus* 68 (1984): 598–610.

Boccaccio on Poetry, Being the Preface and the Fourteenth and Fifteenth Books of Boccaccio's Genealogia Deorum Gentilium. Trans. and intro. Charles G. Osgood. Library of Liberal Arts 82. Indianapolis: Bobbs, 1956.

Bolton, W. F., ed. *An Old English Anthology*. London: Arnold, 1963.

Brewer, Derek, and Jonathan Gibson, eds. *A Companion to the* Gawain-Poet. Cambridge: D. S. Brewer, 1997.

Browne, Thomas. *Religio Medici*. *Sir Thomas Browne: Selected Writings*. Ed. Geoffrey Keynes. Chicago: U of Chicago P, 1968.

Castiglione, Baldassare. *The Book of the Courtier ... Done into English by Sir Thomas Hoby, Anno 1561*. Intro. W. H. D. Rouse. London: Dent, 1928.

Catullus, Gaius Valerius. *Poems*. Trans. F. W. Cornish. *Catullus, Tibullus, [and] Pervigilium Veneris*. 2nd ed. Rev. G. P. Goold. Cambridge: Harvard UP, 1988.

Caxton, William, trans. *The Recuyell of the Historyes of Troye Written in French by Raoul Lefevre*. Ed. H. Oskar Sommer. London: Nutt, 1894.

Chaucer, Geoffrey. *Works*. 2nd ed. Ed. F. N. Robinson. Cambridge: Riverside P, 1957.
De Roo, Harvey. "What's in a Name? Power Dynamics in *Sir Gawain and the Green Knight*." *Chaucer Review* 31 (1997): 232–55.
Douglas, Gavin. *Selections*. Intro. David F. C. Coldwell. Clarendon Medieval and Tudor Series. Oxford: Clarendon P, 1964.
Franklin, Benjamin. *Autobiography and Selected Writings*. Intro. Dixon Wecter. New York: Holt, 1969.
Fulgentius, Fabius Planciades. *The Exposition of the Content of Vergil according to Moral Philosophy*. *Fulgentius the Mythographer*. Trans. and intro. Leslie George Whitbread. Columbus: Ohio State UP, 1971. 103–53.
The "*Gest Hystoriale*" *of the Destruction of Troy*. Ed. G. A. Panton and D. Donaldson. Early English Text Society, os 39 and 56. 1869–74. London: Oxford UP, 1968.
Guido delle Colonne [Guido de Columnis]. *Historia Destructione Troiae*. Ed. Nathaniel Edward Griffin. Cambridge: Medieval Academy of America, 1936.
Highet, Gilbert. *The Classical Tradition: Greek and Roman Influences on Western Literature*. New York: Oxford UP, 1949.
Huizinga, Johan. *Homo Ludens*. Boston: Beacon P, 1971.
The Laud Troy Book. Part 2. Ed. J. Ernst Wülfing. Early English Text Society, os 122. London: Kegan Paul, 1903.
Longsworth, Robert. "Interpretive Laughter in *Sir Gawain and the Green Knight*." *Philological Quarterly* 70 (1991): 141–47.
Lydgate's Troy Book. Ed. Henry Bergen. Early English Text Society, os 103 and 106. 1908–10. Millwood: Kraus, 1975.
Mann, Jill. "Price and Value in *Sir Gawain and the Green Knight*." *Chaucer to Spenser: A Critical Reader*. Ed. Derek Pearsall. Oxford: Blackwell, 1999. 187–205.
Robbins, Rossell Hope, ed. *Historical Poems of the XIVth and XVth Centuries*. New York: Columbia UP, 1959.
Shakespeare, William. *Troilus and Cressida*. *The Complete Works of Shakespeare*. 4th ed. Ed. David Bevington. New York: HarperCollins, 1992.
Sir Gawain and the Green Knight. 2nd ed. Rev. Norman Davis. Oxford: Clarendon P, 1967.
Strite, Sheri Ann. "*Sir Gawain and the Green Knight*: To Behead or Not to Behead—That Is a Question." *Philological Quarterly* 70 (1991): 1–12.
Thomas, Susanne Sara. "Promise, Threat, Joke, or Wager? The Legal (In)determinacy of the Oaths in *Sir Gawain and the Green Knight*." *Exemplaria* 10 (1998): 287–305.
The Trojan War: The Chronicles of Dictys of Crete and Dares the Phrygian. Trans. and intro. R. M. Frazer, Jr. Bloomington: Indiana UP, 1966.

Mortal Hopes: The Trojan Framework of *Sir Gawain and the Green Knight* in a Doctrinal Context

Randi Eldevik

OKLAHOMA STATE UNIVERSITY

The crass wish-fulfillment function that certain kinds of fiction serve for many readers does not often enter into the discourse of literary criticism; it is regarded as something *infra dig*, unworthy of consideration. In examining the appeal that chivalric romances had for medieval audiences—why people read or listened to them, and why poets wrote them (for presumably poets aimed at least in part to attract and please audiences)—wish fulfillment must, however, be taken into consideration. When one reads Georges Duby's account of the *juvenes* in aristocratic society during the High Middle Ages, the younger sons of the gentry and nobility with their frustrated ambitions and aspirations, one can well understand why this eminent historian makes a link between their life experiences and chivalric literature:

> ... the presence of such a group at the very heart of aristocratic society helped to sustain certain ideas, myths and forms of collective psychology. These can be found at once personified and reflected in the literature—and the typical personages depicted therein—of the twelfth century written for the aristocracy. That literature tends to sustain, prolong and stylize the spontaneous reactions, emotional and intellectual, of contemporaries. To begin with, it should be noted that the group of "youths" themselves provided the main

audience for this so-called literature of chivalry which was obviously composed mainly for their amusement.... We should not therefore be surprised if we find that typical events in the life of the "youth"—quest for adventure and feats of arms—provided both the background and theme for epics and romances. Gerald of Avranches, priest to Hugh of Chester's *familia*, found it useful to take as the theme of his sermon, *emendatio vitae*, the lives of the soldier-saints, Demetrius and George, Maurice and the martyrs of the Theban legion. We should certainly not find it unrewarding to consider the themes of the literature of chivalry anew in the light of the tastes, prejudices, frustrations and daily behavior of the "youths."[1]

In this light, we find reasons for the upward movement so typical of chivalric romance—the rewarding of the hero's struggles with victory, exultation, full possession of whatever goal it was he was striving for (some precious treasure, or, just as profitable, a lady's hand in marriage with its concomitant riches and social status), and public recognition of his worth. The more humble and obscure the chivalric hero appears to be in the beginning, as in the widespread motif of the "Fair Unknown,"[2] the greater the satisfaction when the reversal of fortune finally occurs.

Though most *juvenes* would in reality never achieve the same things as these fictional heroes (at any rate, not to such a degree), the vicarious experience of such romances could be enough to keep a younger son going from day to day.

Two objections to this view of the chivalric romance genre immediately arise. In the first place, not all romances display a narrative movement that conforms fully and unequivocally with the upward movement just described: defeat, disappointment, even outright tragedy are not unknown in chivalric literature. (Would the Arthurian mythos be as prominent as it is if the eventual fall of Camelot were not integral to its conception?) To this point we shall return later.

Second, it is quite possible to use a chivalric narrative, even one with the upward movement that is typical of the genre, as a vehicle for conveying other ideas, other concerns, besides the worldly concerns that preoccupied the *juvenes*. Much as these young aristocrats might crave social advancement and success, as church members they could not be oblivious to the Christian doctrine that worldly goods are fleeting and salvation of the soul the only goal truly worth striving for. Granted that cynicism and hypocrisy must have been just as rife in the High Middle Ages as at any other time, and that the proportion of vain worldlings incapable of giving anything more than lip service to such a demanding doctrine must have been just as high in the medieval population as it ever has been[3]—still, it was accepted doctrine, and the literate poets (many of them clerics themselves) who wrote chivalric romances had, of necessity, an education that would make their awareness of Christianity's radical opposition to the pursuit of worldly glory especially acute. Was it not their duty to write lugubrious works full of *contemptus mundi*,[4] rather than stories of worldly glory that surely must inflame the baser appetites of a lay audience?

Even a historical account as materialistic as Duby's mentions churchmen using the *juvenes*' penchant for tales of warrior heroism to make listening youths more attentive to their sermons—the presence of soldier-saints in the sermons being the sugar, so to speak, that coated the doctrinal pill, one way of reconciling Christian duty with worldly pleasure. Obviously, the thirteenth-century emergence of the Holy Grail as the object of fictional quests, rather than some material treasure, can be attributed to the same sort of pious motives. If young men will be *bellatores* in armor rather than *oratores* in ecclesiastical vestments—so the reasoning must have gone—then let us at least try to make sure that they are *bellatores* with some spiritual awareness, *bellatores* who can look beyond the pleasures of the tilting ground, the feast hall, the boudoir, and the throne room to the eternal joys of heaven. So, a literary genre often condemned as immoral (see, for example, Dante's dismissal of the Lancelot romance as mere pandering in Canto V of the *Inferno*)[5] could be made to serve purposes of Christian morality.

In ways that might have been surprising to some medieval *romanciers* themselves, twentieth-century genre theory sometimes goes beyond this kind of didacticism to an even more exalted view of the potential for Christian *sententia* in the romance genre. In writings too well known to require much discussion here, Northrop Frye, while showing a clear understanding of the difference between secular and religious romance and adverting frankly to romance's wish-fulfillment function, points out the typological link that, by virtue of the romance genre's very plot structure, can be seen between chivalric tales of monster-slaying heroes and the master-narrative of Christian scripture:

> [In the Bible we have a sea-monster usually named leviathan, who is described as the enemy of the Messiah, and whom the Messiah is destined to kill in the "day of the Lord." The leviathan is the source of social sterility.... It also seems closely associated with the natural sterility of the fallen world, with the blasted world of struggle and poverty and disease into which Job is hurled by Satan and Adam by the serpent in Eden.... In the Book of Revelation the

leviathan, Satan, and the Edenic serpent are all identified. This identification is the basis for an elaborate dragon-killing metaphor in Christian symbolism in which the hero is Christ (often represented in art standing on a prostrate monster), the dragon Satan, the impotent old king Adam, whose son Christ becomes, and the rescued bride the Church.[6]

Henceforth I shall refer to this particular interpretation of romance plot structure as the anagogic view, since anagoge, in medieval allegoresis, is the level of meaning that deals with "quid speras"—what Christians are to hope for, or look forward to, in the eternity that lies beyond the portals of death. The fact that some medieval writers, too, manifest an awareness of the anagogic possibilities of chivalric tales—Langland, when he speaks of Christ's sacrifice as a chivalric *agon*, with Jesus "jousting in Jerusalem" to save human souls, or the author of the *Ancrene Wisse* when he presents an image of Christian salvation as the rescue of a captive damsel by a chivalric hero—provides interesting support for Frye's view.[7] This is not to say, however, that every medieval *romancier* was conscious of the typological link, or had lofty motives in telling chivalric tales. In the Middle Ages consciousness of the typological possibilities would not have been more than intermittent and would have varied greatly from one writer to the next. The typological possibilities vary from one story to the next, too: insofar as an individual romance diverges from the characteristic narrative pattern of upward movement and successful accomplishment of salvific deeds, and insofar as an individual protagonist diverges from the standard type of the sterling, Christlike hero, the more strained and far-fetched it will seem to try to draw a parallel between that romance and the Christian master-narrative of *agon*, victory, salvation and triumphant entry into the New Jerusalem. Tales of flawed and unsuccessful heroes are just as problematic, of course, from a Dubyesque sociohistorical perspective: how can stories of that sort provide vicarious satisfaction for frustrated *juvenes*?

That brings us to *Sir Gawain and the Green Knight*. As a narrative in which the main character's display of heroism is undercut by lapses in conduct that leave him feeling humiliated, full of self-reproach, and distinctly crestfallen upon his return to court, this romance is highly unusual within the Arthurian canon (cf. the unequivocal triumph of other Knights of the Round Table who are singled out as heroes of their own adventures far from Camelot—Yvain, Gareth). SGGK, it would seem, jars with both the anagogic view outlined above and the worldly concerns of the *juvenes*. With regard to the latter, one could perhaps reconcile *Sir Gawain and the Green Knight* with Duby's ideas by arguing that *SGGK* actually is responsive to the *juvenes*' concerns, but in an unusually sophisticated way that precludes crude, direct wish fulfillment. What the outcome of Gawain's adventure amounts to is a mixture of real heroic achievement and slight failings—slighter than the overwrought and guilt-stricken Gawain himself is willing to concede: he would rather wallow in wretchedness, but the Green Knight and everyone at Arthur's court take a more indulgent attitude that provides readers with a different perspective. By applying Gawain's example to the ups and downs of their own lives, an audience of *juvenes* could end up heartened, fortified by the *consolatio*—for SGGK may provide a kind of philosophical *consolatio*, if not exactly that which Boethius had in mind—that one can't always be the winner and that one must simply buck up, make the best of things, and accept the less-than-perfect realities of self and circumstances. The laughter of the court, making light of Gawain's obsessive perfectionism, could have functioned as a bracing tonic for an audience made up of struggling young knights with tendencies to take themselves too seriously and brood overmuch about their lack of success.

Mention of Boethius, however, brings with it larger concerns than just individual glory. In fact, when one envisions Boethius facing the prospect of a grim death in his prison cell, the anxieties of either a *juvenis* (whether he will win the next tournament, whether he will ever gain an heiress's hand in marriage, whether he will attain any social advancement and prestige) or of Sir Gawain at the end of the poem, pale into triviality. But perhaps Sir Gawain's anxieties at an earlier point in the narrative, when he kneels to endure an axeblow that he thinks will be certain death to him, do not pale. In a way that reinforces Christian soteriology without ever explicitly mentioning Christ, *De consolatione Philosophiae* confronts the problem of human mortality and suffering head-on, and thus complements the master-narrative of Christian scripture: with the turning of fortune's wheel, woe and utter ruination (not just minor setbacks) must always be expected in this world. Thus far, Boethius-Christian doctrine would add that one must look beyond this world to the next for any good that is truly lasting and meaningful. In Augustinian terms the City of God is not the same as the City of Worldly Prosperity, be that Rome, London, Paris, or Camelot. This study proceeds from the assumption that even a romance as full of laughter and *ludus* as SGGK participates, after its own fashion, in the Boethian/Augustinian vision.[8]

If it is objected that the introduction of such weighty matters runs counter to the light and mocking tone of SGGK, the rejoinder must be that the endless fascination of this poem resides partly in its complex mixture of levity and gravity. Seldom has there ever been a work of literature so multi faceted, one that makes such different impressions on different readers. While some would stress the ludic aspects of SGGK, others single out its dark and somber implications.⁹ To Felicity Riddy, for example, the overall effect of the poem is "to make the body's materiality vulnerable and poignant." She adds,

> *Sir Gawain and the Green Knight* is a poem over which death hangs, not abstracted or generalized, but physical and specific: a prospect of steel slicing through your neck. The killing of the animals in the hunts—disembowelled, skinned, cut up—is a reminder of what it is to be flesh.... And the year's gap between Gawain's giving and receiving the blow, which occurs in other versions of the Beheading Game story, is here elaborated into an account of the mutable seasons which seem to circle but in fact move relentlessly forward, taking Gawain with them towards death:
>
> þenne al rypez and rotez þat ros vpon first,
> And þus ȝirnez þe ȝere in ȝisterdayez mony [528–29].¹⁰

Riddy makes a strong case for this reading of the poem. The reader cannot help but feel the cogency of it: there is truth in her view of *SGGK*. To turn from it to other criticism of *SGGK*—critical readings that stress other aspects of the poem and neglect that which Riddy highlights, yet have their own truths to offer—is to experience a strange contrast and a concomitant sense of cognitive dissonance rarely found in the study of English literature. Insofar as any critical commentary on this poem emphasizes one aspect of it to the exclusion of others, that commentary has failed to render an accurate account of what the totality of *SGGK* is. That totality has perhaps eluded all studies of the poem thus far, the present study not excepted. Probably no critic today would dare be as presumptuous as G.V. Smithers was in 1963, when he entitled his study of the poem "What *Sir Gawain and the Green Knight* Is About."¹¹ Yet there are valuable insights in Smithers's study: especially helpful is its highlighting of the "centrality of the tension between the chivalric and the Christian elements in the knightly ethos, and its power and pervasiveness as a theme" (p. 185), which has informed the present study as well. Smithers, Riddy, others: each has an increment of truth to contribute. This study presumes to do no more than add one more increment of truth to our overall understanding of *SGGK*, while bearing in mind that there is more to the poem—much, much more—lying outside the present scope.

Doctrinal considerations, then, are one legitimate avenue of approach to *SGGK*, albeit not the only one. The young aristocrats for whom chivalric romances were written had concerns peculiar to their position, but they also shared in the concern for the state of their immortal souls common to all medieval Christians. Moreover, the Gawain of this poem is not the worldly, sensual Gawain of other Arthurian narratives. Rather, this is a Gawain who carries a shield painted with an image of Mary on one side and a pentacle representing the five virtues on the other side. Clearly the *Gawain* poet has concerns besides the mundane *realia* of knighthood. This is true *a fortiori* if we consider the *Gawain* poet to be also the *Pearl* poet, as he probably is, but even without reference to the other poems of the *Pearl* manuscript, one observes indications in *SGGK* itself of the poet's moral and spiritual concerns in sufficient abundance to justify attention to this aspect of the poem. One of those indications is the poem's ring-composition: the recurrent mention of the fall of Troy, first in line 1 and then again, with the very same phrasing, in the last line of the poem:

> Siþen þe sege and þe assaut watz sesed at Troye,
> þe borʒ brittened and brent to brondez and askez ... [1–2]
> Syþen Brutus, þe bolde burne, boʒed hider first,
> After þe segge and þe asaute watz sesed at Troye ... [2524–25].[12]

Though the alleged Trojan origins of the legendary line of ancient British kings (i.e., Arthur and his ancestors) form the backdrop of all Arthurian romances, a backdrop established firmly by Geoffrey of Monmouth's pseudo-historical *Historia Regum Britanniae*,[13] it is a backdrop tacitly taken for granted and seldom mentioned explicitly in romances of individual knights of Arthur's court. An Yvain, an Erec, a Perceval sets forth on a quest; his travails, his eventual success, his triumphant return to court are what the narrative is concerned with; the doings of the Trojan Brutus so many years prior to that would only be distractions if mentioned in the romance. That the *Gawain* poet should make such a point of evoking an image of the destruction of Troy, so remote in time and space, before narrowing his focus of attention to one particular "outrage awenture" (line 29) involving one particular knight of Brutus's lineage, must be significant: it is a deliberate artistic choice that flies in the face of common practice for *romanciers* of the High Middle Ages and thus calls attention to itself, inviting readers to ruminate on it and its possible pertinence to the adventure of Gawain with which it is juxtaposed.

With varying results, several critics have done that during the last few decades of *Gawain*-poet scholarship. Some of these critics, whether they explicitly mention Duby or not, could be characterized as more or less Dubyesque.[14] They stress the worldly aspects of chivalry, its concern with triumph and glory, and Gawain's loss of face when he must return to court and report his lapse to the courtiers: the fact that the glory of Troy, too, had to suffer eclipse, in a calamity that far outweighs Gawain's minor humiliation, is a way of placing Gawain's distress in proper perspective, and at the same time it is a way of indirectly adumbrating the eventual fall of Arthur and Camelot themselves—events that lie far in the future at the point when Gawain's adventure with the Green Knight occurs, since Arthur and all his court are then in their "first age" (line 54), young and full of the pride and confidence of youth. In this view mention of the fall of Troy serves as a chastening *memento mori*, one that would benefit both Arthur and Gawain in their youthful hubris if they would but hearken to it—but the emphasis is on worldly wisdom, prudence, caution, holding on to the reins of power, making the most of one's opportunities in *this* world, fending off death and ruin for as long as possible. Otherworldly concerns, "the faith that looks through death"—in short, anagoge—do not arise. Other studies, chiefly those of Haines,[15] are more anagogic in orientation and thus more closely allied to the present study, which strives to supplement them by emphasizing certain points that have not yet received due consideration.

In linking the vicissitudes of Gawain, and of his putative ancestor the Trojan Aeneas, and of Aeneas's descendant Brutus, who according to legend founded the realm of Britain, with the Christian doctrine of *felix culpa* (the "fortunate fall"), Haines takes his inspiration from an earlier article by Theodore Silverstein which speaks of "Britain's Fortunate Founding" and makes much of the *Gawain* poet's use of the epithet "Felix," meaning "fortunate" (line 13), for the legendary founder of Britain. Silverstein's concerns are worldly, centered on Aeneas's, Brutus's and Gawain's success or lack thereof: "From tragedy and fall would come a good. Bliss and blunder can be measured both by failure and by virtue, sometimes within the selfsame man or race. For the theater is the shifting scene of history, of accident and fortune, against which human motive and effort play their role."[16] The Christian associations of the key words *felix, fall,* and *virtue* can hardly help but occur to the reader of Silverstein's remarks, but it is left to Haines, years later, to take the obvious next step; Silverstein himself never speaks of *felix culpa,* divine grace, salvation, the Beatific Vision. "History" for Silverstein is the history of Troy, Rome, Britain—earthly history, in short, not the all-embracing cosmic history of Augustine. A close consideration of the title and content of Silverstein's article—"*Sir Gawain,* Dear Brutus, and Britain's Fortunate Founding: A Study in Comedy and Convention"—is revealing. Silverstein not only characterizes *SGGK* as a comedy, he also *writes* comically, with an arch, jaunty tone that seems strangely at odds with the seriousness of the matters he is treating. It is as though, in Silverstein's view, the catastrophe of Troy's fall and later the personal tragedy of Brutus, when he accidentally kills his brother and must go into exile, can be taken lightly just because the legends go on to show how

Rome will rise from Troy's ashes and Brutus will go on to found a splendid kingdom elsewhere, in Britain. It is a tone of Olympian detachment, like that of Vergil's Jupiter who is able to smile at Aeneas's miseries ("olli subridens," *Aeneid* I.254) because he knows they are only temporary, with an upward turn in the hero's fortunes destined to compensate for them.

Olympian detachment—the ability to see the big picture, as opposed to the common experience of struggling human beings immersed in the pains and anxieties of each passing moment—has its Christian counterpart in the Boethian/Augustinian perspective that, recognizing the impermanence of all earthly pleasures and prosperity, refuses to cling to them. Loss and suffering of all kinds are only to be expected in earthly life and therefore are to be accepted in a spirit of resignation—but there is the *consolatio* of an eternity of heavenly bliss to look forward to. The reasoning is parallel to that of Jupiter as he anticipates the "imperium sine fine" (line 279) lying in store for Aeneas and his descendants. Even Christ's suffering on the cross has its place within the overarching vision at which medieval theologians arrived: terrible as that suffering was, it served a greater good, and the resulting state of blessedness, for the saved, will be greater than it would have been if the fall that necessitated Christ's sacrifice had never taken place. So goes the doctrine of *felix culpa*. That this doctrine played an important role in medieval theology cannot be denied. But the *felix culpa* concept is open to criticism: though it might have started out as a commendable attempt to instill gratitude in worshipers by emphasizing the benefits of divine grace, slippage took place (as it so frequently does in religious movements motivated by the best intentions), resulting in an objectionable attitude of jaunty callousness, a brutal cheerfulness that fails to take account of the grisly reality of mutilated flesh. In today's colloquial parlance: "You can't make an omelet without breaking eggs." The alert reader will recognize that such thinking (whether in a Christian or a secular context) merely opens up a slippery slope leading to unbridled atrocities, and it must be questioned and resisted wherever it arises. The idea of Christ's voluntary *self*-sacrifice is not the problem—but there is something horrible when an attitude of cheerful acquiescence in that sacrifice arises in Christian believers whose only concern is how they benefit from it. If one must err, it is surely better to err in the other direction—with the kind of lachrymose piety that, in order to heighten contrition, dwells obsessively on Christ's wounds and the *realia* of crucifixion. That such piety could coexist with *felix culpa* smugness in the same historical period only goes to show that the Middle Ages display as much complexity and inconsistency as any other era.

Every writer is a product of his time, and it is idle to blame a writer for failing to transcend the limitations and distortions of contemporary thinking. When a writer is able to do so at all, however, we recognize that we are in the presence of greatness. It is to Vergil's credit that, in writing the *Aeneid*, he does not limit himself entirely to the serene ruthlessness of Jupiter (which corresponds, in historical reality, to the serene ruthlessness of Augustus Caesar in seizing and holding power throughout his long rule), but rather incorporates into his imperial epic passages of sensitivity and tender compassion that force the reader to ponder the human costs involved in the pursuit of *imperium*. "Sunt lacrimae rerum et mentem mortalia tangunt," says Aeneas (I.462), contemplating images of the atrocities that took place during the sack of Troy—and the reader, feeling the impact of this poignant line, can be certain that no future glory in his destined Italian kingdom will ever dispel the shadows of that past experience from Aeneas's mind. What was lost when Troy fell was, after all, an entire civilization, an entire way of life: as legend has it, the vast majority of the Trojan population was either butchered ruthlessly or enslaved, and if a handful of survivors escaped their enemies' clutches, it was only by an oversight—not because of any humane restraint in the Greek victors. Though the comparison may seem startling, the legend of the fall of Troy could actually be the closest thing to the Holocaust ever imagined by premodern Western man. Ulysses and Neoptolemus, as depicted by Vergil, are as hardened as any Nazis, and their objective is, quite simply, genocide. (Though they are willing that a few Trojan women should remain alive in slavery, they decree that all Trojan males must die, even a child as young as Astyanax, because of the potential threat they pose to the Greeks. And with only a few childless and husbandless slave women remaining, the Trojan people as a people would effectively be extirpated.) That a few of the Trojan people are preserved from destruction and go on to carve out a realm of their own in territory to which they have ancestral links, in the process becoming embroiled in violent conflict against inhabitants unwilling to welcome them there, only strengthens the comparison between ancient Trojans and twentieth-century Jews.

It is a comparison that could occur only to modern readers, of course. What is the relevance of bringing it into a discussion of a fourteenth-century writer's handling of the Troy legends? The comparison is intended to indicate what grave and somber depths there actually are in Vergil's overall vision, and by extension in that of the *Gawain* poet through his allusions to Vergil. It is a vision in which evil and pain are vividly reified, and though Vergil's vision encompasses joy and triumph, too, it does not do so in the shallow, glib manner of Silverstein, or of the worst medieval proponents of the *felix culpa* doctrine. For Vergil, joy and triumph are always costly, as they are for the best Christian theologians. While the comparison between the Fall of Troy and the Holocaust is still under consideration, let us use it to make one further point: is it conceivable that anyone in the world today could be so crass, so insensitive, so hard-boiled as to argue that the terrible ordeal of European Jews at the hands of the Nazis is something to be accepted without regret, *just because* it led to the founding of the State of Israel? The very idea is offensive. But the same kind of thinking is involved when, in classical mythology, the assertion is made that the fall of Troy was "worth it" because it enabled the Roman Empire to come into being (an idea that we might call the *felix lapsus Troiae*)—or when, in Christian theology, the assertion is made that we need have no uneasiness about the enormous total sum of suffering in postlapsarian humanity (including Christ's suffering) because it will be outweighed by the eternal bliss to come. All these instances are blemished by a distorted, unbalanced outlook that denies how "vulnerable and poignant" (to echo Riddy) the "body's materiality" is in actual human experience.

If Riddy is right, though, the *Gawain* poet (like Vergil) has a vision of life that fully takes into account the realities of human suffering, transcending simplistic formulas such as *felix culpa* or *translatio imperii*. Haines is not wrong to concern himself with the *felix culpa* concept in his explorations of SGGK; as we have already conceded, the presence of this concept in medieval theology is a fact, and we may also concede that the concept has a palpable presence in SGGK. The poem is a product of its time. What must be avoided, however, is an over emphasis on the dominance of *felix culpa* in this poem and an underestimation of the *Gawain* poet's ability to press beyond the conventional wisdom of his time. Already we have seen Riddy demonstrate this poet's use of nature imagery to express a poignant sense of the evanescence of life, in the lines about the passing of the seasons into death and decay; equally poignant, in its implications at any rate, is the passage already quoted in which the youth of Arthur and his courtiers is described. Though the *Gawain*-poet never goes on to describe the older Arthur, or the dying Arthur, the mere comment

> For al watz þis fayre folk in her first age,
> On sille,
> þe hapnest vnder heuen,
> Kyng hy3est mon of wylle—
> Hit were now gret nye to neuen
> So hardy a here on hille [54–59].

quietly insinuates to the reader a realization that Arthur and his courtiers have gone the way of all flesh, leaving behind them a standard of magnificence that the feebler generations coming after them can never attain. Notwithstanding all the ludic behavior that goes on in this poem—some of it in close proximity to the quoted passage, for the poet's reflections here are prompted by the need to explain the wildness and frivolity of Arthur's deportment—it is a passage with heart-breaking implications. Its very understatement makes it all the more devastating. The main action of the poem may be comic in its movement, but the backdrop is tragic. Likewise, the master-narrative of Christianity may on the whole be comic, as Dante acknowledged in entitling his epic *La Divina Commedia*—but think of all the tragedies, personal and collective, encompassed within the long timespan of Christian history from Eden to Armageddon. The *Gawain* poet, tragedian and comedian by turns, and more *in toto* than either, displays a breadth and profundity of vision comparable to that of a Vergil or a Dante.

Symptomatic of this fact are the critics' varying views of *SGGK* already mentioned. Equally revealing is the variety to be found within the study of just one critic, Smithers. At one point he states, "The poem is irradiated with the sunniness and gaiety of a polite Christian society and its ideals" (p. 184)—and everyone can think of moments in *SGGK* that bear out the truth of this observation. Only one page further on, however, we find Smithers saying (with reference to the conflict between Christian values and knightly ambition that he forefronts as the poem's central concern), "It is in fact a theme fit for the imaginative expression, in the action of a story, of issues which might touch the heights of *tragic power and pity*" [emphasis added]. That cannot be said of the typical chivalric romance, sunny, sanguine and audience-pleasing. It can be said of *SGGK* (and a few other romances—the *Lancelot-Graal*, for example, with which Smithers is greatly concerned in this study), and the fact that it can stems only in part from the adventure in which Gawain himself is directly involved. That adventure has, to be sure, profound implications. Smithers, Riddy, and Haines have all made important contributions toward laying them bare. The role of the poem's Trojan framework in accentuating and intensifying those profound implications must not, however, be overlooked. By evoking the most extreme and drastic example of human suffering and loss available to the medieval imagination, this framework has the effect of signaling, from the outset, that there is far more at stake, for Arthur and Gawain and their entire society, than the mundane, self-centered concerns that would typically preoccupy an audience of *juvenes*.

Other English poets have since made use of the Trojan catastrophe in the same way. Wordsworth, in one of his few poems based on classical mythology, focused on the personal loss of one woman, Laodamia, whose husband Protesilaus was fated to be the first warrior killed in the Trojan

War. When her pleas to see her deceased husband one final time result in the gods taking pity on her and sending his ghost to visit her, Laodamia's frenzied attempt to renew their conjugal relationship on its old footing meets with an austere rebuke from the ethereal phantom of Protesilaus. Having transcended earthly concerns, he now possesses a quasi-Olympian detachment (properly speaking, an Elysian detachment) and imperturbability: indifferent to Laodamia's human yearnings, he coolly advises her to widen her horizons, adopt a *sub specie aeternitatis* perspective, and let him return to Elysium in peace. Wanting only her old husband back, Laodamia has instead gotten an impersonal adviser comparable to Boethius's Lady Philosophy, or indeed the Pearl-Maiden. But Wordsworth's Laodamia is more than just a sermon in verse. While the words he puts in Protesilaus's mouth have eloquence and cogency, the English poet also sympathizes with Laodamia's bereavement and anguish. Like Vergil, in this most Vergilian of all English poems, Wordsworth compassionately extends the scope of his imagination outward from rarefied heights of Olympian/Elysian detachment to partake of Laodamia's human plight—and he even asserts that Divinity itself does so as well:

> —Yet tears to human suffering are due,
> And mortal hopes, defeated and o'erthrown,
> Are mourned by man, and not by man alone ... [164–66].[17]

"Mortal hopes" is a phrase that sums up what this study has all along been concerned with, from the *juvenes'* hopes of worldly advancement that form such a prominent concern of the romance genre as a whole, to the otherworldly hopes that the realization of human mortality—a realization that is particularly intense in SGGK—is bound to provoke. Anyone who takes a broad view of Arthurian legendary history, encompassing not only its glorious peak but also its catastrophic end, cannot escape this realization. Since the eventual fall of Camelot is only faintly adumbrated in the text of SGGK itself, the addition of the poem's Trojan framework serves as a haunting reminder of how transitory all *gloria mundi* necessarily is. The implications extend beyond concerns of earthly polity—which is why studies of SGGK that focus only on the secular implications of the Trojan framework are unsatisfactory. Like other medieval Christian poems of loss and desolation (e.g., the same poet's *Pearl*, or the Old English *Wanderer*), and like the *Aeneid* itself as seen through medieval Christian eyes,[18] SGGK grounds itself in earthly human experience—the weal and the woe of it both—but finds anagogic intimations therein. What its author has achieved emphatically in *Pearl*, by means of a scenario involving personal bereavement and an explicitly Christian vision of the afterlife, he achieves more subtly in *SGGK* by uniting Gawain's life-or-death adventure with a legendary scenario of near-total devastation, the fall of Troy.

Notes

1. Georges Duby, *The Chivalrous Society*, tr. Cynthia Postan (Berkeley: University of California Press, 1980), pp. 120–21. Duby's concern is, of course, twelfth-century France, while the concern of this study is a late-fourteenth century English poem. It seems reasonable, however, that the conditions of aristocratic life in both of these times and places should bear a close enough resemblance for Duby's comments on the *juvenes* to be pertinent here.

2. In Malory's *Morte Darthur* (Cambridge: Harvard University Press, 1976), p. 92, Larry D. Benson provides a helpful overview of this topos: "In *Gareth* the basic theme is that of the 'Fair Unknown' one of the most widespread of romance themes. It is found not only in the 'Fair Unknown' romances, such as Renaut de Beaujeau's *Li biaus descouneüs* and the English *Lybeaus Desconus*, but in the stories of the *enfances* of romance heroes such as Perceval and Lancelot, in tales of young knights such as La Cote Mal Tayle and Alexander the Orphan, and—in the form of the 'male Cinderella'—it is common not only in romance (as part of the three-day-tournament theme and sometimes of the theme of exile) but in folktale and nonromance genres as well (it appears even in *Beowulf*)." For further information on the topos, see Benson's bibliography.

3. The Lady Meed section of *Piers Plowman* exemplifies this fact of life.

4. The concept of *contemptus mundi* pervades medieval literature, but its most vehement articulation is the treatise *De miseria condicione humane* by Pope Innocent III. It is, however, worth noting that, notwithstanding the distaste for the World and the Flesh he expresses in this treatise, there have been few popes more adroit in manipulating worldly affairs, nor more assiduous in their pursuit of temporal power, than Innocent III. Renunciation of the world was an idea much bruited about during the Middle Ages, but an idea that seems to have had little effect on the actual behavior of medieval churchmen.

5. "Galeotto fu 'l libro e chi lo scrisse," Canto V, line 137. From C. H. Grandgent and Charles S. Singleton's edition of *La Divina Commedia* (Cambridge: Harvard University Press, 1972), p. 55.

6. This passage from Frye's *Anatomy of Criticism* (Princeton: Princeton University Press, 1957), p. 189, concisely sums up ideas that Frye would go on to elaborate in *The Great Code: The Bible and Literature* (New York: Harcourt Brace Jovanovich, 1982). The same chapter of *Anatomy of Criticism*, however, contains a comment on the socioeconomic concerns of romance that strikingly resembles Duby: "The romance is nearest of all literary forms to the wish-fulfilment dream.... In every age the ruling social or intellectual class tends to project its ideals in some form of romance, where the virtuous heroes and beautiful heroines represent the ideals and the villains the threats to their ascendancy" (p. 186). Frye's *The Secular Scripture: A Study of the Structure of Romance* (Cambridge: Harvard University Press, 1976) is where Frye expatiates on "down-to-earth" developments of the romance genre.

7. In the *Ancrene Wisse*, see Part 7, the section beginning "A leafdi wes mid hire fan biset al abuten...." Quoted from Geoffrey Shepherd's edition, *Ancrene Wisse Parts Six and Seven* (Manchester: Manchester University Press, 1972), p. 21.

8. For the impact of Augustine's *City of God* on the medieval understanding of Christian values within the context of secular British history, see Robert W. Hanning's

The Vision of History in Early Britain: From Gildas to Geoffrey of Monmouth (New York: Columbia University Press, 1966), especially pp. 36–37.

9. With regard to a poem that has generated so much critical commentary, comprehensiveness is impracticable. Examples, however, of the emphasis on *ludus* (besides the Silverstein article to be discussed at length below) are: Sacvan Bervocitch, "Romance and Anti-Romance in *Sir Gawain and the Green Knight*," *Philological Quarterly* 44 (1965): 30–37; Arthur Broes, "*Sir Gawain and the Green Knight*: Romance as Comedy," *Xavier Review* 4 (1965): 35–54; J. Finlayson, "The Expectations of Romance in *Sir Gawain and the Green Knight*," *Genre* 12 (1979): 1–24; Arthur Lindley, *Hyperion and the Hobbyhorse: Studies in Carnivalesque Subversion* (Newark: University of Delaware Press, 1996), especially pp. 65–83; Thomas L. Reed, Jr., "'Boþe Blysse and Blunder': *Sir Gawain and the Green Knight* and the Debate Tradition," *Chaucer Review* 23 (1988): 140–61.

10. Felicity Riddy, "The Speaking Knight: Sir Gawain and Other Animals," in *Culture and the King: The Social Implications of the Arthurian Legend*, ed. Martin B. Schichtman and James P. Carley (Albany: State University of New York Press, 1994), p. 151.

11. G. V. Smithers, "What *Sir Gawain and the Green Knight* Is About," *Medium Aevum* 32 (1963), 171–89.

12. All quotations of *Sir Gawain and the Green Knight* are taken from *The Poems of the Pearl Manuscript*, ed. Malcolm Andrew and Ronald Waldron (Berkeley: University of California Press, 1978).

13. Geoffrey, in fact, is not the first to invent this Trojan lineage—one finds the idea as early as the ninth-century *Historia Brittonum* of Nennius—but Geoffrey was instrumental in disseminating the idea far and wide. His *Historia Regum Britanniae* was accepted as authentic history for centuries after its composition in the 1140s.

14. With regard to the Trojan allusions in the poem, perhaps the most insistently secular in emphasis (aside from Silverstein, to be discussed below) is Lynn Staley Johnson, *The Voice of the Gawain-Poet* (Madison: University of Wisconsin Press, 1984); see especially pp. 42–43. Other critics who strike a balance between secular and spiritual concerns, but with considerable emphasis on the former, are Richard Hamilton Green, "Gawain's Shield and the Quest for Perfection," *English Language History* 29 (1962): 121–39, and Donald R. Howard, "Structure and Symmetry in *Sir Gawain*," *Speculum* 39 (1964): 425–33.

15. Most comprehensively, Victor Yelverton Haines, *The Fortunate Fall of Sir Gawain: The Typology of* Sir Gawain and the Green Knight (Washington, D.C.: University Press of America, 1982); see also Haines's "Allusions to the Felix Culpa in the Prologue of *Sir Gawain and the Green Knight*," *Revue de l'Université d'Ottawa* 44 (1974): 158–77.

16. Theodore Silverstein, "*Sir Gawain*, Dear Brutus, and Britain's Fortunate Founding: A Study in Comedy and Convention," *Modern Philology* 62 (1965): 189–206. Quoted from p. 194.

17. Quoted from *The Poetical Works of William Wordsworth*, ed. E. de Selincourt (Oxford: Clarendon, 1944), p. 272.

18. For the medieval Christian interpretation of the *Aeneid*, see Domenico Comparetti, *Vergil in the Middle Ages*, tr. E. F. M. Benecke (New York: Stechert, 1929).

Works Cited

Ancrene Wisse Parts Six and Seven. Ed. Geoffrey Shepherd. Manchester: Manchester UP, 1972.

Benson, Larry D. *Malory's* Morte Darthur. Cambridge: Harvard UP, 1976.

Bercovitch, Sacvan. "Romance and Anti-Romance in *Sir Gawain and the Green Knight*." *Philological Quarterly* 44 (1965): 30–37.

Broes, Arthur. "*Sir Gawain and the Green Knight*: Romance as Comedy." *Xavier Review* 4 (1965): 35–54.
Comparetti, Domenico. *Vergil in the Middle Ages*. Trans. E.F.M. Benecke. New York: Stechert, 1929.
Dante. *La Divina Commedia*. Ed. C. H. Grandgent and Charles S. Singleton. Cambridge: Harvard UP, 1972.
Duby, Georges. *The Chivalrous Society*. trans. Cynthia Postan. Berkeley: U of California P, 1980.
Finlayson, J. "The Expectations of Romance in *Sir Gawain and the Green Knight*." *Genre* 12 (1979): 1–24.
Frye, Northrop. *Anatomy of Criticism*. Princeton: Princeton UP, 1957.
———. *The Great Code: The Bible and Literature*. New York: Harcourt Brace Jovanovich, 1982.
———. *The Secular Scripture: A Study of the Structure of Romance*. Cambridge: Harvard University Press, 1976.
Green, Richard Hamilton. "Gawain's Shield and the Quest for Perfection." *English Language History* 29 (1962): 121–39.
Haines, Victor Yelverton. "Allusions to the Felix Culpa in the Prologue of *Sir Gawain and the Green Knight*." *Revue de l'Université d'Ottawa* 44 (1974): 158–77.
———. *The Fortunate Fall of Sir Gawain: The Typology of* Sir Gawain and the Green Knight. Washington, D.C.: UP of America, 1982.
Hanning, Robert W. *The Vision of History in Early Britain: From Gildas to Geoffrey of Monmouth*. New York: Columbia UP, 1966.
Howard, Donald R. "Structure and Symmetry in *Sir Gawain*." *Speculum* 39 (1964): 425–33.
Johnson, Lynn Staley. *The Voice of the Gawain-Poet*. Madison: U of Wisconsin P, 1984.
Lindley, Arthur. *Hyperion and the Hobbyhorse: Studies in Carnivalesque Subversion*. Newark: U of Delaware P, 1996.
The Poems of the Pearl Manuscript. Ed. Malcolm Andrew and Ronald Waldron. Berkeley: U of California P, 1978.
Reed, Jr., Thomas L. "'Boþe Blysse and Blunder': *Sir Gawain and the Green Knight* and the Debate Tradition." *Chaucer Review* 23 (1988): 140–61.
Riddy, Felicity. "The Speaking Knight: Sir Gawain and Other Animals." In *Culture and the King: The Social Implications of the Arthurian Legend*. Ed. Martin B. Schichtman and James P. Carley. Albany: State U of New York P, 1994. 149–62.
Silverstein, Theodore. "*Sir Gawain*, Dear Brutus, and Britain's Fortunate Founding: A Study in Comedy and Convention." *Modern Philology* 62 (1965): 189–206.
Smithers, G.V. "What *Sir Gawain and the Green Knight* Is About." *Medium Aevum* 32 (1963): 171–89.
Wordsworth, William. *The Poetical Works of William Wordsworth*. Ed. E. de Selincourt. Oxford: Clarendon, 1944.

Ritual Sacrifice and the Pre-Christian Subtext of Gawain's Green Girdle

Peter H. Goodrich

NORTHERN MICHIGAN UNIVERSITY

Were the classical critics of the Western European Celtic-speaking peoples right? Did ritual practice among the Celts include human sacrifice, and does this tradition covertly inform even late medieval works? Arguably they were, and it does. Ritual human sacrifice as practiced in Europe was far from a common event, yet this fact alone makes it more memorable and thus more likely to be mentioned first in the oral literature of the Celtic languages, and subsequently transmitted through written literature. Even dismissing the fanciful inventions of neo–Celtic paganism and reinvented, latter-day Druidism does not necessarily preclude consideration of all prior testimony on which they feed—even fanciful, fictional testimony. Consequently, this essay proposes what may appear to be a heretical reading of *Sir Gawain and the Green Knight*. The *Gawain* poet, I suggest, includes echoes of the ancient practice of ritual human sacrifice among the multiple ambivalences of the poem.

According to my hypothetical reading, Gawain implicitly assumes the mythic Frazerian role of "year-king" when he takes up the Green Knight's challenge to a beheading game, and subsequently experiences the sexual blandishments (for such they appear to be) of Sir Bertilak's wife. This role of the "devoted one" tests his courtly paradigm and devotion to the Virgin Mother, for in the end Gawain must enact either a "pagan" or a Christian paradigm, and in so doing show the true color of King Arthur's court.

This is, however, a conjectural reading suitably hedged with imponderables, qualifications, and paradoxes. As Morton Bloomfield stated in "Sir Gawain and the Green Knight: An Appraisal" 35 years ago, "The poem is fairly and squarely Christian" (45), and it is fair to say that his assessment, rightly, has not been much argued with. But is the poem *entirely* Christian? In terms of its content at least, from its opening classical allusions to the Green Knight to "Morgne þe goddes," it would seem most definitely not. Nevertheless, for approval within the social context of a Christian court, any pagan subtext of preparation for ritual human sacrifice—if indeed intended by the poet—must be rationalized, sublimated, or erased in literary performance. And I would suggest that in this case, it has been. Despite the hints rendered by setting and dialogue, rationalization of the pre–Christian element is achieved by consistently disguising it as a challenge, game, and test rather than as religious observance or ritual sacrifice.[1] Its sublimation is accomplished on the plane of action into courtly dalliance and hunting, "venery" in both major senses of the word, and on the symbolic plane by the suggestiveness of the "green world" summed up in the green girdle that Gawain keeps as a "syngne of my surfet" (l. 2433). Its erasure is accomplished by Gawain's insistence upon survival and the courtly paradigm, by the Green Knight's acceptance of this insistence, and by the attitude of Arthur's court which converts Gawain's baldric from a token of "untrawth" to a badge of "renoun." So much is evaded and left unsaid in the poem that it is left to the audience to comprehend fully the girdle's ambivalent ritualistic import. Gawain himself encrypts the old ritual by excusing his near-acquiescence to the ancient forms as "þe faut and þe fayntyse of þe flesche crabbed" (l. 2435), aroused and fed by female seductiveness: "How tender hit is to entyse teches of fylþe" (l. 2436). And even the poet, although not averse to entering the text with comments on other matters, never breathes a word about the old ritual union of the tribal king and the land that Gawain so narrowly escapes. The subtext of ritual human sacrifice must therefore be defined by its very absence—a difficult strategy at best.

Reading pagan ritual into the text therefore confronts serious obstacles. Not the least of these has been the strategic marginalization of myth criticism by acknowledging its "suggestiveness" while demeaning its anthropological literalness. C. S. Lewis, for example, tolerates mythic readings like that of John Speirs, but discounts anthropological "ferlies" as an unnecessarily "roundabout" reader construct which "rejects the fiction as it was actually written" (71). Even more damning has been the resolute skepticism of critics like Bloomfield, who states,

There is no doubt that pagan rituals were still alive in the fourteenth century, as they are today, but there is much doubt that the participants had any notion of their meanings. And besides, these ritual relics were to be found among the folk. *Sir Gawain* is one of the few undoubtedly aristocratic poems of the English Middle Ages extant. It would be surprising if in this courtly and Christian atmosphere of a poem perhaps written entirely or partly in high style, we could find alive mythic and ritualistic elements [43].

Nevertheless, I will attempt this surprising act. Bloomfield is right to the extent that, as archaeologist R. C. Turner admits, "Religious belief and religious ceremony leave little tangible remains in the archaeological record" (203). Yet, as Turner also observes, preservation of such rituals in oral tales "formed the core of an illiterate society's history and myth. They may have undergone little change over the centuries but they are available to us in written forms, which are easier to manipulate and embellish, and where new elements can be more easily introduced into the texts" (204). If one grants their persistence and eventual mutability, they still "must be treated with great care" (Turner 204) because one cannot be certain about the extent to which the analogues of *Sir Gawain and the Green Knight* may constitute the *Gawain* poet's sources or attest to some common original source. Thirty years ago, Bloomfield could be so sure of his assumptions that he apparently felt no discomfort with a waffling term like "atmosphere." To the New Critics, the notion that an absence could denote presence, that part of what is intended to be "read" could be what remains tantalizingly unwritten, was laughable. Yet more recent critical trends have taught us that a text inscribes more than meets the eye (or ear) of any given reader, no matter how expert and informed that reader may be. We can no longer be sure, as Lewis and Bloomfield were, that the *Gawain* poet and his audience did not actually have such "ferlies" to exorcise. Lewis himself admits that pagan attitudes, even without clear "antecedents," can be "presuppositions, still alive in the completed product" (62). So even if the Celtic practice of human sacrifice was already conjectural for the poet and his audience, it could constitute a meaningful subtext.

Ross Arthur explains the implications best when he says that "the Gawain poet was intensely concerned with the productive possibilities of controlled ambiguity" and that "this multivalence must be now accepted as a fact of the text" (ix, 3). We now accept many radically different interpretations and value the poem so highly because of its dynamic plurisignification: its words remain the same but its meanings, like Morgan and Bertilak, are shape-shifters. Rather than one more "confrontation of complementary reductions" like those Arthur goes on to decry, I would like to show that the presence of a pagan subtext involving ritual human sacrifice is not only plausible, but consistent with other, more conventional interpretations within the poem's system of controlled ambiguity. Blended with the *Gawain* poet's Plantagenet culture are classical, Biblical, Scandinavian, Anglo-Saxon, and British elements. That much we may see simply from the poem's vocabulary.[2] And while the *Gawain* poet's precise knowledge of pre–Christian rituals is problematical, there can be no doubt of antecedents for human sacrifice in all four of those earlier cultures.

Classical literature offers many examples of ritual human sacrifice for the propitiation of the gods, not least within the matter of Troy with which the *Gawain* poet frames his poem, and with which cultivated medieval audiences were familiar. The Greek fleet sails, so to speak, upon the winds generated from the ashes of its admiral Agamemnon's daughter, Iphigeneia.[3] In Vergil's *Aeneid* the concept of ritual human sacrifice is again invoked in the passages describing Turnus's killing of Pallas and Aeneas's savage response to it: the Trojan sacrifices eight hostages, the four sons of Sulmo and the four sons of Ufens, on Pallas's funeral pyre. While single combat differs from ritual human sacrifice in that the loser does not passively submit to death, but dies under martial conventions rather than religious ones, it is similar in that he participates willingly and that the aura surrounding his death may carry quasi-religious implications due to the epic prestige of such combats in heroic society. Aeneas's culminating defeat of Turnus carries with it this quasi-religious aura, but Turnus wears a different kind of trophy or girdle than Gawain, the belt not of a lady but of the slain hero Pallas, and for it he receives his death blow. In Rolfe Humphries's translation, "now Pallas, / Pallas exacts his vengeance, and the blow / Is Pallas, making sacrifice!" (ll. 1023–25). Both heroes were suitors of the same woman, King Latius's daughter Lavinia, and the outcome of this killing is the establishment of the Trojans, the marriage of Aeneas and Lavinia, and the eventual merging of Trojan and Latin stock into a new people. The situation is inventively and quadruply reversed by the *Gawain* poet. While it is King Arthur and his court who inherit the mantle of Aeneas and his descendents in his poem, it is Morgan le Fay's challenge through the transformed Bertilak that imperils Arthur's knight. Rather than being sacrificed, he is spared. Rather than having sexual relations with Bertilak's lady, Gawain resists her advances and thus retains the role of unsuccessful "suitor" as well as his head. And rather than merging, the entourages (and implicitly the cultures) of Arthur's court and Morgan's remain separated.

We can say, therefore, that the tradition of ritual human sacrifice is part of the classical literary inheritance of the *Gawain* poet, although in classical sources it is rarer than other kinds of sacrifice and always treated as exceptional either for its divine ordination or its barbarity. Classical references to human sacrifice among the Celtic-speaking tribes of Northern Europe are also numerous and significant, despite being founded more on hearsay than on direct observation. Moreover, they are colored by the writers' senses of cultural superiority and their propagandistic purposes. Such descriptions occur in Diodorus Siculus (V 31, 32), Strabo (*Geography* IV 4.5), Julius Caesar (*De Bello Gallico* VI 16), Pomponius Mela (*De Situ Orbis* III 2.18–19), Lucan (*Pharsalia* III 399–452), Pliny the Elder (*Natural History* XXX 13), Tacitus (*Annals* XIV 30), and Dio Cassius (*Histories* LX 11.2).[4] These classical writers refer to Druids divining from the death throes and entrails of their victims—who were usually criminals or prisoners of war; Strabo and Tacitus refer specifically to this practice among the Welsh (Green 183). According to J. R. Magilton, "There may have been little distinction between ritual and judicial deaths in Celtic society" (184), yet both kinds were regarded as strange and beknighted by the Romans. Writing about the Roman invasion of Anglesey in 60 C.E., Tacitus deliberately foregrounds the transgressive nature (to the Romans) of both the British women and Druids:

> Standing on the shore was the opposing army, a dense formation of men and weapons. Women in black clothing like that of the furies ran between the ranks. Wild-haired, they brandished torches. Around them, the Druids, lifting their hands upwards towards the sky to make frightening curses, frightened [the Roman] soldiers with this extraordinary sight. And so [the Romans] stood motionless and vulnerable as if their limbs were paralysed. Then their commander exhorted them and they urged one another not to quake before an army of women and fanatics. They carried the ensigns forward, struck down all resistance, and enveloped them in [the enemy's own] fire. After that, a garrison was imposed on the vanquished and destroyed their groves, places of savage superstition. For [the Druids] considered it their duty to spread their altars with the gore of captives and to communicate with their deities through human entrails [Koch and Carey 28].

Closely related to ritual human sacrifice was the cult of the human head, considered by many Indo-European cultures to be the locus of the personality or soul. Heads were offered to Celtic gods in temples, which could be open-air sacred groves or buildings (Green 116). Archaeology provides material corroboration of the practice, although this evidence is scarce because it is difficult to distinguish between bodies ritually sacrificed and bodies ritually treated after death from battle or natural causes (Green 184) or even those subsequently disturbed in nonritual ways (Briggs 181). Moreover, a pervasive belief in the immortality of the soul has been documented by classical writers about the Celtic-speaking peoples. Ammianus Marcellinus, Hippolytus, and Clement of Alexandria establish an explicit connection between this belief and the Pythagorean doctrine also espoused by Ovid's *Metamorphoses*, a frequent source of medieval writers that would likely have been known by the *Gawain* poet; according to Ammianus: "The [Vþtes (diviners)] endeavored to explain the sub-mysteries of nature. Between them were the Druids, an intimate fellowship of greater ability who followed the doctrine of Pythagoras. They rose above the rest by seeking the unseen, making little of human mortality as they believed in the immortality of the soul" (Koch and Carey 25). In the *Pharsalia*, the Roman poet Lucan addresses them directly: "...The same spirit controls the limbs in another realm. / Death, if what you say is true, is but the mid-point of a long life" (I: 457–58, Koch and Carey 26). Such a belief is the essential implication of the Green Knight's (and Morgan's) test of Gawain's "trawþe": not merely a point of commonality between Druidical and Christian belief in the immortality of the soul, but a crucial difference between the doctrines. The pre–Christian concept of the soul's transmigration into another body in this world, or into an "otherworld" that is essentially a reified vision of natural physical processes, is not the same thing as the Christian resurrection of the soul or of the body at the end of history itself through direct mediation of the Godhead. Through his manner of leaving this world and theological orientation towards the ultimate self-sacrifice, Gawain must either embrace material nature fully—seeing little discontinuity between it and spiritual nature—or reject it for a radically different reality.

Since the poem uses the motif of decapitation with an axe, the cult of the head is especially significant. Ananda K. Coomaraswamy tells us that Indo-European tradition considers decapitation not only "a disenchantment of the victim" but "a consummation desired by the victim himself ... the release of all the imprisoned principles" (109). As representations of the new chivalric order, Arthur's knights are sworn to combat the old superstitious order which constantly threatens to release itself from courtly and Christian bonds. And while the Green Knight as representative of the old order is not disenchanted by decapitation, Gawain certainly knows *he* would be. Cosmographically, "the final purpose of the sacrifice is ... not merely to continue the creative process ... but also to reverse it, by building up again the divided deity, whole and complete, and therewith the sacrificer himself" (111–12). The pagan subtest is thus a "re-enchantment" and nothing less than Morgan's cultural restoration.

The archaeological evidence for British ritual sacrifice is most important, scant though it may be, given the accepted localization of the poem and its poet in the northwest Midlands not far from Wales. Infant burials under building foundations at Springhead in Kent and Alcester in Warks—the second one Romano-Celtic—show decapitation, and adult male skulls have been found in grain pits at a Danebury, Hants hill fort, a Cosgrove, Northants shrine, and other sites (Green 126, 117; see also Turner 189). Numerous examples of severed heads as war trophies have been referenced in literature and found throughout Europe. A closely related use of the axe is illustrated by the discovery in 1984 of Lindow Man (more technically known as Lindow II), a 25 to 30-year-old Briton preserved in bog-peat at Lindow Moss south of Manchester. Lindow II suffered a ceremonial triple death: first stunned by a poleax, then bled from a cut throat, and finally garroted. While the axe-blow was not intended to decapitate, both the cut throat and garroting suggest decapitation and all three deaths concentrate on the head. According to R. C. Turner, radiocarbon dating situates the corpse between 2 B.C.E. and 119 C.E. Another Lindow body in two parts, Lindow I (a head) and Lindow III (the remainder, although both were at first thought to be from different individuals), was discovered in May 1983, and dated between 25 and 230 C.E. It, too, is now considered to be a ritual sacrifice (Turner 189). The similar threefold death of Borremose Man in Denmark supports the commonality of Iron Age Celtic and Germanic rituals and the interpenetration of Celtic and Germanic enclaves.[5]

Commonality and interpenetration are important because they help to explain how the memory of such rituals could survive the twelve-hundred-year gap between Lindow II's death—and possibly that of Lindow I and III, as well—and the composition of *Sir Gawain and the Green Knight*. During the Roman period, the Lindow area was settled by the Brigantes, whose rebellions in the 60s C.E. severely threatened the Roman conquest. Although the Midlands near Lindow Moss later came under the Anglo-Saxon rule of Mercia after the Cornovii were driven westward, some British enclaves likely continued among the Saxon conquerors as they did among the Romans. Indeed, it seems likely, for the area remained sparsely settled throughout the Middle Ages. The antiquarian W. H. Norbury even noted in 1884 that the local residents of Lindow had remained distinctive in their physiognomy and culture (Ross and Robins 63).[6] If true, such distinctiveness could therefore well have been present for the poet to remark upon and contrast with the high courtly culture of King Arthur's court.

It would also be appropriate to the Green Knight's isolated castle and nearby "chapel" in the poem's northerly wilderness. Tantalizing evidence for locating the poem in this region are Gawain's wanderings in the Wirral peninsula not far west of Lindow Moss, and the "king-in-the-ground" tradition of a sleeping Arthur buried under Alderley Edge just southeast of it. While they disagree about the precise locations of the Green Chapel, R. E. Kaske and Ralph Elliott conclusively locate them within the same few square miles of the Peak District near the juncture of Cheshire, Derbyshire, and Staffordshire, not far southeast of Lindow and Alderley.[7] The *Gawain* poet's apparent love of numerology could suggestively span this tripartite junction, triple death, triple goddess and Holy Trinity. Such interests also consorted well with royal politics in the late 1390s, when, according to Michael Bennett, Richard II's "apparent interest in the older regional centres [such as Chester] and their cults is striking" (86).[8]

For all these reasons, the tradition of human sacrifice could plausibly have been remembered in the area long enough to influence the nearby court of the *Gawain* poet and his original audience. Though incidental, other minor but provocative congruences exist to link the historical evidence and *Sir Gawain and the Green Knight*. For example, stone heads have been found in the area (Ross and Robins 77–78), and in the Boxing Day sword dance at Handsworth-Grenoside near Sheffield a "chief" wearing a fox fur hat is decapitated in mime (Ross & Robins 58). Lindow II himself died wearing nothing but a fox fur armband, for which Anne Ross and Don Robins have dubbed him "Lovernios" (53–59). While foxes may readily be expected in an area as wild as this was during the Middle Ages, the insignia seems apt for a tribal totem or a sacrificial victim (especially a victim as resourceful as Gawain). In an equally controversial conjecture, they date Lindow II's sacrifice not just within the window of radiocarbon dating, but to the Beltain or spring festival of 60 C.E. (17, 101ff), and claim that it may well have been motivated by Roman suppression of the Druids and Boudica's failed rebellion (87–91).[9]

Another suggestive connecting element is mistletoe, of symbolic importance to druidism. Pliny the Elder describes its ceremonial use by the Gauls (*Natural History* XVI 27):

> In their language the mistletoe is called "the healer of all." When preparations for a sacrifice and a feast beneath the tree have been made, they lead forward two white bulls with horns bound for the first time. A priest in white clothing climbs the tree and cuts the mistletoe with a golden sickle, and it is caught in a white cloak. They then sacrifice the bulls while praying that the god will grant the gift of prosperity to those to whom he has given it. They believe that mistletoe, when taken in a drink, will restore fertility to barren animals, and is a remedy for all poisons [Koch and Carey 26].

His description dovetails with the "golden bough" that gives Aeneas passage to the underworld, and is plucked in the "year-king" ritual of Diana at Aricia.[10] Vergil, Pliny, and Frazer all associate the mistletoe with the oak tree, sacred to the Druids. They also describe how it symbolizes the solar fire and life force persisting through the winter solstice, and thus serves as an "all-healer" or conveys the soul or element of continuity in both nature and the individual human life. The "gold" berries and green foliage consort well with the motival color schemes of *Sir Gawain and the Green Knight*. Mistletoe is seldom found on oak trees in Britain, but is frequently part of herbal remedies; four grains of mistletoe pollen were among the stomach contents of Lindow II's last meal (Turner 193). According to Magilton, "as a parasitic plant, it is a 'betwixt and between' substance, belonging neither on the earth nor in the sky nor in the water" (186). This liminality suits the bog of Lindow Moss and the Green Knight's chapel, also "betwixt and between" places in terms of the physical world as neither earth nor water (or both together) and the interface they represent as "entrances and exits to the Otherworld" (Magilton 187). Such liminalities between natural and supernatural inform the still-popular "courtly" custom of kissing under a seasonal sprig of mistletoe, and the Herefordshire farmhouse practice of burning and replacing it in the kitchen on the first day of the New Year (Frazer 183) suggests the continuance of this signification in folk practices relevant to Gawain's roles, both overt and covert, in the Christmas festivities of Bertilak's court. Altogether, it would not be too fanciful to agree with Ross and Robins's conclusion that "significant Celtic customs survive in the folk memory to hint at the role of human sacrifice in the former Celtic religion of the region" (78).

Recent scholarship, then, provides evidence to combat Bloomfield's twin contentions that the *Gawain* poet and his audience did not understand the meaning of pagan rituals and that they were in any case too far removed from the "folk" to care. There is really no reason to think that pagan rituals must survive in their pure form in order to be understood, or must continue to be understood only in their earliest sense. Also, the researches of literary ethnologists like Keith Richards amply demonstrate that both peasants and aristocrats, while possessing quite different cultures in some ways, were far from mutually exclusive in others. Not only did the nobility live in Norman castles and manors, but also the common folk. And the ties between folk and nobility were necessarily close in sparsely populated rural areas. In all likelihood the folk were present in the hall where the poet spoke and the nobility were acquainted with their customs and superstitions. Moreover, orthodox Christianity did not have the exclusive grip on people's imaginations that Bloomfield seems to assume, even if we take the devoutness of the aristocracy and the literate at face value. After all, the Christian faith did not succeed by outlawing pre–Christian beliefs and practices, but by furnishing alternative rationales and subsuming many "paganisms" into Christian rituals and doctrines. And key, connotation-fraught terms such as "trawth" and "surfet" admit more than strictly aristocratic and Christian interpretation. The "erasure" of paganism is thus only apparent.

All this would be beside the point if the Gawain poem's allusiveness did not somehow suggest the pagan subtext of human sacrifice and a "re-oralizing" of local traditions. But it does. As previously stated, the *Gawain* poet girdles his narrative at beginning and end with references to pre-Christian legendary history—in the siege of Troy. This strategy not only invites comparison between pagan and courtly models of culture, but indicates that the former lies at the very root of British royal ancestry. The most obvious pagan outcroppings within the frame thus created are of course Morgan Le Fay, the Green Knight and beheading game, the Green Chapel, and the "green world" they all represent.[11] Each in turn provides insights into the pagan subtext summed up in the green girdle, the insignia that contrasts most clearly with Mary's image inscribed upon Gawain's shield, and worn significantly closer to the body.

Although the *Gawain* poet describes Morgan in hypertrophied form as a hideous beldame overdressed in obsolete mode (ll. 947–69), Bertilak praises her as "Morgne the goddes" (l. 2452). That phrase, together with the extreme contrast between her appearance and that of Bertilak's lovely wife who apparently shares her licentiousness, suggests that Morgan indeed represents the British triple goddess whose iconographic opposite and perhaps third complement may be found in Guenore herself, "grayþed in the myddes" (l. 74) of Arthur's Christmas feast. Yet the poet himself neatly sidesteps that viewpoint by consigning it to Morgan's scion. Morgan's shape-shifting powers are nonetheless apparent in the transformation of her scion Bertilak into the Green Knight, though not, perhaps, of herself into the tempting spouse.

The appearance of this goddess as the instigator of the plot implicates not only her dangerous femaleness but also its celebration in some festival of procreation and renewal. Associated with her are the motifs of annual kingship and ritual marriage with the land. Christmas and New Year provide the main Christian counterpart that is active in the poem; what the poet does not tell us but might well have been thinking is that they fall neatly between the Celtic festivals of Samhain on November 1—during which the dangerous release of the spirit world foreshadows the start of winter—and Imbolc on February 1—which celebrates the procreative power of the triple goddess and the renewal of spring. Just as the courtly and Christian Guenore presides over Arthur's Christmas feast, so may the hag Morgan be associated with Samhain and Bertilak's fresh young wife with Imbolc. Samhain itself is the date when Gawain leaves Arthur's court to enter a liminal wilderness and honor his pledge, and this beginning of the Celtic New Year is subsumed by the poet in making the pledge come due on the Christian New Year. The underlying myth is the union of male and female divinities to ensure the well-being of tribe and land. While we do not know that human sacrifice necessarily accompanied these festivals, it could well have been possible for the *Gawain* poet and his audiences both to make such associations and to leave them pointedly unsaid. The period between Christmas and New Year's Day telescopes, concentrates, and effectually erases this symbolic action which attacks Gawain—whether we choose to see him as solar hero or ladies' man—at his most vulnerable point.

Such a strategic displacement also demonstrates what one feminist analysis regards as the poem's "revisionist agenda" of marginalizing the dangerous female, which remains "uneasy and incomplete" because "if women were legally and politically marginalized within feudal society, they were nonetheless central, biologically, economically, and politically, to its continuation" (Fisher 129, 146). Women had been more clearly central to pre-Christian Britons, not only in literature but history, as figures like the Amazonian Cartimandua and Boudica demonstrate. Indeed, Boudica's nearly successful challenge to the Roman occupation was launched from the same region as Bertilak's castle, and could easily be interpreted as analogous to Morgan's challenge against the international power and renown of her Romano-Celtic half brother. Although *Sir Gawain and the Green Knight* is indeed about *Gawain*, there is reason in the text to think that Arthur himself may have been Morgan's preferred target, for he is the first to take up the Green Knight's proffered axe and nearly fulfills the year-king archetype himself. It is Morgan too who eventually ferries him to Avalon, as the *Gawain* poet's audience were surely aware. Like the triple goddess, her mood can be either destructive or benign, and at times in this seriously comic poem it seems both simultaneously. Morgan not only pulls strings, but they are often expressed sexually and attached to human puppets—even, one finds, to self-confident males like Gawain who think they have no strings attached. This dangerously powerful influence of the female motivates the actions of courtly knights despite the male forces that suppress and marginalize it to the castle of Hautdesert.

The intended sacrifice, displaced to the courtly paragon Gawain, is played by him in deadly earnest. Arthur's sister's son, a significant relationship in the often matrilineal Celtic line, is an appropriate substitute for the king. Thinking to avoid the return bout, he decapitates the Green Knight in the most lurid manner, with the medieval literary equivalent of a kung fu movie's sound effects. That the civilized knights and ladies of the Round Table are not too squeamish to cheer the gory stroke ironically shows how near their society, the ideal of the *Gawain* poet's audience, really is to the Druidical sacrificial "gamen" so deplored by the Latin historians. Against the court's expectation, the Knight displays the marvelous ability to survive this ritualistic death, just as pre–Christian Celtic religion apparently recognized no significant difference between life and afterlife, no end to the natural circle of being. A momentary discontinuity, or a scarcely recognizable crossing of tribal boundaries, and one is in the otherworld. And so Gawain is committed to his quest.

At the end of a year whose joys are movingly described, the appointed time of this reluctant year-king comes. He sets out amidst the public mourning of the court, as blithe on the surface as if he really is glad to accept the role, although we are unmistakably told that he doesn't expect to live past his assignation. The meaning of a human sacrifice follows an essentially circular pattern analogous to that of the quest. One hemisphere is that of the god-made-man, in which, according to Jean Markale, "the original act of sacrifice ... was a process of self-identification with the deity" (224). The other hemisphere is that of the hero-made-god, in which "the victim was a messenger for the community fulfilling the ritual" (Markale 125). Thus the sacrificial ritual of beheading, severing what the Celts regarded as the seat of the spirit and vital powers from the body, signifies a process of transcendental self-discovery.

Ross Arthur persuasively reads the device of the pentangle on Gawain's shield in this way; it signifies his semi-divine status, though protectively in terms of the Christian ethos which commands the fourteenth-century audience's sympathies. "The pentangle is best seen," he says, "as a sacramental badge, a visible indication of the inward spiritual grace granted to Gawain before his departure on the quest. It is also, because of its ambiguous meaning, an excellent focus for meditation on the relationship between the limited and fragile faith that may be our possession temporarily in this life and the endless truth in which we may participate in the life to come" (105). Outwardly signified by this sign for God and inwardly faced by the image of Mary, the Christian sign for the Goddess, Gawain wishes to break with the pre–Christian tradition of material sacrifice. From the pagan perspective, however, there is little difference between the corporeal and the spiritual, and thus great difference in attitude toward human sacrifice.

The complex signification of the pentangle and Mary's image, functioning as symbolic dimensions of his complex (but in this case, useless) physical armor, may indeed be preferable to the pagan triplicity of hunts, axe blow and anticipated death. Yet readers have often remarked how little mention is made of them once he arrives at Bertilak's castle. Perhaps that is because his testing may be understood to confirm which paradigm he ultimately will consent to—the pagan or the Christian—since both are ambiguously intertwined in the courtly. His tempting at the castle occurs only after he lays the shield and armor aside, and covers up with symbolic courtly discourse the low blows delivered by the very material desire sacred to a different Goddess. If surviving practices or at least memory of pre–Christian sacrificial rites were known to the *Gawain* poet and his audience, then they could not fail to make such a mental connection. In that case the poet need not mention it, but only create the narrative conditions that would elicit this awareness.

As for the Green Knight, Marie Borroff observes that he is presented "as, on the one hand, emanating from the real world, that is, the mutable and transitory world in which we live out our lives as human beings, and on the other hand, as representing an illusory view of that world" (120). Even in the final scene his alteration from monstrous to human shape is suggested only through his conversation. Our view of him becomes more realistic as he is "demystified" by assuming the role of boisterous, even manic host during the holiday season and strict but sympathetic judge in the closing scene. Our views of his wife and of courtly morals are correspondingly "demystified" by the gleeful anticipation at Hautdesert that Gawain will put on an edifying display of manners, by the exchange of winnings, and by the remarkable metonymy of the Lady's all-but-forthright seduction with the forthright venery of her husband's hunts.

Here again the subtext of pagan sacrifice operates ironically through its very erasure. The decorum of sacrificial victim would almost require him to accept the blandishments of Bertilak's wife and join her in the procreative ritual of the momentary death as a foreshadowing of the greater ritual to follow. As the one devoted to the Goddess, all things would be granted to him but the staying of the sacrifice itself. Yet Gawain, obtusely, resists and is ironically saved by his very obtuseness as better suited to Christian chivalry than to the pagan variety of self-sacrifice and sacred prostitution—the sort in which "surfet" or excess is not also a sin, the sort firmly yet wryly excluded by the *Gawain* poet's ethos. The tension between Gawain's superhuman exercise of self-restraint here and the comparatively uninhibited randiness he is known for in other romances adds to the rich ironies of a work in which he is more concerned with looking out for his own head than for the fairer sex, and in which the green girdle betokens how close he comes to losing it—in other words, of what mortals still owe to the old gods.

Even the animals hunted by Bertilak and laughingly awarded to

Gawain in exchange for his kisses have an iconographic pagan role. Stag and boar were sacred to the Celts, and their killing might well foreshadow the divine victim in a poem where nothing can be taken simply at face value. In Celtic religion, animals are regularly identified with male and female divinities, and such hunts typically relate to the eternal cycle of life and death embodied in the triple goddess. Lindow Man's triple death possibly indicates his successive ritual dedication to Taranis, Esus, and Teutates (Ross and Robins 97–99; Magilton 184). The three attempts on Gawain in the feminine precinct of the bedroom perhaps demonstrate that he is neither stag nor boar, but he does have a bit of fox in him. And both Morgan and Bertilak's wife seem to have a bit of the vixen.

Finally, the Green Chapel itself serves as reminder that different cultures have different temples. This chapel is green because it is in nature. The clearest reference in the poem to pre–Christian religion next to "Morgan the goddess," it possesses a suggestively feminine and fairy combination of mound and spring, and clearly recalls the tumuli, Druidical open-air sanctuaries, and votive shafts of Celtic religious practices. If nothing else in the poem confirms the pagan subtext of ritual sacrifice, the chapel and the grinding of the giant's axe do; as in a *Star Wars* movie, the hero has "a bad feeling about this." Yet here, too, the poet erases the pagan subtext with the Green Knight's surprising lenience, which indicates that the ancient forms are little more than another game created in envy of the courtly sort, and thus no longer revered even by the Goddess herself. It is apparently only Gawain who, while accepting this explanation from Bertilak, has really expected death and cannot "lighten up."

So while Gawain leaves Arthur's court bearing a shield, he returns wearing a girdle, a sign among other things of his guilty concession to materiality. Moreover, his "cowarddyse" relates to his inability to fully adopt either the pagan or the Christian sacrificial paradigm; and either way, his "covetyse" ambiguously undercuts his supposed perfection in both faith and conduct. As the sign of this "untrawth" or wavering, the girdle is generally taken to mean what Gawain claims it does: his sin or frailty of the flesh. He is too human, it seems, to be adequate as divine intermediary, moving between life and death as though they were the same element or "gamen," joyful game of being. If as R. A. Shoaf proposes, the green girdle which Gawain calls a "syngne of surfet" signifies also the plurality of signs and interpretative possibilities within the poem (153), then the exclusivity of any interpretation is uneasy and unstable. And so is the exclusivity of either Morgan's or Arthur's cultural ideology. That Camelot converts the baldric to a bright badge of honor suggests the court's peculiar idolatry, which translates its "surfet" of meanings, including its potential identity with mistletoe bough, into a form of self-congratulation. Their idolatry nevertheless sustains the unresolved tension between the old and the new paradigms in which the old, however redefined and erased, continually infiltrates and remains active within the new. Weaving the ritual of human sacrifice into Gawain's green girdle, we too may wear it as an unstable sign of shifting paradigms.

In this way the girdle and its reception suggest that Gawain and Camelot have humanly failed both old and new modes of sacrificial perfection. Again Ross Arthur comments, "If Gawain is to be seen as an example to the audience, part of the message is that all men, no matter how outstanding and no matter what special advantages they may be given, naturally put self-preservation and love of self higher than spiritual perfection" (134). Gawain preserves his head not because of perfect "trawth" to Christian God, Celtic goddess, or feudal lord or lady, but because an equivocal courtly code equips him with the means to fail and succeed simultaneously, and slip out of a tight spot with a little nick in place of an apotheosis.

Notes

1. For example, the chronological centering of events on religious holidays common to both Christian and pre–Christian calendars, the suggestive "chapel" setting of Gawain's final test, and the near-priestly way in which the unordained Green Knight, ministering for "Morgne þe goddess" (l. 2452) "confesses" and "absolves" Gawain, permitting him to retain a penitential token

2. There are numerous studies, not all of them in agreement about the proportion of word origins. See the summary on pages 238–9 in H.N. Duggan, "Meter, Stanza, Vocabulary, Dialect."

3. An alternative classical tradition in the lost epic poem *Cypria* and Euripedes's *Iphigeneia in Tauris* has her replaced on the altar by a deer and carried off by the goddess Artemis/Diana to be her priestess in the land of the Tauri, where she consecrates the victims for their practice of sacrificing all strangers who enter their country. Interestingly, the sacrificial victim in this alternative account, like Gawain in *Sir Gawain and the Green Knight*, is connected to the motif of a deer hunt: there is an implied parallel between Iphigeneia, Gawain, and the deer that is sacrificed or hunted. And in both versions of Iphigeneia's fate, the sacrifice is initiated to appease the goddess of the hunt to whom Morgan le Fay, whose court is located in the midst of the wilderness, could be loosely likened. Artemis/Diana, the woodland goddess of wild nature and protector of women, is the same whose cult at Arisia in Italy purportedly involved ritual combat for the golden bough, which is described in Vergil's *Aeneid* VI ll. 220–27 as like mistletoe in winter. The metaphorical matrix of venery, sexuality, and sacrificial death is also supported by well-known myths such as that of Actaeon (who is transformed into a deer and torn apart by her hounds) and Orion, both victims of Artemis/Diana, as well as the revenge of her sentinel Opis on the Trojan Arruns for the killing of her warrior handmaiden Camilla in the *Aeneid* XI ll. 856–958. Gawain's status as a virile "woman-killer" suggests why he, too, might become a welcome target.

4. These are written in the tradition of the Stoic philosopher Poseidonius, whose lost *Histories* described the Celts in its twenty-third book, and specify a variety of techniques for execution. Most are translated in John T. Koch and John Carey, *The Celtic Heroic Age*, 13–14 (Diodorus Siculus), 18 (Strabo), 22 (Julius Caesar), 25 (Pomponius Mela), 27 (Pliny), 28 (Tacitus). Quotations are also frequently retailed by modern studies of the Celtic world and of druidism in general.

5. An early, influential examination of Northern European bodies deposited and preserved in peat bogs, P. V. Glob's *The Bog People* (1969), concluded that many of these bodies likely attested to pan–European rituals of annual kingship.

6. Ross and Robins report that Norbury considered these local residents "the remnants of an ancient race," but admit that his lack of specifics constitutes no more than a "slender clue" (63).

7. Elliott proposes Ludchurch, a natural rift on the former lands of Dieulacres Abbey which was active in the Gawain poet's day, and two miles from Swythamley park, his candidate for the castle Hautdesert, "where the earls of Chester once owned a hunting lodge on an eminence recorded as Knight's Low ("on a lawe")" ("Landscape and Geography" 116–17). Responding to Elliot's original monograph, Kaske prefers the cave at Wetton Mill, nine miles away. The local scenery is also clearly reminiscent of the otherworldly cliffs described in *Pearl*. Elliot's conjecture currently predominates.

8. Bennett also speculates about possible locations for Hautdesert, as well as describing Richard II's visits to the area.

9. Boudica's campaign against Roman colonization was apparently motivated by maltreatment from the *procurator* (financial secretary) and other officers of the Roman governor C. Suetonius Paulinus. The death of Prasutagus, the Iceni king, left his succession in almost Lear-like disarray, with the Emperor and his two daughters (one of whom was Boudica) as co-heirs. When Boudica was flogged and her daughters raped, the Iceni revolted and soon were joined by the Trinovantes and other neighboring tribes. The Britons, led by Boudica, sacked and burned Colchester, St. Albans, and London before being destroyed by Suetonius' army.

10. See especially the *Aeneid* VI, ll. 156–67, 219–28, and Frazer (in *The New Golden Bough*) 674–77, 690–95. (Frazer is cited here in the abridged New American Library edition for its ease of reference.) Vergil, Pliny, and Frazer all associate the mistletoe with the oak tree, sacred to the Druids. Moreover, it symbolizes the solar fire and life force persisting through the winter solstice, and thus the soul or element of continuity in both nature and the individual human life.

11. Even the physical description of the Green Chapel bears some resemblance, especially when Kaske's or Elliott's conjectures about its location are granted, to the site of Turnus's death, between cliffs and a watery plain or marsh (see *Aeneid* XII ll. 806–7).

Works Cited

Arthur, Ross G. *Medieval Sign Theory and* Sir Gawain and the Green Knight. Toronto: U of Toronto P, 1987.

Bennett, Michael J. "The Historical Background." In *A Companion to the Gawain Poet*. 71–90.

Benson, Larry D. *Art and Tradition in* Sir Gawain and the Green Knight. New Brunswick, NJ: Rutgers UP, 1965.

Bloomfield, Morton W. "Sir Gawain and the Green Knight: An Appraisal." *Critical Studies of Sir Gawain and the Green Knight*. Ed. Donald R. Howard and Christian Zacher. Notre Dame: U of Notre Dame P, 1968. 24–55.

Bog Bodies: New Discoveries and New Perspectives. Ed. R. S. Turner and R. G. Scaife. London: British Museum Press, 1990.

Borroff, Marie. "Criticism of Style: The Narrator in the Challenge Episode." *Critical Studies of* Sir Gawain and the Green Knight. Ed. Donald R. Howard and Christian Zacher. Notre Dame: U of Notre Dame P, 1968. 125–43.

Briggs, C. S. "Did They Fall or Were They Pushed? Some Unresolved Questions about Bog Bodies." In *Bog Bodies.* 168–82.

Brewer, Derek, and Jonathan Gibson, eds. *A Companion to the Gawain Poet.* Cambridge: D. S. Brewer, 1997.

Coomaraswamy, Ananda K. "*Sir Gawain and The Green Knight*: Indra and Namuci." *Speculum* 19 (1944): 104–25.

Duggan, H. N. "Meter, Stanza, Vocabulary, Dialect." In *A Companion to the Gawain Poet.* 221–42.

Elliott, Ralph. "Landscape and Geography." In *A Companion to the Gawain Poet.* 105–18.

Elliott, R[alph]. W. V. *The Gawain Country.* Leeds Texts and Monographs N. S. 8. Gen. Ed. Stanley Ellis and Peter Meredith. Leeds: University of Leeds, 1984.

Fisher, Sheila. "Taken Men and Token Women in Sir Gawain and the Green Knight." In *Seeking the Woman in Late Medieval and Renaissance Writings: Essays in Feminist Contextual Criticism.* Eds. Sheila Fisher and Janet E. Halley. Knoxville: U of Tennessee P, 1989: 71–105.

Frazer, Sir James. *The New Golden Bough: A New Abridgement.* Ed. Theodor H. Gaster. New York: NAL, 1964.

Glob, P. V. *The Bog People.* London: Faber and Faber, 1969.

Green, Miranda J. *Dictionary of Celtic Myth and Legend.* London: Thames and Hudson, 1992.

Kaske, R. E. "Gawain's Green Chapel and the Cave at Wetton Mill." *Medieval Literature and Folklore Studies: Essays in Honor of Francis Lee Utley.* Ed. Jerome Mandel and Bruce H. Rosenberg. New Brunswick: Rutgers UP, 1970. 111–21.

Koch, John T., and John Carey. *The Celtic Heroic Age: Literary Sources for Ancient Celtic Europe and Early Ireland and Wales.* Second Ed. Andover, MA: Celtic Studies Publications, 1995.

Lewis, C. S. "The Anthropological Approach." *Critical Studies of* Sir Gawain and the Green Knight. Ed. Donald R. Howard and Christian Zacher. Notre Dame: U of Notre Dame P, 1968. 59–71.

Magilton, J. R. "Lindow Man: The Celtic Tradition and Beyond." In *Bog Bodies.* 183–87.

Mandel, Jerome and Bruce H. Rosenberg, eds. *Medieval Literature and Folklore Studies: Essays in Honor of Francis Lee Utley.* New Brunswick: Rutgers UP, 1970.

Markale, Jean. *The Celts: Uncovering the Mythic and Historic Origins of Western Culture.* Tr. C. Hauch. Rochester, VT: Inner Traditions, 1993. First ed. *Les Celts et la Civilisation Celtique.* Paris: Payot, 1976.

Ross, Anne, and Don Robins. *The Life and Death of a Druid Prince.* New York: Simon and Schuster, 1989.

Shoaf, R.A. "The 'Sygne of Surfet' and the Surfeit of Signs in *Sir Gawain and the Green Knight.*" *The Passing of Arthur: New Essays in Arthurian Tradition.* Ed. Christopher Baswell and William Sharpe. New York: Garland, 1988. 152–69.

Turner, R. C. "The Lindow Man Phenomenon: Ancient and Modern." In *Bog Bodies.* 188–204.

Vergil. *The Aeneid of Vergil: A Verse Translation by Rolfe Humphries.* Ed. Brian Wilkie. New York: Macmillan, 1987.

Treasonous Founders and Pious Seducers: Aeneas, Gawain, and Aporetic Romance

Nicholas Haydock

UNIVERSITY OF PUERTO RICO–MAYAGÜEZ

> The storm within your head, Aeneas, is known to me. Your journey is mine. And when the goddess Diana prophesied of Britain, he awoke and found the vision to be holy.
> —Peter Ackroyd, Milton in America

After protracted skirmishes spanning a period many times longer than the Trojan War itself, a clear consensus has emerged as to the identity of the treasonous "tulk" mentioned in line 3 of *Sir Gawain and the Green Knight*. That it was "Ennias the athel" who not only settled the West but who also—in one way or another—betrayed the East is now widely accepted by editors and scholars of the poem. The most succinct and incisive summary of the relationship between Gawain and Aeneas is Vantuono's note on lines 3–5 in his 1999 edition:

> The analogy between Gawain and Aeneas is twofold. Firstly, both failed in loyalty out of a desire for self-preservation. Gawain keeps the green girdle because he thinks it will save his life (1856–58). Aeneas, when the Trojan War was going badly, joined with Antenor in advising King Priam to negotiate for a settlement; when Priam accused them of disloyalty and plotted to have them murdered, they ran away. Secondly, both Gawain and Aeneas shielded a woman. Gawain promises Bertilak's wife that he will conceal the green girdle from her husband (1862–65). When, after the fall of

Troy, Hecuba reproached Aeneas for his betrayal and beseeched him to seize her daughter, he tried to conceal Polyxena from the Greeks, but Antenor betrayed him and her. Aeneas was then banished by the Greeks, and he became the leader of the Trojans after the defeat [149].

I would argue, however, that the consequences of this identification for our appreciation of the poem's complexities are still a vast and unsettled province of *Gawain* studies.[1] Alfred David's article (1968) on Gawain and Aeneas is a trenchant exposition of the syntactical and literary historical issues raised by the ambiguity of the lines but, like almost every critic before or after him, David backs away from drawing any but the most general parallels between the two. While he maintains that "the poet ... wants us to connect the Troy legend with the theme of the poem and to see in Aeneas a *figura* of his own hero" (404), he quickly retreats from the kind of reading such a connection would seem to demand, concluding that "the poet has (not) worked out a detailed analogy between Troy and Britain or Aeneas and Gawain. The correspondence is never made explicit, and after the opening stanzas Troy, Aeneas, and Brutus are forgotten until the very end" (407).

In a similar example of faint-hearted figuralism, Ad Putter notes the verbal echoes in *Patience* of the storm scene in Book 1 of *Aeneid* and then fails to trace how Jonah's *catabasis* into the belly of the whale and his later subduing of the aggressive inhabitants of Nineva parallels the journey of Aeneas in Vergil's poem (124–25). That the *Gawain* poet should wish to compare the translation of empires and religions in the *Aeneid* with Jonah's mission to bring the word of God to the Ninevites is not insignificant. For Putter, though, the verbal reminiscences of the *Aeneid* do not establish any intertextual complexities worth noting; they simply demonstrate familiarity with classical literature "which the *Gawain*-poet would have read in school" (124).

That even such meticulous readers as David and Putter should slight the importance of the *Gawain* poet's use of the *Aeneid* is perhaps a function of the poet's un-allusive style. As Putter himself notes, the *Gawain* poet tends to hide his learning: he seldom refers to specific sources, nor does he weigh the sometimes conflicting authority of earlier writers in the ways Chaucer is wont to do (4–17). His deployment of ancient sources is often figural rather than verbal, but these unflagged allusions are no less integral to the meanings of the poems for their being inexplicit. While the fact that the *Gawain* poet was influenced by Vergil's *Aeneid* has never seriously been doubted—at least not since Chapman's article of 1945—the consequences of his indebtedness for our understanding of *Sir Gawain and the*

Green Knight have never been systematically traced. Chapman enumerates a number of verbal parallels between the two poems, many of which to me seem tenuous or even fanciful. More than 30 years later, in a brief article, Sanderlin suggested a connection between Gawain's sparkling appearance in lines 864–68 and the godlike radiance bestowed upon Aeneas by his mother Venus before he is revealed to Dido in Book 1. Thus far the yield of verbal parallels is embarrassingly sparse, but if we are to attend to the question of the relationship of the two poems with anything like the care this question deserves, we must be prepared to explore the possibility of figural imitations as well as verbal echoes.

Figurae in *Sir Gawain* are intimately related to—indeed they descend directly from—the conventional myth-history of Western civilization which traces settlement and ethnogenesis from the splintering of peoples that purportedly occurred during the period of the Trojan diaspora. The careers of Aeneas, Romulus, Brutus, and Gawain are not accidentally parallel, nor are the similarities of the cycles of bliss and blunder in Troy and Camelot a matter of happenstance. Put simply—and in a way that applies as well to the *Aeneid*, itself—genealogy *is* destiny. Typological and figural readings of the *Aeneid* like those of Fulgentius and Bernardus Silvestris, which seem to modern audiences so contrived actually comprise richly textured admixtures of imposed and intrinsic allegory. Vergil's ancient readers understood that his poem included elaborate, structural parallels with Homer's *Iliad* and *Odyssey*, and that the meaning of Vergil's poem was to a great extent a feature of the variations within these repetitions.[2] Within the poem characters themselves think figurally; Aeneas is twice called a "second Paris" (in Carthage and in Latium). The last six books of the *Aeneid* comprise "Vergil's *Iliad*," a complex drama of rival typologies, as Aeneas and Turnus contend to play the role of Achilles and to turn their opponents into Hector (see Gransden). More crucially, commentators from Servius through our own contemporaries have realized that Aeneas at different times in the poem figurally embodies his later Roman descendents. When he dallies with Dido in Carthage, he is like Anthony with Cleopatra; when he sacrifices Turnus, he is like Augustus whose ruthless justice established the *pax Romanum*.

The combination of *in bono* and *in malo* figural parallels represented by Aeneas's similarities to Anthony and Augustus should remind us that in Parry's terms there are least "two voices" in Vergil's *Aeneid*: one which celebrates the creation of an empire and another that speaks poignantly to the costs of that process of ethnogenesis. Certainly one can and should distinguish between Vergilian and Ovidian Aeneases, or between the classical and the medieval Aeneas, but one should not hypostatize or rarify

Vergil's text in the process. Both Aeneases are present in Vergil's poem, although Vergil is, like the *Gawain* poet, at pains to temporize and justify his hero's flaws. Therefore Gerald Morgan is certainly wrong about the *Aeneid* and about *Sir Gawain* when he says:

> The fact of a medieval tradition associating Aeneas with the treachery of Troy cannot, of course, be denied. But over against it has to be set the Vergilian tradition in which Aeneas is celebrated for his public virtues as the founder of the Roman Empire. Which of the two traditions is relevant to the *Gawain*-poet? Both cannot be. The literary problem is to set the poem in one context that makes sense. There is no value in evoking a tradition that is at odds with the sympathies of the poem [1991, 43].

Deciding ahead of time that the poem can make only one, univocal kind of sense drawn from one, univocal source is about as far from the "sympathies of the poem" as one can get. Nevertheless, I share Morgan's frustration with the vagueness that characterizes most discussions of the aporetic identities of Gawain and Aeneas. If the parallel between these treasonous founders and pious seducers is crucial for our understanding of the poem, then we must establish a more extensive intertextuality between the two works than the lone, vague reference at the beginning of the poem. I can only begin to suggest here the outlines of such an analysis. I offer figural readings of details like the "holly bob" and a tree simile, as well as more crucial symbols such as Gawain's shield and the infamous girdle. From these figural echoes I move to *Sir Gawain*'s radical revision of the ending of the *Aeneid*, which manages to reconcile what Vergil himself could not, the contrary impulses toward justice and mercy.

Golden Bough and Holyn Bobbe

> *I reach to touch the next oak but draw back.*
> *Where I thought to touch hangs a head.*
> —Anne Eliot Crompton,
> *Gawain and the Lady Green*

The final elements spotlighted in the *Gawain* poet's lavish description of the Green Knight in Fitt 1 are two objects which he holds in either hand:[3]

> Bot in his on honde he hade a holyn bobbe,
> That is grattest in grene when greueȝ ar bare,
> And an ax in his other, a hoge and vnmete,
> A spetos in sparthe to expoun in spelle, quoso myȝt [206–9].

A number of critics have been struck by the stark juxtaposition of the sprig of holly and the terrible axe. Many have seen the pair as representing a choice that is open to Gawain between a peaceful gesture (i.e., striking the Green Knight with the holly bob or refusing to play his "gomen") and senseless violence (see Weiss; Arthur, 184; Clark and Wasserman, 6; Shoaf, 158; Blanch and Wasserman, 103–10; cf. Vantuono's ed., 164). The ambiguous image is also characteristic of a consistent strategy in the poem to represent the identities of its characters in aporetic terms. Is the Green Knight a guest or an invader, friend or foe, teacher or tempter, monster or man? Certainly there is something almost Grendel-like about his entrance to and exit from the hall. Yet however terrifying ("aghlich") and other-worldly, he also cuts the svelte and fashionable figure of a well-mannered lord. He is both insulting and courteous. Of course his identity is also double in a more obvious sense: as the Green Knight and as Lord Bertilak, as both guest and as host, he plays festive games that are both deadly and comic. Bertilak's lady is also doubly doubled: the perfect *femme fatale*, she is both *ami* and enemy, lover and killer. She also is doubled by the queerly apposite figure of Morgan le Fay, who means her nephew no harm yet arranges an elaborate scheme that puts his life in serious jeopardy. Most notably, Gawain himself at the end of the poem is both the pentangle knight and the knight of the girdle, both the paragon and violator of "trawþe." For Gawain and for the audience the trick seems to be to embrace contradictions or at least to survive in a world beset by troubling and destabilizing aporias.

The moral choice between good and evil or between peaceful amity and reckless violence which many readers have thought implied by the holly sprig and the axe is remarkably akin to the influential Servian interpretation of the golden bough as a representation of the Pythagorean *bivum*. For Servius and, *mutatis mutandis*, later commentators on Book 6 of the *Aeneid* such as Macrobius, Fulgentius and Bernardus Silvestris the golden branch is an image of the Pythagorean Y which represents education and the awakening of moral discretion in youth. As Christopher Baswell has pointed out, such interpretations of the golden bough play a consistent role in glosses of *Aeneid* 6. 136–37 found in manuscripts produced and circulated in medieval England (Baswell 67–68, *et passim*; see also Chance 222–24 and 478–80). Generally, the branch was thought to schematize and symbolize the fork in the road of one's life which occurs in adolescence where one chooses the path of virtue or vice.

The ultimate result of such a choice is confirmed in the road-plan of Hades where the road divides, one way leading to the blessed afterlife of Elysium and the other to the torments of Tartarus (6. 540–43). In Tartarus

Rhadamanthus and Tisiphone scourge tormented shades who are guilty of *dolos ... superbos* (arrogant deceits, 567–68) and who in their life on earth postponed atonement for their sins (569). The greatest number of these tortured souls are those

> quique ob adulterium caesi, quique arma secuti
> impia nec veriti dominorum fallere dextras,
> inclusi poenam expectant ne quaere doceri,
> quam poenam, aut quae forma viros fortunave mersit.
>
> (who were slain for the sin of adultery; or who followed the standard of treason, and feared not to break allegiance with their lords—all these immured await their doom) [6.612–615].

Priests, poets and artists populate Elysium but the first group to be mentioned as residing there is the troop of men who received wounds fighting for their country (*Hic manus ob patriam pugnando vulnera passi*, 660). The choices Gawain makes in the course of the poem and the results of his actions are decidedly more equivocal or aporetic than those of souls in Vergil's Hades. At the beginning of the poem, Gawain steps forward to protect Arthur and Camelot from the playful menace which the Green Knight's challenge represents. He is willing to sacrifice himself for his country and like the blessed warriors in Elysium he suffers a "wound" in their defense. He manages (just) to avoid adultery, but by his own admission is guilty of treason—although unlike the damned of Tartarus he does confess and make atonement for this sin. Gawain ends the poem still on earth, between heaven and hell and between the roles of patriotic redeemer and treasonous fraud.

The Green Knight enters Camelot as Aeneas enters hell, with a weapon in one hand and a branch in the other. In response to Charon's boisterous challenge, the Sybil assures him that the sword does not represent a threat and as proof of their peaceful intentions shows the ferryman the golden bough (see 6.400–410). The Green Knight also assures the beardless boys on the benches and their leader, the "sumquat childgered" Arthur, that he comes in peace and that the branch he carries is proof of his kind intentions:

> 3e may be syker bi this braunch that I bere here
> That I passe as in pes and no ple3t seche [265–66].

Arthur, however, is harder to mollify than Charon. He takes umbrage at the Green Knight's provocative offer of peace and insists that "Here fayle3 thou not to fy3t" (278). The Green Knight, though, holds to his purpose: both the year and the court are young, the season and the age of Arthur's knights more suited to a game than a battle. His reply that the benches of Arthur's hall are filled with "berdle3 chylder" (280) echoes the poet's earlier, more positive characterization of the court as a "fayre folk in her first age" (54) and his more equivocal portrayal of Arthur as "sumquat childgered" (86). The age of the court has provoked a great deal of critical comment. Defining the age precisely is difficult, but the emphasis is surely on the combination of innocence and recklessness in Arthur and his court. Phillipa Tristram saw the court as figure of Youth (28–34), and Mary Dove thought "first age" signified *first youthe*, the age that comes between childhood and maturity. Whichever precise age is meant, however, it is clear that Arthur and his court have reached—perhaps only just—the stage when moral choices must be made that will determine the path their lives will take. Hence, the tone of the poem as whole: we are presented with a dry run, a preseason scrimmage, a war game that mimes the same moral choices the court of Arthur will later be offered under live-fire conditions. As a two-fisted embodiment of the Pythagorean *bivum* the Green Knight represents just such a choice. Of course the choice itself is ambiguous, but Arthur's headlong acceptance of the Green Knight's challenge is ominous. Perhaps this is only a "gomen," but it is a game with fatal overtones, a game which admits, albeit improbably, the possibility of mutual destruction. The blow-for-a-blow game will be played in deadly earnest at "The Day of Destiny" when Mordred willingly pulls Arthur's spear through his own body in order to kill the king.[4]

Perhaps in the opening fitt, as in the third, Gawain could have chosen not to accept the gift which is offered. Both gifts, axe and girdle, seem to hold power over life and death, yet both are curiously impotent in performing their supposed function. The girdle clearly is not a talisman which allows one to cheat death. But what about the "holyn bobbe"? In the *Aeneid* the golden bough makes it possible for Aeneas to descend to Hades and to return alive to the world above. When Aeneas first sights it gleaming in the dark forest the bough is compared to mistletoe: "quale solet silvis brumali frigore viscum / fronde virere nova" (just as in forests the mistletoe is wont in the dead of winter to grow green with new leaves, 205–6). The holly bob too has this strange property of flourishing in the midst of a dead forest: "that is grattest in grene when greue3 ar bare" (207). The similarity between the two is intriguing. Conventionally, someone entering a foreign court would carry an olive branch, not a sprig of holly, as a sign of peace. The Green Knight's choice is certainly in keeping with the Christmas season, but he has to tell the court that the holly bob signifies peaceful intentions, presumably because the significance is not conventional. Much later the Green Knight will explain his supernatural resistance to death as an enchantment performed by "Morgan the goddes," a witch famed for prophecy. Wherein does this enchantment lie? Perhaps the sprig of holly, like the golden bough which the Sibyl makes Aeneas take on his journey, is a talisman that allows the Green Knight to survive death. If this is so, then Gawain certainly chooses wrongly when he takes the axe instead of the branch.

Trees and Men

> Vergil informs us that a race of men came from the trunks of trees.
> —Peter Ackroyd, Milton in America

In both the Aeneid and Sir Gawain the headlong career of individuals and empires is punctuated by moments of awe-inspiring stillness. The dilations in Sir Gawain provoke both suspense and wry frustration; we pause to experience our own emotional investment in the narrative as well as to appreciate the author's manipulation of our emotions. Such suspensions of activity often mark crises of indecision or hesitation within the characters themselves. The Green Knight's arrival in Camelot produces such a pause: "Ther watz lokyng on lenthe the lude to beholde" (232).[5] His challenge provokes another: "And al stouned at his steuen and stonstil seten / In a swoghe sylence thurgh the sale riche; / As al were slypped vpon slepe so slaked hor lotez" (242–44). The poet's breathless, droll aside, "What thenne?" (462), after the Green Knight rides out of Camelot, marks another pause pregnant with excitement, mystery, and humor. Such pauses entail miraculous survivals that trouble identity even as they preserve life. In the fourth fitt, at the center of the return match of the Beheading Game, such a still point is reached when Gawain, having flinched at the first feint, stands firm in response to the second:

> Gawayn graythely hit bydez, and glent wyth no membre,
> Bot stode stylle as the stone, other a stubbe auther
> That ratheled is in roché grounde with rotez a hundreth [2292–94].

The compound simile is unusually elaborate for the Gawain poet. The comparison drawn between Gawain's wholehearted, unflinching courage ("now thou hatz thi hert holle," 2296) and the unmoved stone and tree appears rocksolid, but the image is also anchored in the poem by a complex tangle of connections. The vehicles of stone and tree seem less alternatives in a compound comparison than a progressive elaboration where the simple "ston" gives way to the more fully developed simile of the stump with roots that clutch the stone-studded earth. In this echo chamber of a poem images reverberate. One can trace correspondences with the resounding cave ("in a hard roche," 2199) where the Green Knight sharpens his axe. Gawain's perception of this sound is described via another simile ("As one vpon a gryndelston hade grounden a sythe," 2202), implicitly connecting the Green Knight's coming stroke with the Grim Reaper's deadly harvest and his iconic scythe. Such reverberations make for a complex piece of music, filled with counterpoint. Is the fate of Gawain's rock-solid resolve to be like the grindstone that the axe grazes but does not destroy, or like the stump that stands firm but headless? Also, how does Gawain's bravery at this point compare with the timid courtiers who "stonstil seten" (242) in response to the Green Knight's initial challenge in Camelot? Just as their apparent cowardice may be alloyed with self-control ("I deme it not al for doute / Bot sum for cortaysye," 246–47), it is difficult to discern to what extent Gawain's seemingly staunch immobility is alloyed with sheer, bloodcurdling fear. While the simile seems to add retrospective significance to earlier details, it also functions as a grisly—albeit misleading—hysteron proteron. Its sources in the *Aeneid* (discussed below) depict living trees resisting (or failing to resist) an assault, while the tree in *Sir Gawain* is already a stump ("stubbe"). The change tends to undercut Gawain's heroic resolution with a macabre joke at his expense: he is not yet like a stump, but he soon may resemble one. The compound simile which places stone and stump in a pair forms an eldritch silhouette of a dead hero, an image of Gawain's head lying at his feet. After all, stones and stumps are neither courageous nor resolute; their fixedness is not an act of will but a condition of their (non)existence. Their stillness is characteristic of inanimate things, and it is that kinship with a dead and unregenerate natural world that the simile implies. Like Eliot's "son of man," neither Gawain nor the audience can know:

> What are the roots that clutch, what branches grow
> Out of this stony rubbish? Son of man,
> You cannot say or guess, for you know only
> A heap of broken images, where the sun beats,
> And the dead tree gives no shelter, the cricket no relief,
> And the dry stone no sound of water.

The *Gawain* simile's two sources in the *Aeneid* provide patterns of imagery that link this gravid pause in the Beheading Game with the fall of cities and the dangers of women. While the fates of the trees in the *Aeneid* similes are diametrically opposed, one falls and the other survives, both similes mark instances of miraculous escape by Aeneas from forces which threaten his life and mission. Interestingly, both escapes, from Troy and from Dido, will provoke the charges of cowardice and treason hurled at Aeneas later in the Middle Ages. In Book 2, Venus removes the cloud of mortal things from his eyes so that he can see through his fear and rage to the reality of what is happening. The gods are taking the ancient city apart and the towering citadel crashes down in flames.

> Tum vero omne mihi visum considere in ignis
> Ilium et ex imo verti Neptunia Troia;
> Ac veluti summis antiquam in montibus ornum
> Cum ferro accisam crebrisque bipennibus instant
> Euere agricolae certatim, illa usque minatur
> Et tremefacta comam concusso vertice nutat,
> Vulneribus donec paulatim evicta supremum
> Congemuit traxitque iugis avulsa ruinam
> Descendo ac ducente deo flammam inter et hostis
> Expedior, dant tela locum flammaeque recedunt [2.624–34].

(Then, truly, all Ilium seemed to me to sink down into the flames and Neptune's Troy to be toppled from its base. It was just as when farmers contend with each other to bring down an ancient ash tree in the mountains, hacked repeatedly with sword and with many blows from the two-headed axe, it leans, threatening to fall at any moment, and nods with trembling leaf and shaking crown, until little by little, overcome by its wounds at last, it makes a loud grown, and torn from the hillsides, falls in ruin. A god leads me. I descend and am pulled safely through flames and foes. Weapons give way and the flames retreat.)

Ostensibly this simile equates the gods' destruction of Troy with the *agricolae* (farmers) who batter the ancient ash. It foregrounds the irresistible will of the gods which serves to render the city helpless. What had seemed a human conflict of indeterminate outcome is revealed as a *fait accompli*: Juno, the sworn enemy of Troy and Venus, holds open the Scaean Gates and directs the invading force (2. 612–614). Note how the metaphors of the *Aeneid* simile personify the falling tree (*comam*, head; *vertice*, top of the head, crown; *vulneribus*, wounds; *minatur*, to lean over, bend; *nutat*, to nod or waver; *congemuit*, to yell). Metaphors personify the tree while the simile explicitly connects the tree with Troy. The complexity of reference is not capricious: the city is falling, and Aeneas as an individual is also in great danger at this point. In fact, like the tree, he is being battered by his enemies and vacillates between the impulses toward fight and flight, putting in jeopardy not only his own life but also that of the new city it is his destiny to establish. More immediately, the personification of the tree connects its fall with the decapitation of Priam whose headless and nameless trunk now lies abandoned on the sands ("*iacet ingens truncus / avulsumque umeris caput et sine nomine corpus,*" 2. 557–58).

In the scene at the Green Chapel further implications are grafted onto Vergil's already complex image. Like the tree in the *Aeneid*, Gawain has quivered in response to the Green Knight's first (feigned) blow. The stump of the *Gawain* simile implies that Gawain, like Priam, may be rewarded for his courage with an ignominious defeat; he too could well end up a headless, nameless trunk. Like Aeneas, Gawain must somehow find his way past this mortal danger to the city that awaits him. Most compellingly, Gawain's situation draws a similar parallel between the fates of the hero, the king, and his city. As the axe hovers poised above Gawain's head, its duplicate hangs ominously above the dais back in Camelot. The axe in Camelot, perhaps a type of Damocles' sword, symbolizes the precariousness of Arthur's rule, a significance retrospectively precipitated by our knowledge that, but for the graceful courage of Gawain, Arthur's neck would now be beneath the Green Knight's blade.

Roger Hornsby's (1970) systematic exploration of Vergil's similes in the *Aeneid* emphasizes the profound ways in which similes interact across the surface of the narrative to point out contrasts and to express development symbolically. Such an interaction is clearly at work in the tree similes of Books 2 and 4. As Hornsby notes, the movement for Aeneas is from acceptance to stoic resistance: "passivity has become patient endurance" (26). Dido's pleas, carried to Aeneas by her sister, Anna, shake him but do not topple his resolve:

> Talibus orabat, talisque miserrima fletus
> fertque refertque soror. Sed nullis ille movetur
> fletibus, aut voces ullas tractabilis audit;
> fata obstant placidasque viri deus obstruit auris.
> Ac velut annoso validam cum robore quercum
> Alpini Boreae nunc hinc nunc flatibus illinc
> eruere inter se certant; it stridor, et altae
> consternunt terram concusso stipite frondes;
> ipsa haeret scopulis et quantum vertice ad auras
> aetherias, tantum radice in Tartara tendit:
> haud secus adsiduis hinc atque hinc vocibus heros
> tunditur, et magno persentit pectore curas;
> mens immota manet, lacrimae volvuntur inanes [4. 437–49].

> (She [Dido] pleaded for these things, and her sister carried her pleas back and forth. But Aeneas is not moved by tears, nor does a yielding man hear her words. The fates stand against it, and a god plugs the man's sympathetic ears. Just as when the Alpine

winds, blowing now here and now there, strive among themselves to uproot an oak tree staunch with the strength of many years; a cracking sound issues forth, and from the battered tree the highest leaves thickly strew the ground, the oak clings to the rock and just as far as its head stretches into the windy heavens, just so far does its root stretch down into the underworld: even so the hero is battered on both sides by incessant arguments, in his mighty heart he suffers these agonies; his mind remains unmoved, tears are useless.)

I have cited the two *Aeneid* similes in their entirety because I believe the *Gawain* simile draws from both and participates in a complex interaction with them.

Superficially the *Gawain* simile has more affinities with the passage just quoted: Gawain stands firm like a tree anchored by its roots to the stony ground ("That ratheled is in roché grounde with rotez a hundreth," 2294). The attack does not destroy him, but it does damage him. In the *Aeneid* simile the storm causes leaves to fall from the tree, a detail which symbolically figures the tears which fall (presumably) from Aeneas (*lacrimae volvuntur inanes*, 4.449). In *Sir Gawain* it is drops of blood, not tears, which fall to the ground, but in both images there is a poignant sense of suffering experienced and withstood. Yet the tenor of the similes in *Gawain* and in *Aeneid* 4 are hardly apposite; in *Sir Gawain* the hero's resolution demonstrates physical courage, and in the *Aeneid* Aeneas holds fast to his mission despite the pleas and charms of a woman. Still, once the real nature of Gawain's test has been revealed and we learn that this has in fact been a test of chastity and "trawþe" rather than courage, the parallels between the two poems shift in our perception like a figure/ground diagram. Gawain's ability to resist the enticements of Lady Bertilak—his chastity, not his courage—is the real issue here. That he manages while lying in bed to withstand the Lady's charms is what leaves him still standing at the end. However, the *Gawain* simile's "stubbe" implies not only, as suggested above, a grisly beheading joke, but also the severely truncated nature of Gawain's act of courage. In keeping the girdle as a talisman against harm, Gawain has diminished himself even before he arrives at the Green Chapel. Like the stump, Gawain has already been toppled before the axe falls. The simile in *Sir Gawain* situates its image between the fallen tree of *Aeneid* 2 and the resistant tree of *Aeneid* 4. The interactions of the *Gawain* simile with its sources in the *Aeneid* combine to symbolize Gawain's mixed, aporetic success in the poem; he stands an already fallen hero.

The tree simile in *Aeneid* 4 played a significant role in Stoic discussions of virtue and human emotions like fear. Augustine's synthesis of philosophical ideals of resistance to the passions in *The City of God* (Book

9, Chapter 4) cites the line "*mens immota manet, lacrimae volvuntur inanes*" as proof of Aeneas's virtue:

> Both schools (Stoic and Peripatetic) certainly maintain that if they were urged to any disgraceful or criminal act by a threatened danger to these "goods" or "advantages" as the only way to ensure their retention, *they would prefer to lose all that guarantees the life and health of the physical body rather than commit any violation of justice.* Thus the mind in which this principle is fixed does not allow any of those disturbances to prevail in it against reason, even though they may occur in the lower parts of the soul. On the contrary, the mind exercises dominion over them. Far from consenting to them, it resists, and by that resistance establishes the reign of virtue. Vergil describes Aeneas as such a man when he says: "Unmoved his mind: the tears roll down in vain" [348, emphasis added].

While a great deal has been written on the precise nature of Gawain's fault, one could do worse than to gloss Gawain's withholding of the girdle in the terms Augustine outlines here. Gawain commits a "disgraceful or criminal act" in order to keep a "good or advantage" that he supposes will "guarantee the life and health of the physical body." Thus while he seems a paragon of stoic virtue and, like Aeneas, to have mastered his fears at the Green Chapel—his head remains still—his mind has already been turned by the ploy of the magic girdle. In Augustine's synthesis of ancient theories of emotion, fear is natural. Its presence in, for instance, a Stoic philosopher whose ship is threatened by a storm (Augustine here recounts a story from Aulus Gellius's *Attic Nights*)—or, for that matter, in a knight who quivers beneath the axe of a supernatural foe—is no argument against their virtue. Virtue *is* compromised, though, when one gives in to one's fears and commits an unjust act to retain a worldly advantage that will ensure or prolong one's life. Gawain's retention of the girdle is just such an act. He manages to hold his head still beneath the axe and, against all odds, to keep his head when lesser men would be losing theirs, yet in his battle of wits and wills with the lady it is she who manages "his mode for to remwe" (1475).

I want to append here a few more general and speculative remarks about the influence of Vergil's similes on the structure of *Sir Gawain and the Green Knight*. The third fitt is perhaps the most intricately organized episode in all of Middle English literature. Certainly one can find analogues for the alternation of hunting and bedroom scenes in the interlace structure of French romance as well as in the appositive style of the English alliterative tradition. While both traditions must certainly have affected the *Gawain* poet's invention, the structure of the third fitt for me resembles nothing so much as an epic simile. Similes manufacture unexpected affinities between disparate worlds. The vehicles of Vergil's similes in particular often assert a kind of proleptic influence on events in the narrative. Ostensibly, the famous simile in Book 4.69–73 which compares Dido to a hind accidentally wounded by a shepherd (*pastor ... nescius*) points to Aeneas's ignorance of the effect he has had on her. But there is also a grim excess significance (*letalis ... harundo*, deadly shaft) that anticipates Dido's tragic death. Of course this simile also represents an important *locus classicus* that helped to establish what would become a conventional association in medieval literature between hunting and loving, Venus and venery—a tradition so beautifully traced in Marcelle Thiébaux's now classic study *The Stag of Love: The Chase in Medieval Literature*.

Another of Aeneas' foes, the indomitable and impious Mezentius is compared to a boar:

> Just as a boar that, for long years, found shelter
> within Mount Vesulus' pine forests or
> among the marshlands of Laurentum, where
> he pastured on rich reeds, when driven down
> from his high hills by gnashing dogs and caught
> by rings of netting, halts and fiercely roars
> and bristles up his shoulders; not one hunter
> has heart enough to show his anger or
> move in against him; but far off and safe
> they hound and harry him with shafts and shouts:
> then, even so, no one, however just
> his indignation, dares to meet Mezentius
> with drawn sword; they provoke him from a distance
> with missiles and loud shouts. He hesitates
> from side to side; but unafraid, gnashing
> his teeth, he shakes their lances from his shield [10. 707–19,
>   trans. Mandelbaum].

While the *Gawain* poet's description of the boar hunt is richly and realistically detailed, many of these details are notably close to the *Aeneid* simile. Both boars are old beasts (*multos ... annos*, 10. 708; "that wi3t fol olde," 1440). Both poems emphasize that the boar's fierceness keeps men and dogs at bay, they shout at the boar and shoot at him from afar, but to no avail (compare *Aeneid*. 10. 711–18 and *Gawain* 1454–63). Like a boar Mezentius shakes spears from the "hide" of his shield (*tergo decutit hastas*, 10.718), and like a man protected by a shield the boar's hide in *Sir Gawain* is impenetrable ("Bot the poynte3 payred at the pyth, that py3t in his schelde3," 1456). Finally, both boars (the one in *Sir Gawain* and Mezentius himself in the *Aeneid*) are impervious to the hoards of lesser men that harry them from a safe distance, though they are finally killed, after a break in the narrative, by a leader who steps forward to engage them one on one at close quarters (*Aeneid* 873–908 and *Gawain* 1581–96).

The *locus classicus* for the theme of the love chase itself is the scene in *Aeneid* 4 where Aeneas and Dido are driven by a storm from their hunting party and into a cave where they have sex—an interlude apparently orchestrated (as is that in *Sir Gawain*) by a goddess. Structurally, the hunting scene interrupted by lovemaking in the *Aeneid* provides a fascinating parallel—if it is not a source—of the *Gawain* poet's more subtle and extensive exploration of this compound theme. In the deer simile discussed above Dido certainly takes on the role of prey, hunted by the gods and driven in panic by her own emotions. But in the battle of wills between the two lovers it is also suggested that Aeneas may fall prey to Dido. His first glimpse of her in Book 1 compares her to Diana whom Aeneas watches Acteon-like from his hiding place (494–504). Later in Book 4, as he prepares to leave, Dido in her frenzy contemplates all manner of Bacchic carnage on Aeneas, his son Ascanius, and the whole Trojan fleet. The reverberations of this theme throughout the *Aeneid* are acutely summarized by Marcelle Thiébaux:

> Dido is now both huntress, and figuratively, smitten prey. The love of Dido and Aeneas, of which she is the victim, serves to effect Aeneas' development from a heedless sensual delectation to his stinging self-examination and a renewed sense of duty. He knows Dido's love for a time, and survives it. The love chase in which these two are temporarily caught up is part of the epic's larger hunt. Aeneas, a hunter of his own destiny, a hunter after Rome and the hunter of Turnus, is himself a man whom Juno and the fates toss and harry (*jactant, impellunt, agunt*) [95].

A similar aporetic figuralism has also been noticed by many writers on *Sir Gawain* (see, for instance, Burnley, Green, and Morgan [1987]). Gawain too knows the Lady's "love for awhile and survives it," albeit in a more chaste fashion. She like her lord in the forest is clearly hunting in the bedroom, but as in the *Aeneid* the theme of the hunt has multiple and complex applications. Despite the extended interlude at Hautdesert, Gawain spends the majority of the poem hunting the Green Knight, although he pursues him through the forests of Wirral only to yield himself up as defenseless prey. And while most readers draw connections between Gawain in the bedroom and the three animals in the forest, the Lady's behavior on successive days also appears to mirror the stag's lurking meekness, the boar's dauntless, frontal assault, and the fox's use of deception. She too, we must remember, is at her lord's mercy, driven by him to do what she does with apparent reluctance. After all, although such speculation is perhaps idle, what might the Lady's fate have been if she had succeeded in seducing Gawain?

Epic similes provide us with intellectual challenges. Their abundant detail forces readers to negotiate intricate patterns of dissimilar similitudes. The structure of *Gawain* as a whole demands precisely this sort of attention from its readers. In many ways the third fitt with its envelop pattern of hunting/temptation/hunting scenes resembles the structure of such similes. The hunting episodes, like a simile's tenor, are interrupted by the eerily apposite scenes in the bedroom which take up the position of a simile's vehicle, and then we pick up the action in the forest just where we left it. But we are left to draw our own parallels and conclusions from the juxtaposition. How are Gawain or the Lady like beasts of prey or like hunters; and how is flirtatious conversation like a hunt? And what of the apparent excess information provided by the slaughter of the beasts? Does it presage Gawain's death, as the fatal shaft fixed in the flank of the deer in *Aeneid* 4 presages the death of Dido? The genius of the structure is that it allows Gawain to control the extent to which he resembles the slaughtered beasts. Only Gawain's resolute insistence on his identity and his mission prevent him from falling prey to Bertilak's advanced hunting strategies of misdirection and ambush. Gawain avoids repeating the pattern of chase, death, and mutilation; he resists the regressive pull of deadly implication provided by simile patterns of the third fitt.

What is true of the microcosmic structure of the daily hunts is also true of the macrocosmic ring structure of the poem as a whole. Readers cannot but puzzle over the dissimilar similarities between the two Christmas games, between the guest in Camelot and the host in Hautdesert, and finally between the flourishing civilization in Camelot and the references to the destruction of Troy which frame the entire poem. To read *Sir Gawain* is to pass through a series of concentric rings, each one mirroring and enclosing its predecessor, like the annual rings which mark the growth of a tree. We read like an axe blade, exposing the intricate design of this tough, beautiful poem as we hack our way through, back to the fall of Troy where we began.

Shields and Belts

Dolus an virtus, quis in hoste requirat?
—*Aeneid* 2.390

One definition of the word "knot" in Middle English is 'the meaning or gist of a story" (see, for instance, Chaucer's "Squire's Tale" V, 401-8). Few readers would disagree that the two knots of *Sir Gawain*, the pentangle depicted on Gawain's shield and the "gordel" or "belt" which he knots around his body, are integral to the meaning of the poem. The narrative transitions from the iconic pentangle, a multifaceted sign of perfection and "trawþe," with its elaborate, fixed denotations to the multifarious girdle, a "token of untrawthe," whose connotations are unstable, protean, aporetic. It is surprising, then, that no critic has pointed to an analogous interaction of shield and belt in the second half of the *Aeneid*. Superficially, the shields and belts of the two poems are not very much alike, yet their narrative function, their significance, and the role they play in defining the hero's identity are remarkably similar.

In Book 8 of the *Aeneid* Venus, seeking to protect Aeneas against harm in the coming conflict, makes Vulcan construct divine armor for her son. In a long *ekphrasis* (8.608–731) Vergil describes tableaux of Roman history proleptically displayed on the shield. The history of the city of Rome from Romulus and Remus to Augustus Caesar is portrayed there as a kind of promise to Aeneas of the civilization he will found but not live to see. If we wish to give sufficient critical attention to the parallels between the shield in *Sir Gawain* and the one in the *Aeneid*, we must recognize that imitation may be based on figural readings of a source text as well as on verbal echoes or specific details. Definite parallels between the two shields are few, although the schematic depiction of Gawain's shield as an "endeles knot" (630) of interlocking gold lines does bear a superficial resemblance to the "*clipei non enarrabile textum*" (the indescribable texture of the shield, 8.625) of Aeneas. Servius thought the phrase referred to the interweaving of the pictorial images on the shield (quoted in Williams, volume 2, 267), a reading perhaps encouraged by the fact that Vulcan separates the panels on the shield by the representation of a golden ocean: "*haec inter tumidi late maris ibat imago aurea*" (the golden image of the surging sea flowed between these [pictures] throughout, 8.671–72). The analogy between the *Gawain* poet's "endeles knot" and the *textum* of scenes which signify Rome's *imperium sine fine*, bordered and interwoven by the golden sea, may be no more than an accidental resemblance, but that both shields represent a coherent pattern of interdependent virtues is most probably not an accident.

The allegorical reading of the *Aeneid* as the journey of an Everyman through hardship and error to wisdom is a definitive strain in Vergil commentaries from late antique scholars such as Servius and Macrobius, through the more exclusively allegorical commentaries of Fulgentius (sixth century) and Bernardus Silvestris (twelfth century), down to early modern theorists like Petrarch, Boccaccio, Christoforo Landino, and Edmund Spenser. The *Expositio Vergilianae Continentia* of Fulgentius marks the first thoroughgoing attempt to reduce Vergil's narrative to an ethical system—a mode of understanding that was to have an enormous influence on the reading of Vergil for more than a millennium. Fulgentius's gloss on the armor of Aeneas ignores the historical tableaux of the *ekphrasis* and concentrates instead on the shield's ethical content:

> Then he (Aeneas) puts on the armor of Vulcan (VIII. 621ff.); that is, the protection of the alert intelligence against all the temptations of evil. Vulcan is *bulencauton* (*boule* + *kautes*), or, as we say, "ardent wisdom." All the virtues of the Romans are displayed on this armor because all happiness is either provided by or foreseen through the careful protection of wisdom. To act well is the harbinger of future good, and he who acts well insures good for himself. Thus wisdom both produces good things and can look forward to them [trans. Hardison, in *Classical and Medieval Literary Criticism*, 340].

Fulgentius's characterization of the shield as a *summa* of Roman virtues is hardly far-fetched; many modern scholars interpret the scenes in analogous ways. R. D. Williams, for instance, sees in the shield "the presentation of Roman virtues, of *exempla* of the Roman character" and goes on to equate particular scenes with specific Roman virtues like *fides, libertas, fortitudo*, and *pietas* (vol. 2, 265).

Obviously, the virtues represented on Gawain's shield bear only incidental resemblance to those purportedly depicted in the *Aeneid*; the two shields represent *summae* that schematize two different—albeit contiguous—moral universes. The schema of virtues in *Gawain* embodied in the five senses, the five fingers, the five wounds of Christ, the five joys of Mary and the final pentad of "fraunchyse," "fela3schyp," "clannes," "cortaysye," and "pité" is drawn from a wealth of Biblical and medieval sources (for an overview of critical opinion, see Vantuono, 178–85). Yet, taken in its entirety as a symbol functioning within the narrative, there is a profound analogy between what Ross G. Arthur (1987, 45–46) calls "The Shield of Truth" and the shield of "*pius Aeneas*." Both represent a pattern of virtues by which one opposes, in Fulgentian terms, "all the temptations of evil." Fulgentius's allegorization of the shield description in the *Aeneid* helps us to superimpose the function of the two shields in their respective narratives in other ways as well. His fanciful etymology of Vulcan as *boulekauton* or "ardent wisdom" aligns the creator of this *textum* with the proverbial wisdom of Solomon who established the pentangle as the sign of "trawþe." More importantly, Fulgentius's allegorization of Vulcan's shield confines its significance to a single lifespan: "To act well is the harbinger of future good, and he who acts well insures good for himself." Just such a moral equation between actions and consequences is in fact what *Sir Gawain* so precisely and deliberately establishes. The *Gawain* poet does not imitate his source in the *Aeneid* so much as he makes an ethical translation of its contents from ancient to Christian culture, a *translatio virtutum*.

But the influence of spiritual readings of the armor of Aeneas on the *Gawain* poet's refashioning of his hero's shield could also be more direct and precise. In two important articles Phillip F. O'Mara (1992a and 1992b) has emphasized the influence of Robert Holcot's scriptural exegeses on the *Gawain* poet's numerological poetics. Holcot's work "On Twelve Prophets" (Bodleian Library MS. Bodl. 722, fol. 199r) analyzes the armor of Aeneas in terms of its five component raw materials (gold, silver, brass, iron, and wood), and then goes on to suggest how these five materials can be understood to signify other fives, such as the five physical senses or the five wounds of Christ.

> Et iste Eneas fingi potest habuisse arma aurea, argentea, enea, ferrea, et lingnea. Nota quod applicari possunt ad custodiam quinque sensum et ad quinque vulnera Cristi [quoted in Allen 92].

Holcot provides a schema for understanding Aeneas's armor allegorically, which the poet seems to have adopted in fashioning the fivefold significances of Gawain's shield. Both of Holcot's suggested *significationes* (the five senses and the five wounds of Christ) are taken on board, and the pattern of symbolic fives is completed by the addition of the five joys of Mary, the rather inapposite five fingers, and the five virtues. The *Gawain* poet uses Holcot's suggestions about reading the armor of Aeneas allegorically as a template for an imitation of the *Aeneid* which is modeled on a spiritual, not literal, understanding of it.

The shields of Aeneas and Gawain have only a minor role in the fortunes of their owners, yet in both poems belts play a much more integral role in determining the fate of their wearers. The belt is loaded with multiple and sliding significance in both narratives: it serves as sign of recognition and reversal—and also as a focal point for an ambivalent exploration of the themes of identity, guilt and justice. Indeed, that the parallels between the endings of both poems should have escaped attention by critics is surprising. In each poem an adversary (Aeneas and the Green Knight, respectively) pauses, standing over his defenseless victim, delaying the final, fatal blow. But when the adversary does strike, it is because of a belt that the victim wears. For the adversary, the belt in both poems is a sign of guilt; it signifies a crime which merits a just, even judicial punishment. Both poems emphasize that while the belt was taken from another, it belongs to the adversary, and the victim's possession of it is evidence of the breaking of an oath. Mythically speaking, the belt-wearer represents a sacrificial victim whose sacrifice marks the beginning of a new age, a new dispensation. Yet both poems also use their climactic scene to pose ultimately aporetic questions about justice and mercy, about the virtue of their heroes, and about the worthiness of the societies they represent.

In Book 10 of the *Aeneid*, Turnus strips from the dead body of Pallas a sword-belt decorated with an infamous *nefas*.

> ... et laevo pressit pede talia fatus
> exanimam rapiens immania pondera baltei
> impressumque nefas: una sub nocte iugali
> caesa manus iuvenum foede thalamique cruenti,
> quae Clonus Eurytides multo caelaverat auro;
> quo nunc Turnus ovat spolio gaudetque potius.
> nescia mens hominum fati sortisque futurae
> et servare modum rebus sublata secundis!
> Turno tempus erit magno cum optaverit emptum
> intactum Pallanta, et cum spolia ista diemque
> oderit [10.495–505].

(Having said these things, he stepped on the corpse with his left foot, tearing away the terrible weight of a belt on which an impious deed was embossed: a slaughter, carved in relief by Clonus, son of Eurytus, in thick gold, on a single wedding night a band of young men shamefully slaughtered and bloody bridal beds; now Turnus exalts and rejoices all the more in these spoils. Oh, how ignorant are men's minds of fate and fortunes to come, or how to stay within bounds when lifted up by success! For the great Turnus a time will come when he will wish to purchase Pallas untouched, when he will detest this day and these spoils.)

The necessity of maintaining the element of surprise in *Sir Gawain* prevents the poet from engaging in such clear foreshadowing, but in retrospect the Lady's insistence about the special properties of the girdle, "the costes that knit ar therinne" (1849), has much the same resonance. She assures Gawain that he would "prayse it at more prys" (1850) if he understood these "costes" (magical properties, but also costs, penalties)—a significance (again in retrospect) analogous to the price Turnus would be willing to pay (*emptum*) not to have taken the girdle from Pallas' corpse. Of course Gawain, like Turnus, does have occasion to detest the "spoils" he takes from the Lady for, in his estimation, they spoil him. Once apprised of the real significance of the girdle, he tears it from his body like an unclean thing, despoiling himself of the thing which has spoiled him. He returns the hated object to Bertilak to whom it belongs by right and from whom he has criminally despoiled it (see lines 2376–85).

At the Green Chapel Gawain initially treats the girdle as a *nefas*, a sacrilegious, impure thing. He later deigns to wear it as a sign of "surfet" (2433) and "the faut and the fayntyse of the flesche crabbed, / how tender hit is to entyse teches of fylthe" (2435–36). Yet if—as I have been arguing throughout this essay—the *Gawain* poet's response to Vergil encourages us to understand the significance of symbols like trees, shields or girdles as a product of negotiation between context and subtext, then we are perhaps obliged to interrogate further the relationship of the two belts. The story depicted on the belt of Pallas is one not only of *nefas* but also of miraculous virtue and survival. Danaus, frightened by a prophecy that he would be murdered by a son-in-law, sends his fifty daughters to their bridal chambers to murder their newlywed husbands. Forty-nine of his daughters comply with the order; only the virtuous Hypermnestra, celebrated in Ovid's *Heroides* and Chaucer's *Legend of Good Women*, does not pollute her marriage bed in this way. The Lady's visits to Gawain's bedroom have, because of the intercalated hunts and especially because of the real nature of her attempted seductions, something of the menace of the Danaids about them. She is there, apparently, under orders to murder him by having sex with him. Gawain thinks she is after his body, when what she really wants is his head. In the *Aeneid* the *ekphrasis* on the belt suits Turnus whose claim as the intended bridegroom of Lavinia brings him into a fatal conflict with the destiny of Aeneas. In the story of the Danaids only one prospective bridegroom survives; Aeneas makes it clear that the belt belongs by right to him and his allies ("*meorum*" 12. 947). By taking the belt, Turnus has doomed himself to the fate of the slaughtered bridegrooms depicted on it.

The final, culminating blow in both works is deeply implicated in questions of justice and mercy. Both the Green Knight and Aeneas forestall what would be a killing blow, hesitate, and then strike a blow which they deem to be just recompense for the stolen belt worn by their adversary. The final scene in the *Aeneid* contains Vergil's most masterful use of the rhetorical device of *amplificatio*. The belt is denominated no less than six times in seven lines—an effect analogous to a prolonged close-up in cinematography—it magnifies the importance of the belt, even as it parses a vast array of significance and consequences:

> ... stetit acer in armis
> Aeneas volvens oculos dextramque repressit;
> et iam iamque magis cunctantem flectere sermo
> coeperat, *infelix* umero cum apparuit alto
> *balteus* et *notis* fulserunt *cingula bullis*

> Pallantis pueri, victum quem vulnere Turnus
> straverat atque umeris *inimicum insigne* gerebat.
> ille, oculis postquam saevi *monimenta* doloris
> *exuviasque* hausit, furiis accensus et ira
> terribilis: "tune hinc *spoliis* indute meorum
> eripiare mihi? Pallas te hoc vulnere, Pallas
> immolat et poenam scelerato ex sanguine sumit."
> [12.938–49, my emphasis]

> (Aeneas stood, ferocious in his armor;
> his eyes were restless and he stayed his hand;
> and as he hesitated, Turnus' words
> began to move him more and more—until
> high on the Latin's shoulder he made out
> the luckless belt of Pallas, of the boy
> whom Turnus had defeated, wounded, stretched
> upon the battlefield, from whom he took
> this fatal sign to wear upon his back,
> this girdle glittering with familiar studs.
> And when his eyes drank in this plunder, this
> memorial of brutal grief, Aeneas,
> aflame with rage—his wrath was terrible—
> cried: "How can you who wear the spoils of my
> dear comrade now escape me? It is Pallas
> who strikes you, who sacrifices you, who takes
> this payment from your shameless blood"
> [trans. Mandelbaum, 335–36].

The shifting denominations of the belt provide an important analogue to the *Gawain* poet's own exploration of the belt as a polysemous sign. It is first named an *infelix balteus* (ill-fated or unhappy baldric)—a phrase interesting for a number of reasons. Its location (*umero*, over the shoulder) as well as the word *balteus* suggest that Turnus is wearing the belt as a trophy, hooked over one shoulder and fastened on the opposite side at his waist. The semantic range of *infelix* is even more interesting for our purposes. It refers perhaps most immediately to the sense that the belt is invested with bad luck or that it is cursed. Of course the adjective makes more sense if we treat it as a transferred epithet: it is Turnus who is *infelix*—he is about to be spared when the sight of the belt rekindles the rage of Aeneas. The sense that Turnus is unlucky or unhappy sorts well with the dynastic sense of the word *felix*. As an epithet the word is a traditional way of designating the founder of a civilization (e.g., the "Felix Brutus" in *Sir Gawain*, line 13). Turnus had thought to be the patriarch of Italy, but becomes instead the sacrificial victim upon whose corpse Aeneas founds (*condit*, 950) a new civilization. Gawain ultimately wears his belt as a baldric ("abelef, as a bauderyk, bounden bi his syde," 2486), but not as a trophy (the Green Knight returns it to him suggesting he treat it as a "pure token / of the chaunce of the Grene Chapel at cheualrous kny3tez," 2398–99). Instead Gawain wears the baldric "in syngne of my surfet" (2433) and as a "token of untrawthe" (2509). The Gawain who had advertised his own spiritual perfection gives way to a new Gawain who pursues a life of penance: the Knight of the Pentangle becomes the Knight of the Girdle. This personal gesture of penance by the "fyne fader of nurture" (919) is co-opted by the lords and ladies of Camelot and also by a late medieval reader who set the motto of the Knights of the Garter ("*Hony soyt qui mal pence*") as a postscript to the poem. The sympathetic reactions of the Camelot faithful as well as the approval implied by the appended motto seem to adopt Gawain as the (in)*felix* founder of a chivalric ideal.

The phrase *inimicum insigne* ("hateful sign," 12.945) turns on the notion of an alliance spoiled by the sign of the belt. For Aeneas the belt is *inimicus* because it signifies that Turnus, despite his offer of peace and friendship, is still his foe, by virtue of his having killed Pallas. For Turnus the belt is *inamicus* because it is a prize he now scorns, a sign which, as the poet had predicted in Book 10, he has come to hate (cf., 10.504–05). Gawain too comes to despise a belt he had once prized, calling it a "falssyng" and cursing it, "foule mot hit falle" (2378). Yet it ultimately becomes for him as it does for Aeneas a *saevi monimenta doloris* ("memorial of bitter grief," 945). Both Gawain and Turnus must pay a penalty, pay with their own guilty blood (*poenam scelerato ex sanguine sumit*, 949) for wearing the sign of a warrior they thought they had slain. Both the "slain" adversaries have their revenge: the Green Knight through his miraculous survival and Pallas as his spirit works out its revenge using Aeneas as its instrument: "*Pallas te hoc vulnere, Pallas immolat*" (Pallas gives you this wound, Pallas sacrifices you, 948–49).

To the victors go the spoils. But as Roger Hornsby (1971) has pointed out, in a fascinating article on the despoiling of the dead in Homer and the *Aeneid*, wearing "the armor of the slain" is usually a fatal mistake. In a warrior society, archaic or medieval, things like shields or belts are visible markers of the wearer's personal identity as well as his allegiances. In Book 22 of the *Iliad* Hector dies because he wears the armor of Achilles, which he had despoiled from the dead body of Achilles' comrade Patroclos. The scene provides the source of the passage in the *Aeneid* discussed above. It may be that the belt Gawain receives from the Lady is the very same "belt" (130) which the Green Knight wore on his visit to Camelot— he tells Gawain at the Green Chapel "hit is my wede that thou werez, that ilke wouen girdel" (2358). Certainly the green and gold color scheme would seem to go with the outfit! Like the Homeric warriors before him, Gawain trusts in the talismanic power of an item stolen from a foe he has 'killed.' That the Green Knight does not in fact die, even though his head is severed from his body, and that Gawain receives the belt from his wife point to the kind of concessions romance makes to the supernatural and the amatory, but it does not fundamentally alter the symbolic substructure. In donning the "armor of the slain," Gawain, like Hector and Turnus before him, wears the "sign" of someone else. In doing so he puts his own identity in jeopardy.

Justice and Grace

We often say as a matter of convenience that the poem begins and ends with the translations of imperial power after the destruction of Troy, but of course that is technically and perhaps significantly inaccurate. The poem begins "Siththan the sege and the assaut watz sesed at Troye" but ends in the eternally present possibility of Christ's grace which the poet wishes for himself and his audience. The fall of Troy and the crucifixion of Christ mark not only crucial moments in the history of the West, but also distinct moments of ethnogenesis. The myth-history of the Trojan diaspora justifies the ethnic and national identities of Western peoples and the crucifixion unites these nations—at least ideally—as one people. This slight imperfection in the poem's circular and numerical structure (it does not end where it began nor does its total number of lines resolve to the numerological music of the number 25) is created by the supernumerary and superstructural prayer for Christ's blessing—a final five lines which make all the difference. Human perfection is not only unattainable, but also insufficient; the addition of Christ and the grace he brings presents a final *figura* which both throws human imperfections into sharp relief and transcends them. Like its hero the poem is imperfect; it overshoots the completion of a perfect circle only slightly, just as the arc of the axe swing at the end of the poem falls only inches short of duplicating exactly Gawain's decapitation of the Green Knight in Camelot. Those five extra lines provide a supplement, an addition of the possibility of grace which fundamentally alters the revenge justice that dominates not only the end of Vergil's poem but also the view of history that underwrites ancient imperial epic.

The justice dispensed in *Sir Gawain* is both the poetic justice of low comedy and the divine justice tempered by mercy that is the hallmark of Christian "comedy." The Beheading Game plot employs a prevalent topos in medieval tragic poetics to manufacture an outrageously precise poetic justice. A number of late medieval poets, Chaucer, Lydgate and Henryson in particular, were influenced by the backhanded definition of tragedy in Boethius's *Consolatio Philosophiae*. In Book 2, prose 2 of this work Lady Philosophy exclaims: "Quid tragoediarum clamor aliud deflet nisi indiscreto ictu fortunam felicia regna vertentem?" (What else is the cry of tragedy but a lament that happy states are overthrown by the indiscriminate blows of fortune?). The trope of the *indiscretus ictus* (which Chaucer felicitously translates "unwar strook") is often employed in late medieval tragedies to stress the unexpected and sometimes undeserved nature of tragic blows. One can see the trope deployed as a consistent feature of the poetics of medieval tragedy in Chaucer's *Troilus* and "The Monk's Tale," in Lydgate's *Troy Book* and *The Fall of Princes*, and in Henryson's *Moral Fables* and *The Testament of Cresseid*.[6] The "unwar strook" also plays a distinct role in the poetics of late medieval comedy, especially those highly literate comedies, like Chaucer's "The Miller's Tale," which seem to mirror or parody tragic plots.

The bargain for an exchange of blows struck by Gawain and the Green Knight at first seems to obviate both senses of the word *indiscretus* (unexpected/undiscerning) and to replace Fortune's game with one controlled completely by men themselves. Gawain strikes the initial blow fully expecting that by this act he will decide both the Green Knight's fate and his own. The upshot, though, is *indiscretus* in both the literal and figurative senses of the word. Gawain succeeds in beheading the Green Knight, but head and body do not remain separate for long (*indiscretus* literally means "not separate," "inseparable"). And Gawain's failure of discretion (both physical and intellectual) has doomed him to receive a return blow that is both expected and deserved.

> To the Grene Chapel thou chose, I charge the, to fotte
> Such a dunt as thou hat3 dalt—disserued thou habbe3
> To be 3ederly 3olden on Nw 3eres morn [451–33].

Knowing the time, date, place and means of one's death introduces a fatalism that would seem to negate both free will as well as the power of Fortune. Yet, when the axe is hung above the dais, a wary medieval reader would see this as a sign of Fortune's impending power over earthly dynasties.

> "Now sir heng vp thyn ax, that hat3 innogh hewen,"
> And hit wat3 don abof the dece, on doser to henge,
> Ther alle men for maruayl myght on hit loke,
> And, bi trwe tytle therof, to telle the wonder [477–80].

Boethius's *Consolatio* cites the exemplum of King Damocles, who used the specter of a sword hanging by a thread above his throne to signify the impending doom under which all earthly reigns exist. As such the hanging axe in Camelot should encourage wariness, the hope that kings may forestall or delay the "unwar strook" of Fortune through vigilance. Yet among the young and reckless of Camelot, this pendulous weapon is taken for a conversation piece, not as a warning of the immanent danger that threatens earthly kingdoms. In their folly Arthur's courtiers unwittingly rear a symbol of Fortune's impending but unexpected blow.

The return match at the Green Chapel a year later explores the complexities inherent in the theme of the "unwar strook" even further. Gawain's expectation of the blow is heightened by the sound of the grinding stone and the two feints. But he cannot know with what subtle discretion the axe will finally fall. The precision of the Green Knight's stroke is miraculous, a blow that he at least deems measured, accurate and deserved. Gawain's response to the glancing blow shows that he assumes the stroke to have been unintendedly errant: he jumps back and prepares to defend himself. His relief at the narrow escape is based on the assumption that the blow was an *indiscretus ictus*, a mistake which grants him an unexpected and perhaps undeserved reprieve. Subsequently he learns that in the "chance of the Grene Chapel" nothing has been left to chance. The two feints as well as the meticulously discrete glancing blow represent precise responses to Gawain's conduct. Of course the implication that Fortune uses a scalpel rather than a blunt instrument is perhaps even more daunting than the idea that people are prey to a universe of irrational, random forces. Gawain's embittered sense that he has failed in a rigged game may reflect late medieval anxieties about increasingly regulated and calibrated systems of assessing and punishing human transgression. The increased importance of confession and penitence, as well as the promulgation of the doctrine of purgatory offered Christians a world and a hereafter wherein the specter of a deliberate blow hung poised with terrifying accuracy above every sin.

Gawain's state of mind at the end of the poem is in many ways no different from that of Turnus in the last line of the *Aeneid*: his is also a *vita indignata* (12.952). However, the addendum of Christ's passion offers an alternate and transcendent *figura* for Gawain. In its concatenation of symbols the poem moves from pentangle to girdle to Christ's crown of thorns— a triad of symbols which like other triads in the poem is characterized by repetition and variation. Like the girdle the crown is a sign of shame that comes later to represent an heroic ordeal. But in its woven branches and points the crown also recalls the endless knot once set by Solomon as a token of "trawþe." The crown of interwoven points represents a new covenant, a new bond of fidelity, a second sign of "trawþe" that completes and fulfills the first. To the Camelot faithful, Gawain's defeat seems a miraculous victory, his suffering a cause for commemoration. Like Christ, Gawain's success is aporetic; it can only be accurately expressed via oxymora such as "a victorious defeat" or "a shameful triumph." Like Christ and like Aeneas, the mixed nature of Gawain's success, the suffering and doubt which beset him, make him an even more potent figure of ethnogenesis. He becomes the self-sacrificing patron of an ethos, the father of a chivalric ideal which survives not only Gawain's mixed success but also the destruction of Camelot. It survives into the contemporary world of the poet's audience; they pay their "worship" to an ancestor who founded their way of life and who provides an ideal pattern by which his followers can rule and measure their own lives. Of course, Christ's followers seldom got it quite right either: they had trouble knowing how to praise him properly. They let their fears and their enthusiasms get the better of them at times. The same is true of the Camelot faithful who misappropriate Gawain's miraculous return from certain death, yet their reactions ultimately must guide those of the poem's audiences, medieval and modern. This is not to say that finally Gawain becomes a "Christ-figure" or anything so trite, but rather that the figure of Christ supplies a pattern and a purpose to Gawain's anguished penance. That is why we are only partially correct to think of Gawain as an alienated figure at the end of the poem. He is alienated from all the things that a Christian knight should be alienated from: pride, fame, and trust in the things of this world. At the end of the poem Gawain is a sad penitent, but he receives a great deal more at the Green Chapel than a scar, a belt, and a healthy dose of self-loathing; he also receives mercy. And having experienced mercy from so unlikely a source in this world, he may be more hopeful of it in the next. The last of the *felix* founders named in the poem is Christ himself; it is his eternal city and his "blisse" (2530) to which all may come who complete the poem's cycle of history that began in the ashes of Troy.

Notes

1. See the editions of Tolkien and Gordon, Davis, Andrew and Waldron, and Vantuono. Important articles which contribute to the debate about the identity of the "tulk" and the relevance of the first stanza to the work as a whole include Chapman, Silverstein, David, Hunt, Burnley, Andrew, and Stevenson. On the myth of the translation of empires, see Gertz and Silverstein. For two important book-length studies of the effect of the myth of the translation of empires on modern history, see MacDougall and Geary.

2. The most extensive example of such an interpretive strategy is Macrobius's *Saturnalia*, Books 5–6. For a recent, brief introduction to modern scholarship on Vergil's use of Hellenistic and Byzantine sources, see Farrell.

3. My notion of the importance of aporias for understanding the poem is in many ways parallel to the approaches of Ganim, who emphasizes "disorientation" and contradiction, and Stanbury (96–115), who traces the ways in which shifts of point of view alter our perceptions and judgements. I prefer the term aporia because it has a firm hold both in medieval rhetorical poetics (where it is called *dubitatio*) and in contemporary, post-structualist discourse.

4. I refer, of course, to Sir Thomas Malory's version of Arthur's death in "The Most Piteous Tale of the Morte Arthur Saunz Guerdon" in *Malory: Works*, ed. Eugène Vinaver, p. 714.

5. All quotations of *Sir Gawain and the Green Knight*, hereafter cited by line number only, are taken from the edition of William Vantuono.

6. For a fuller discussion of medieval tragedy and the trope of the *indiscretus ictus* see Kelly.

Works Cited

Ackroyd, Peter. *Milton in America*. London: Vintage, 1997.

Allen, Judson B. *The Friar As Critic: Literary Attitudes in the Later Middle Ages*. Nashville: Vanderbilt UP, 1971.

Andrew, Malcolm. "The Fall of Troy in SGGK and Troilus and Criseyde." In *The European Tragedy of Troilus*. Ed. Piero Boitani. Oxford: Oxford UP, 1989. 75–93.

Arthur, Ross G. "A Head for a Head: A Testamental Template for *Sir Gawain and the Green Knight* and *The Wife of Bath's Tale*." *Florilegium* 6 (1984): 178–94.

———. *Medieval Sign Theory and Sir Gawain and the Green Knight*. Toronto: Toronto UP, 1987.

Augustine. *Concerning the City of God Against the Pagans*. Trans. Henry Bettenson. London: Penguin Books, 1972.

Baswell, Christopher. *Vergil in Medieval England: Figuring the Aeneid from the Twelfth Century to Chaucer*. Cambridge: Cambridge UP, 1995.

Blanch, Robert J., and Julian N. Wasserman. *From Pearl to Gawain: Forme to Fynisment*. Gainesville: UP of Florida, 1995.

Boethius, Anicius Manlius Severinus. *Tractates; De consolatione Philosophiae*. Trans. H. F. Stewart et. al. Loeb Classics. Cambridge, MA: Harvard UP, 1978.

Burnley, J. D. "*Sir Gawain and the Green Knight*, Lines 3–7." *Notes and Queries* Mar. 1973: 83–84.

Chance, Jane. *Medieval Mythography: From Roman North Africa to the School of Chartres, A.D. 433–1177*. Gainesville: UP of Florida, 1994.

Chapman, Otis. "Vergil and the *Gawain*-poet." *PMLA* 60 (1945): 16–23.

Clark, Susan L., and Julian N. Wasserman. "The Passing of the Seasons and the Apocalyptic in *Sir Gawain and the Green Knight*." *South Central Review* 3 (1986): 5–22.

Classical and Medieval Literary Criticism: Translations and Interpretations. Eds. A. Preminger, L. Golden, O.B. Hardison, and K. Kerrane. New York: Fredrick Ungar Publishing, 1974.

Crompton, Anne Eliot. *Gawain and the Lady Green: A Novel*. New York: Donald I. Fine Books, 1997.

David, Alfred. "Gawain and Aeneas." *English Studies* 49 (1968): 402–9.

Dove, Mary. "Hyghe Eldee in *Sir Gawain and the Green Knight*." In *The Perfect Age of a Man's Life*. Cambridge: Cambridge UP, 1986. 134–40.

Farrell, Joseph. "The Vergilian Intertext." In *The Cambridge Companion to Vergil*. Ed. Charles Martindale. Cambridge: Cambridge UP, 1997. 222–38.

Ganim, John. "Disorientation, Style and Consciousness in *Sir Gawain and the Green Knight.*" *PMLA* 91 (1976): 367–84.

Geary, Patrick J. *The Myth of Nations: The Medieval Origins of Europe.* Princeton: Princeton UP, 2002.

Gertz, Sunhee Kim. "*Translatio Studii et Imperii*: Sir Gawain As Literary Critic." *Semiotica* 63 (1987): 185–203.

Gransden, K. W. *Vergil's Iliad: An Essay on Epic Narrative.* Cambridge: Cambridge UP, 1984.

Green, Dennis Howard. "Structural Irony." In *Irony in the Medieval Romance.* Cambridge: Cambridge UP, 1979. 326–58.

Hornsby, Roger. "The Armor of the Slain." *Philological Quarterly* 45 (1966): 347–359.

———. *Patterns of Action in the* Aeneid: *An Interpretation of Vergil's Epic Similes.* Iowa City: U[of Iowa P, 1970.

Hunt, Tony. "Irony and Ambiguity in *Sir Gawain and the Green Knight.*" *Forum for Modern Language Studies* 12 (1976): 1–16.

Kelly, Henry Ansgar. *Chaucerian Tragedy.* Cambridge: D. S. Brewer, 1998.

MacDougall, Hugh A. *Racial Myth in English History.* Hanover: UP of New England, 1982.

Macrobius. *Macrobius.* Ed. Jacob Willis. 2 vols. Bibliotheca Scriptorum Graecorum et Romanorum Teubneriana. Leipzig: B. G. Teubner, 1963.

Malory, Thomas. *Malory: Works.* Ed. Eugéne Vinaver. 2nd ed. Oxford: Oxford UP, 1971.

Morgan, Gerald. "The Action of the Hunting and the Bedroom Scenes in *Sir Gawain and the Green Knight.*" *Medium Aevum* 56 (1987): 200–26.

———. Sir Gawain and the Green Knight *and the Idea of Righteousness.* Dublin: Irish Academic Press, 1991.

O'Mara, Phillip F. "Robert Holcot's 'Ecumenism' and the Green Knight." *Chaucer Review* 26, no. 4 (1992a): 329–42.

———. "Holcot and the *Pearl*-Poet." *Chaucer Review* 27, no. 1 (1992b): 97–106.

Parry, A. "The Two Voices of Vergil's *Aeneid.*" In *Vergil: A Collection of Critical Essays.* Ed. S. Commager. Englewood Cliffs, NJ: Prentice-Hall, 1966. 66–80.

Poems of the Pearl Manuscript: Pearl, Cleanness, Patience, Sir Gawain and the Green Knight. Eds. Malcolm Andrew and Ronald Waldron. Berkeley: U of California P, 1978.

Putter, Ad. *An Introduction to the Gawain-Poet.* New York: Longman, 1996.

Sanderlin, George. "Two Transfigurations: Gawain and Aeneas." *Chaucer Review* 12 (1978): 255–258.

Shoaf, R. A. "The 'Syngne of Surfet' and the Surfeit of Signs in *Sir Gawain and the Green Knight.*" In *The Passing of Arthur: New Essays in the Arthurian Tradition.* Eds. Christopher Baswell and William Sharpe. New York: Garland, 1988. 152–69.

Silverstein, Theodore. "*Sir Gawain*, Dear Brutus, and Britain's Fortunate Founding: A Study in Comedy and Conventions." *Modern Philology* 62 (1965): 189–206.

Sir Gawain and the Green Knight. Eds. J. R. R. Tolkien and E. V. Gordon. 1st ed. Oxford: Clarendon Press, 1925, 1936.

Sir Gawain and the Green Knight. Ed. Norman Davis. Rev. 2nd ed. of Tolkien and Gordon. Oxford: Clarendon Press, 1967.

Sir Gawain and the Green Knight, Revised Edition. Ed. and trans. William Vantuono. Notre Dame, U of Notre Dame P, 1999.

Stanbury, Sarah. *Seeing the Gawain-Poet: Description and Act of Perception.* Philadelphia: U of Pennsylvania P, 1991.

Stevenson, Sharon. "Aeneas in Fourteenth-Century England." In *The Classics in the Middle Ages.* Ed. Aldo S. Bernardo and Saul Levin. Binghamton, NY: Center for Medieval and Early Renaissance Studies, 1990. 371–78.

Thiébaux, Marcelle. *The Stag of Love: The Chase in Medieval Literature.* Ithaca, NY: Cornell UP, 1974.
Tristram, Philippa. *Figures of Life and Death in Medieval English Literature.* New York: New York UP, 1976.
Vergil. *Opera.* Ed. R. A. B. Mynors. Oxford: Clarendon Press, 1969, 1980.
_____. *The Aeneid of Vergil: A Verse Translation.* Trans. Allen Mandelbaum. New York: Bantam Books, 1961.
_____. *The Aeneid of Vergil.* 2 vols. Ed. R. D. Williams. London: St. Martin's Press, 1973.
Weiss, Victoria L. "Gawain's First Failure: The Beheading Scene in *Sir Gawain and the Green Knight.*" *Chaucer Review* 10 (1976): 361–66.

The "Tresounous Tulk" in Sir Gawain and the Green Knight

E. L. Risden

ST. NORBERT COLLEGE

Sir Gawain and the Green Knight begins and ends with references to Troy. The more famous opening lines make what may seem an innocuous allusion, but that illusion provides a guiding metaphor for the whole poem—the siege and burning of Troy—and imposes some difficulty of explanation. After razing of the city, the poet writes,

> þe tulk þat þe trammes of tresoun þer wroȝt
> Watz tried for his tricherie þe trewest on erthe
> Hit watz Ennias þe athel & his highe kynde
> þat siþen depreced prouinces & patrounes bicome
> Welnege of al þe wele in þe west iles... [ll. 3–7].

The closing reference in the very last stanza of the poem comes after Gawain's return to Camelot, as the members of Arthur's court agree to wear the green sash, and the poet again specifies the assault and siege as well as honorable adventures and lineage: all the lords and ladies will, for Gawain's sake, wear a green baldric, and they shall feel honored in doing so:

> þus in Arthurus day þis aunter bitidde
> þe Brutus bokez þerof beres wyttenesse;
> Syþen Brutus þe bolde burne boȝed hider fyrst
> After the segge & þe asaute watz sesed at Troye
> iwyse

> Mony aunterez here-biforne
> Haf fallen suche er þis
> Now þat bere þe croun of þorne ... [2522–29].

Here the allusion seems almost more gratuitous: "Since Brutus came hither after the siege and assault of Troy ended, many earlier adventures have befallen so before this one [Gawain's adventure, or the current time?]," the poet reminds us. Obviously he wants us to depart with the same idea clearly in mind as that with which we began because he offers an interpretive strategy by referring to the Troy story. Why is that story so important, and who is that treasonous tulk?

Traditional wisdom argues that the man is Aeneas and that the reason for his importance lies in the bloodline he establishes which, according to early British historians such as Geoffrey of Monmouth, leads to Brutus and to Arthur and to all the true monarchs of England. Presumably the double reference to the fall of Troy serves as a reminder to the audience of England's noble heritage and how from tall Troy's ashes grew a greater empire, Rome, and perhaps from there another young one on the rise, England. Though referred to as "traytor," as Tolkien and Gordon point out, in *The Gest Hystoriale of the Destruction of Troy*, the *Scottish Troy Fragments*, and Lydgate's *Troy Book*, Aeneas remained a hero to the English, and not just because of their love for Vergil.

Aeneas as symbol suggests the warrior whose cause at first fails, yet who rises above failure to achieve a new and better quest by piety, courage, and devotion to duty, accomplishing all the gods ask of him, including the founding of an empire. Thus *Sir Gawain and the Green Knight* is encased by a metaphor that casts a Classical (both learned and flattering) comparison upon Gawain's journey, adventure, and significant but imperfect success: Gawain returns home alive and serves as a model to Arthur's court and all would-be nobles to come.

Many scholars (see, for example, Frederic Madden and Alfred David) have commented on the parallels, noting that both Aeneas and Gawain undergo a complete, if slightly blemished, quest, shield a lady, and establish a role model. Further, both embody *trawþe*, perhaps the major theme of *Sir Gawain and the Green Knight* and one we may associate in retrospect with the pious/dutiful Aeneas.

Other scholars (see, for example, Israel Gollancz and A. C. Cawley), suggest Antenor, not Aeneas, as the real traitor and the referent for *tulk*; Aeneas may have been a traitor against the *Greeks* for concealing Polyxena, or perhaps to a small degree against Troy's honor because at one point he urged Priam to settle with the Greeks or because he escaped the city's fall (though even Trojans probably wouldn't hold that against him), but Antenor betrayed Polyxena and Aeneas and Troy by unveiling her hiding place to the Greeks, by conspiring with the conquerors. But, then, why would the *Gawain* poet mention Antenor? Aeneas serves as a better parallel to Gawain, and if *Sir Gawain and the Green Knight* has a parallel to Antenor, it might more readily appear in Morgan le Fay, the motive force behind the plot, the character who betrays Arthur's court, but surely no tulk. Other than to foreshadow Morgan, Antenor seems a superfluous allusion, while Aeneas at least serves as a productive one.

But Aeneas fails in one respect where Gawain does not: in romantic love. Aeneas loses his wife in the confusion during the burning of Troy, and his dalliance with Dido provokes her suicide. By way of comparison, Gawain's chastity is tested by Morgan's retinue, and he proves himself true, if not fully Christlike. Further, Aeneas's goal is to found an empire, but Gawain's is to preserve his king's honor, his own life, and his profession's virtues. But beyond the comparison with Aeneas, what has the burning Troy to do with Gawain and Arthur's court that it merits such foregrounding?

I would like to suggest, as a parallel reading to Professor Haydock's, an alternative referent to said tulk: not Aeneas or Antenor, but *Odysseus*; I'd also like to argue the applicability of the *Gawain* poet's allusion to the burning of Troy: the ultimate fall of Camelot, brought on in some tales (such as Malory's) by Gawain's insistent challenge against Launcelot, which splits the court, allows Mordred to mount a threat, and weakens Arthur's forces so that he will ultimately fall. That challenge, finally, is a kind of treason, and it parallels activities of Odysseus better than those of Aeneas.

One of our problems in deriving the meaning of the "tulk" allusion comes from the difficulty in translating the text and in determining its proper punctuation—not at all clear in the original. Translation of the lines might run something like this (cf. Tolkien, Borroff, and Vantuono):

> Since the siege and the assault had ceased at Troy,
> The burg broken and burnt to brands and ashes,
> The leader who the works of treason wrought there
> Was tried for his treachery, the trewest on earth.
> It was Aeneas the prince and his high family
> That after pressed the provinces and became patrons
> Of well-nigh all the wealth in the west isles.

Now if we place a colon after the fourth line, as do Tolkien and Gordon, we are bound to equate the tulk with Aeneas, but the manuscript has no such clear mark. A colon is reasonable, but so is a period, and if we end the sentence at line 4, the next line may begin a new sentence contrasting the previous one, the reading I suggest as an option: the treasonous man is likely a counselor of some sort (ON *tulkr*, spokesman), who wrought (built) there the trewest "tricherie," perhaps *trickery* rather than treachery, on earth. What better trickery of the ancient world do we know than the Trojan Horse, built by Odysseus to allow the Greeks to burn Troy to ashes?

And who met greater trials after the assault at Troy than Odysseus, whose adventures take him farther astray and through greater tribulation even than Aeneas's?[1] Tolkien's translation of *Sir Gawain and the Green Knight* has a dash at the end of the fourth line, also appropriate and telling because of what the dash signifies: an abrupt change in thought or rhetorical purpose. And, to the English, Odysseus is a traitor, because he created the ruse that brought down the city of their ancient ancestors, who believed the Greeks had sailed away, leaving them in peace and with a gift as compensation. Odysseus's true and successful trickery contrasts with Aeneas's uprightness: the founder-to-be of Rome seeks to save his old city, then serves the gods by building a new one, even at the expense of his own wishes (leaving Dido). However, unlike Aeneas, Odysseus remains true in his heart to his beloved; though untrue in the modern sense with Calypso and Circe, he never gives up hope of returning to Penelope, and his dalliances are imposed by the gods and by circumstance rather than by his own choice.[2]

Gawain, too, has his brief flirtation, remaining technically sinless, but he does pay for the kisses with the Green Knight's second feigned blow in their encounter at the Green Chapel, where the Green Knight serves as a kind of proxy confessor, absolving Gawain of his fault so he may return to Camelot in that same state in which the Romans saw Aeneas, blessed. Does he, like Aeneas, leave a lady he loves (Lady Bertilak), or does he, like Odysseus, leave a lady who tries to seduce him so that he may continue to follow a duty more personal than political (to get home alive)?

Is Gawain, like Odysseus, too eager in his martial duty, or does he undertake a swing of the axe simply to save his king? In the name of a "game" he willingly strikes the Green Knight's head from his shoulders, while the Green Knight repays that stroke with only a feint. Does Odysseus go too far in his trickery (the Greeks call him "resourceful," literally, "of many turns," but the Romans apply a pejorative "crafty" or "cunning"), or does he simply find a way to bring a seemingly endless war to its necessary conclusion? Odysseus, like Aeneas and Gawain, undergoes in the *Odyssey* a long journey, but his goal is not Aeneas's, to found an empire, but rather it matches Gawain's goal, to return home.

Again like both Aeneas and Gawain, Odysseus serves in battle because honor requires it, and he best succeeds when he relies on divine guidance rather than tools or his own strength. Odysseus runs into trouble when he offends Poseidon and trusts in his own ability and strength of will to get home; Gawain fails when he trusts in the green sash rather than in God to save his life. Odysseus finds himself in an impossible position, having offended the god of the sea, yet needing to reach home by sea; Gawain, too, deals with an impossible situation: he agrees to share everything he gets with Bertilak, but the Lady requires that he keep the gift of the sash secret—he simply cannot keep both promises.

Of course, Odysseus reaches home because he is resourceful and persistent, other gods help him, and Poseidon's wrath is eventually eased, and Gawain survives because he is brave enough to try, God does not abandon him, and Bertilak lets him off the hook, since no murder was actually done. Aeneas, by comparison, faces no similar impossibility: though he does not wish to leave Dido, shortly he willingly turns to Lavinia when the new opportunity presents itself. Aeneas builds a new home, while both Odysseus and Gawain return home, where they will find honor and appreciation.

W. B. Stanford notes of Odysseus "the inherent ethical ambiguity of his distinctive character among the Homeric heroes—which is intelligence" (7); one may say the same of Gawain (and also of Aeneas), both in this story and in some others, as Gawain's intelligence, like Odysseus's, may work for him or against him. As Stanford also points out (6), Odysseus has created for authors who have taken up his story a problem of "self-identification": one tends to invest the character with oneself or to subsume that character as an aspect of one's identity, and authors have done the same with Gawain, making him hero or villain as politics dictated. The "greatest knight" in Arthuriana varies with the heritage of the writer.

So while Vergil did "contrive to blacken Ulysses's character for some fifteen hundred years of the Western literary tradition" (Stanford 137), the Middle Ages saw a rehabilitation in progress: "in Benoit [de Sainte Maure, circa 1170] Ulysses begins his slow climb back into literary favour" (285). Similarly, while Malory depicts Gawain as a good knight and sworn friend of Launcelot, Gawain does turn on his friend, and more than any knight other than Mordred, Gawain causes the fall of Camelot. The *Gawain* poet, though, returns to earlier Cymric tradition and makes Gawain, even above Launcelot, the flower of Arthurian chivalry—though not flawless. Aeneas loses at Troy only to win in Italy; Odysseus wins at Troy, returns home, and may or may not move finally to infamy (cf. Dante's *Inferno*); Gawain both loses and wins, doing, as the Green Knight assures him, the best one could, and returning home—to a Camelot that will one day fall.

Another possible parallel appears if we look at our heroes' subsequent stories. Later tales, cited for instance by Dante, suggest that Odysseus's wanderlust finally won out, urging him from home to more adventures during which he was finally killed far away, his loyal followers with him. Similarly, Malory tells of the events leading up to the death of Arthur, how Gawain would not reconcile with Launcelot for the inadvertent killing of his brothers, and how Arthur's siege of Joyous Garde, upon which Gawain insisted, permitted Mordred the foothold into military power that costs Arthur dearly in the final battle. I have no evidence that the *Gawain* poet would have known either the story of Odysseus or an earlier Arthurian work from which Malory might have drawn that tells this Gawain story; I suggest only that this additional connection completes an interesting comparison, a comparison furthered by the closing allusions in *Sir Gawain and the Green Knight*.

The final sixteen lines translate something like this:

> Those lords and ladies that belonged to the [Round] Table,
> Each warrior of the brotherhood a baldric should have,
> A band obliquely about him of bright green,
> And that, for the sake of that man, in [like] suit to wear.
> For that was accorded the renown of the Round Table,
> And he who had it honored evermore after,
> As it is declared in the best book of romance.
> Thus in Arthur's day this adventure occurred:
> The Brutus books bear witness thereof,
> Since Brutus, the bold warrior, first turned hither,
> After the siege and the assault was ceased at Troy,
> I believe,
> Many adventures before now
> Have fallen out such as this.
> Now he who bore the crown of thorns
> Bring us to his bliss. Amen.

Those lines bring closure, structural circularity, and thematic repetition. They appear in context after Gawain returns to court: he tells his story, blemishes and all, accusing himself of "couardise and couetyse" (line 2508). The cowardice is only briefly and minimally true: he flinches at the first blow. The coveting at first seems inaccurate. Nothing in the poem tips it off, but since Gawain declares it, it must be true. Though the sash is thrust upon him by the Lady, likely he intended to keep the sash beyond the encounter with the Green Knight, using it in battle to gain further renown and assurance of success. Such coveting, desiring to keep what was given him beyond the supposed purpose for which it was given, suggests that had the sash served its purpose with the Green Knight and afterward, Gawain would have forgotten even his shield, with its endless knot and St. Mary, and he may have exchanged his faith in God for faith in magic—a sin even he apparently cannot confess explicitly.[3] The lords and ladies laugh, but comfort him, and they choose, where our quotation picks up, to wear the green sash or baldric, men and women both, *for Gawain's sake*. They should wear it *for their own sake*, as a reminder of human sinfulness, as a spur to humility. Instead, the green baldric becomes a symbol of pride, of belonging to King Arthur's court, and the bearer thus shares in the court's renown.

The image suggests more than mere appreciation of the romantic, heroic past. These two failures must have entered the mind of our clerical author and invoked images of Judgment and Apocalypse, for he returns in reverse order through images raised at the beginning of the poem to Brutus, the founder of the potential Eden or New Jerusalem of England, to the images of the burning and destruction of Troy, a clear Doomsday metaphor and parallel to the fall of Camelot. He concludes that many such adventures have occurred before *this*: the ambiguous pronoun may refer either to Gawain's adventure or to "this time," that is, the poet's time. The ambiguity condenses time around the adventures of Troy, Aeneas, Brutus, Gawain, and anyone else who has had similar tests of endurance, dedication, courage, and loyalty, a technique typical of apocalypses and apocalyptic reference, to telescope to the "end time" when the world is burnt to ashes, Judgment occurs, and a new and better world arises, the good rewarded and the sinful punished.

The apocalyptic resonance fits with the last two lines of the poem: may Christ bring us to bliss—so be it. They refer directly to Judgment and salvation and come rather abruptly after the Troy allusion—a reminder that, as we see throughout the Middle Ages and as we witnessed with the arrival of the year 2000, Western culture has an obsession with ends and a persistent concern—or for some, even a hope—that "the end is near." Such reminders, like any apt symbol or allusion, draw from the closure of a poem a wish to act, or at least to act better. The resulting circularity of the poem leaves us with a renewed or continuing concern for salvation, or perhaps a simple, Thomas Browne–like *memento mori*: the *theta*, a circle crossed by a line, a symbolic *thanatos* and the circular narrative crossed by the line of Gawain's quest.

Thematically, the English poet may have seen in Odysseus not his own history, but that of the Greeks, with their limitations, and his audience would find a better (or parallel) model in Gawain, and a better one yet in Christ. In the story of Troy and the adventures of heroes, we see the vanity of human wishes, the inevitable fall of the greatest of earthly cities until we see its eventual replacement with the New Jerusalem. Only courage, truth, and faith, the *Gawain* poet suggests, protect us, along with the basic goodness of heart that Gawain mostly shows and partly learns. Neither skill nor magic will suffice. "Hony Soyt Qui Mal Pense," "Ill be to who thinks evil": the concluding posy suggests we bring evil upon ourselves when we think evil of others. And yet Bertilak admits that while Morgan staged the adventure to challenge Gawain's wits and test the best of Arthur's court, she did so also to frighten Gwenevere to death. Apparently, the audience's goal, in the poet's estimation, is to follow our quests, avoid thinking evil thoughts to the degree we are able, and yet protect ourselves against it, as evil lurks where we least suspect, so that we may avoid the burning of our own Troy and instead find the salvation that, in his best moments, Gawain sought as well.

Notes

1. Support for the notion of Odysseus as treacherous knight appears often through the medieval romance tradition. From the fourth-century Latin "history" of Dares and Dictys derive Benoit de Sainte-Maure's twelfth-century *Roman de Troie*, John Lydgate's fifteenth-century *Troy Book*, and particularly Guido della Colonne's thirteenth-century *Historia Troiana*, translated into Middle English in the fourteenth century as *The Gest Hystoriale of the Destruction of Troy* (EETS 1869, reprinted by Greenwood in 1969). The *Gest* refers to Odysseus ("Ulexes") so: "Ulexes the lefe kyng was loueliest of other, / He was the fairest by ferre of all the felle grekes, / And falsest in his fare, and full of desseit" (lines 3786–88). Later, Telamon accuses Odysseus of showing ever a false character: "This Vlixes, þat vtwith aunterit hym neuer / With no course for to come, as a knight shuld; / But with falshed & flatery, feynyng of wordes, / And callis hym the cavse of cacchyng þis toune, / But with treason & trauntis of his untreu fare / He fortherit neuer a fyge with his fight yet" (lines 12201–06). In Book 34, "How hit happit Ulixes aftur the Sege," Odysseus, captured by King Nauplius of Crete, who "purpost with pyne to put hym (o) lyve, / for the tale of the treson, I told you before,/ Of the prise kyng Palomydon, his aune pure son" (lines 13124–26), escapes "thurgh wiles & wit" (13118). These passages clearly associate Odysseus, rightly or not, with the idea and the word *treachery*.
2. Notice also how among the opium-eaters Odysseus "doesn't inhale."
3. Gawain again parallels the "resourceful" Odysseus, who like Gawain does what he must to survive and return home. Though Odysseus may offend Poseidon, he remains true to Athena, "wisdom," and Gawain aims to act wisely according to human wisdom, if impiously, in trusting the magic of the sash.

Works Cited

Borroff, Marie, trans. *Sir Gawain and the Green Knight.* In *The Norton Anthology of English Literature.* 6th ed., vol 1. M. H. Abrams, gen. ed. New York: W. W. Norton, 1993. 202–54.
Cawley, A. C., ed. *Pearl and Sir Gawain and the Green Knight.* New York: Dutton, 1962.
David, Alfred. "Gawain and Aeneas." *English Studies* 49 (1968): 402–9.
The Gest Hystoriale of the Destruction of Troy: An Alliterative Romance Translated from Guido

de Colonna's "Hystoria Troiana." Eds. Geo. A. Panton and David Donaldson. EETS, 1869 Rpt. New York: Greenwood, 1969.

Gollancz, Israel, ed. *Sir Gawain and the Green Knight*. EETS, O. S., 210. London: Oxford UP, 1940.

Madden, Sir Frederic, ed. *Syr Gawayne and the Grene Knygt*. In *Syr Gawayne: A Collection of Ancient Romance-Poems by Scottish and English Authors, Relating to That Celebrated Knight of the Round Table*. The Bannatyne Club 61. London: Taylor, 1839. Rpt. New York: AMS P, 1971.

Sir Gawain and the Green Knight. Eds. J. R. R. Tolkien and E. V. Gordon, rev. Norman Davis. 2nd ed. Oxford: Clarendon, 1967.

Stanford, W. B. *The Ulysses Theme: A Study in the Adaptability of a Traditional Hero*. 2nd ed. Ann Arbor: U of Michigan P, 1968.

Tolkien, J. R. R., trans. *Sir Gawain and the Green Knight, Pearl, and Sir Orfeo*. New York: Ballantine, 1975.

Vantuono, William, ed. and trans. *Sir Gawain and the Green Knight: A Dual-Language Version*. New York & London: Garland, 1991.

The Fierce Achilles in Chaucer, Gower, and the Gawain Poet

Rosanne Gasse

BRANDON UNIVERSITY

In Chaucer's *Troilus and Criseyde*, Achilles makes two brief, yet nevertheless important appearances, both in Book 5: the first to slay Hector,[1] and the second to kill Troilus.[2] The narration of these events, unlike much of the poem, is sparing in detail. Achilles is given no lines of dialogue and only two descriptive words are used of him. First is the adverbial comment that he "despitously" killed Troilus, attributing to the Greek hero not the presence of callousness so much as the absence of compassion. Second is the adjective "fierce." "Fierce" Achilles kills the hapless Troilus without compassion. Yet, while he appears in the text only briefly as the one who brings closure to the lives of both the Trojan heroes, the presence of Achilles, rather like the war itself, haunts the love story of Troilus and Criseyde throughout. When Criseyde is first told that Pandarus expects her to return Troilus's love, she complains,

> Allas! I wolde han trusted, douteles,
> That if that I, thorugh my disaventure,
> Hadde loved outher hym [Troilus] or Achilles,
> Ector, or any mannes creature,
> Ye nolde han had no mercy ne mesure
> On me, but alwey had me in repreve [2.414–19].

The linkage here of Troilus and his brother, Hector, is not unexpected, because Chaucer makes much of the "Troilus as a second Hector" motif.[3] But the reference to Achilles, the killer of both brothers, may seem curiously out of place in Criseyde's complaint, given that the context is not martial.

And certainly Diomede may seem to the reader to be the more appropriate choice of Greek hero for Criseyde to allude to here, given the later events in the story. And yet Chaucer clearly had his reasons for bringing Achilles into the equation at this point, because he has Troilus do the same thing when he swears not to betray Pandarus and Criseyde's trust in his good intentions:

> But natheless, by that God I the swere,
> That, as hym list, may al this world governe—
> And, if I lye, Achilles with his spere
> Myn herte cleve, al were my life eterne,
> As I am mortal, if I late or yerne
> Wolde it bewreye, or dorst, or sholde konne,
> For al the good that God made under sonne [3.372–78].

Certainly one can brush these off as examples of what Barry Windeatt has called "patterns of doubling and concatenation ... worked into the structure of *Troilus*" (190). Troilus's expression of his potential fate is balanced by his actual fate; Criseyde's use of Achilles's name is balanced by Troilus's use. Yet given that Achilles does later kill Troilus, although the exact means and manner of the slaying are unknown, are we meant to interpret such as confirmation that he did indeed betray the trust of Pandarus and Criseyde somehow? Or did Chaucer place the reference to Achilles here for some other reason? How did English writers of the medieval period, including the *Gawain* poet, view Achilles, best of the Achaeans?

In Homer's *Iliad* Achilles is the tragic figure who destroyed all he held dear, including his own essential humanity, because of pride. His medieval reputation, to say the least, is often less exalted. His reputation was the victim, first, of the post–Homeric tendency such as we see in Euripides to view the Greek heroes of the Trojan War as treacherous, violent, and lacking in moral compass. Roman (and in the medieval period, royal) genealogical links to the Trojans also contributed to a steady degeneration of his character (Patterson 91–94).

As Hector's stature grew so that he became one of the Nine Worthies, so his slayer's, Achilles, fell. It became obvious that Achilles could only have triumphed over Hector by taking unfair advantage, as he does in Chaucer, killing Hector when he is "unwar" of Achilles's presence and off his guard.

But the medieval tradition of the Trojan War also owes much to the late classical "eyewitness" accounts of Dares Phrygius and Dictys Cretensis, from whom, especially Dares, the full medieval tradition later blossomed. Dares first foregrounded what became one of the key aspects of Achilles's narrative in the medieval period: Achilles as the ill-starred lover of the Trojan princess, Polyxena.[4] This story has its roots in the classical period—the story of Polyxena's sacrifice on the tomb of Achilles is told, for example, in Euripides's *Hecuba* (518–82), Ovid's *Metamorphoses* (13.441–526), and Seneca's *Troades* (1138–68), but without any reference to a love story. Achilles's unrequited love for Polyxena was first fully formulated by Benoit de St. Maure (who romanticized it) and then later Guido de Columnis (who ironized it). The typical elements of the story as found in Benoit are straightforward: on the first anniversary of Hector's death, at his tomb in a temple, Achilles sees Polyxena for the first time and, struck by her beauty, immediately falls in love. He withdraws from the fighting lovesick, but also plans to use the withdrawal of his services to the Greeks in war as a bargaining point with the Trojans to negotiate marriage between himself and Polyxena: if his desire to marry Polyxena is granted by the Trojans, he will end the war and Troy will be safe. A trusted friend acts as the intermediary between Achilles and Hecuba, who agrees to the marriage, but only so as to set up the ambush at Hector's tomb in which Achilles, expecting to marry Polyxena, is killed by Paris's arrow instead. Hecuba's motive is revenge for the deaths of Hector and Troilus. When Troy falls, Pyrrhus sacrifices Polyxena on his father's tomb, because of Achilles's love for her. She dies, in Gower's later words, "gulteles / For love, and yit was loveles" (8.2595–96).

Love, or at least a relationship with a woman, features in two more episodes in Achilles's narrative known to medieval readers from the classical tradition. The first is the story of Deidamia as told by Statius in the *Achilleid* (1.318–440). She was impregnated by Achilles while, at the instigation of Thetis, he was dressed as a woman. By disguising her son as a girl, Thetis hoped to prevent Achilles's participation in the Trojan War and thus his inevitable early death. Nevertheless, when his identity is revealed by Ulysses, he abandons Deidamia to go off to the war. She gives birth to Neoptolemus (Pyrrhus). The other story is that of Briseis, the slave girl demanded of Achilles by Agamemnon at the beginning of the *Iliad* (1.184–85). A pleading letter from Briseis to Achilles is the subject of the third letter in Ovid's *Heroides* in which she begs Achilles to accept Agamemnon's offer of reconciliation, which would include the return of Briseis to Achilles, untouched.

In these two stories the emphasis is on Achilles as the betrayer of women. He enters Deidamia's bed on the false pretense that as a woman, he poses no threat to her virginity. Then he abandons her, leaving her to the fate of an unwed mother. Briseis's story could be taken as a story of male sexual betrayal. Indeed in Gower's *Confessio Amantis*, Achilles and Troilus both are briefly mentioned as victims of supplantation in love, Achilles by Agamemnon and Troilus by Diomedes (2.2451–58). However, in Ovid's version Achilles betrays Briseis when he hands his beloved over too quickly, without sufficient protest, to the other man. Briseis accepts that she must be handed over, yet still complains "differri potui; poenae mora grata fuisset" (13).[5] His silence is particularly hurtful and interpreted as a denial of their love:

> nam simul Eurybates me Talthybiusque vocarunt,
> Eurybati data sum Talthybioque comes.
> Alter in alterius iactantes lumina vultum
> quaerebant taciti, noster ubi esset amor [9–12].[6]

And then, worse, Achilles refuses the settlement which would restore the happy couple. Like Deidamia, Briseis has been betrayed by abandonment. As Chaucer says in *The House of Fame*,

> Eke lo how fals and reccheles
> Was to Breseyda Achilles [397–98].

This quick summary of the classical tradition reveals that the parallels between Achilles and Troilus in Chaucer's *Troilus and Criseyde* are more careful, deliberate and manifold than at first glance they may appear. Both are examples of doomed youth: the fate of Troy depends on the lives of both men.[7] Both must die before Troy will fall, and the death of the one will lead to the death of the other. Both fall in love in a similar manner, in a temple at an annual religious service, and immediately fall lovesick. Both are supplanted in love by public circumstances which necessitate the unwilling handover of the woman to another male. Both make no public protest to prevent or delay the transaction. Both are destroyed for the love of a woman. And finally the lovers of both men are destroyed in turn: Polyxena sacrificed on Achilles' tomb and Criseyde ruined in name and reputation. The story of Achilles, then, is clearly the mirror image of Troilus's narrative, and understanding the horizon behind his figure in medieval literature generally can help readers to better understand Chaucer's *Troilus and Criseyde* as a whole. Gower's *Confessio Amantis* and the anonymous *Sir Gawain and the Green Knight* will serve as the illustrative examples of this medieval horizon.

Gower refers to Achilles ten times throughout the *Confessio Amantis*, in seven brief allusions and three fully developed episodes. Gower chooses to push Achilles the unhappy lover into the background of his text, allowing this aspect of his narrative expression but only in brief mentions. He is noted among the company of lovers:

> The worthy Grek also was there,
> Achilles, which for love deide [8.2544–45].

There is the mention of Agamemnon's supplantation of Achilles, another quick reference to Achilles in tandem with Troilus again, falling in love in a temple (5.7591–602), and two mentions of Achilles withdrawing from the battle for the love of Polyxena. The point of these two mentions is illustrative of Gower's attitude. In the first (4.1693–1701), Amans uses the example to support his view that a man need not perform feats of arms to prove his worth to his lady but the Confessor counters by repeating the narrative of Achilles in love with a moralized slant:

> And for thou makst an argument
> Of that thou seidest hiere above,
> Hou Achilles thurgh strengthe of love
> Hise armes lefte for a throwe
> Thou schalt an other tale knowe,
> Which is contraire ...
> Whan that knyhthode schal be werred
> Lust mai noght thanne be preferred;
> The bedd mot thanne be forsake
> And Schield and spere on honde take,
> Which thing schal make hem after glade,
> Whan thei ben worthi knihtes made [4.1798–1810].

The critical attitude expressed here is a clue to Gower's conception of Achilles: he is a man capable of such human weakness, but it is not characteristic of him and not worthy of him. The other references concentrate on his martial prowess. His opposite in character therefore is not the lovelorn Troilus with whom Gower three times associates him, but rather the indolent and, by tradition, common Thersites.

> Orace to his Prince tolde,
> That him were levere that he wolde
> Upon knihthode Achillem suie
> In time of werre, thanne eschuie,
> So as Tersites dede at Troie.
> Achilles al his hole joie
> Sette upon Armes forto fihte;
> Tersites soghte al that he myhte
> Unarmed forto to stonde in rest:
> Bot of the tuo it was the beste
> That Achilles upon the nede
> Hath do, wherof his knyhtlihiede
> Is yit comended overal [7.3581–93].[8]

Gower's portrait of Achilles as the epitome of knighthood is not unproblematic, because it reflects his concerns expressed elsewhere about the unchristian nature of war (3.2260–69). Achilles after all is presented as a warmonger who finds joy in the killing and subjugation of others, even if the Trojan War is arguably a just one. Nevertheless, his opposite, Thersites, does not stand for peace; and in time of need, in the practical day-to-day accounting of human affairs, the continued safety of the realm depends upon the heroic code of conduct as represented by Achilles. Gower takes some care, in fact, to model something other than simple bloodlust in the figure of his princely Achilles. In "Telaphus and Teucer," Achilles is "cruel and fell," but also "worthi" and "among all othre ches" (3.2653–55). Not a mindless killer, he withholds his hand at the request of his son to show mercy to a fallen foe.[9] In the "Education of Achilles," the 12-year-old boy is taught to hunt only the lion and the tiger, to be the killer of killers rather than the weak and the innocent, whereby he learns fearlessness:

> And that hath mad him forto passe
> All othre knihtes of his dede,
> Whan it cam to the gret nede ... [4.2010–12].

The most interesting of the three full episodes is "Achilles and Deidamia." This passage certainly has the potential to effeminize and mock the manly image, for in this story, of course, Thetis dresses Achilles as a girl and transforms him into a woman:

> And thus, after the bokes sein,
> With frette of Perle upon his hed,
> Al freissh betwen the whyt and red,
> As he which tho was tendre of Age,
> Stod the colour in his visage,
> That forto loke upon his cheke
> And sen his childly manere eke,
> He was a womman to beholde [5.3014–21].

There is something amusing in the idea of the fierce Achilles, the terror of the battlefield, being shown as a skillful cross-dresser. In fact, he is so good at passing as a woman that those two ladies' men, Ulysses and Diomede, when they come to fetch Achilles to Troy, cannot, "be his vois ne be his pas" (5.3151), pick him out of the group of young ladies, even though they have been told that is where he is hiding. Yet the point of the episode is not to demonstrate that Achilles has a feminine side, or to deride the macho image as caricature. The central question of the episode is identity: as Ulysses and Diomede must come to identify Achilles for the Greeks to win the war, so Achilles must come to identify himself as a man. Thus the nocturnal activities of Deidamia and Achilles result in pregnancy, as what might have appeared to be lesbianism is identified as heterosexuality. Achilles' identity is revealed even more dramatically by his choice of the gifts Ulysses offers to the group of young ladies. Faced with having to pick between the things of women and the things of men,

> Achilles thanne stod noght stille:
> Whan he the bryhte helm behield,
> The swerd, the hauberk and the Schield,
> His herte fell therto anon;
> Of all that othre wolde he non,
> The knihtes gere he underfongeth,
> And thilke aray which that belongeth
> Unto the wommen he forsok [5.3168–75].

The helm, sword, hauberk, and shield obviously represent Achilles' outer, public representation of himself as a man and a knight. But the message is deeper. Achilles takes the equipment of battle with him to his chamber, where he arms himself in private before making a grand public entrance in his new guise as a knight. But before that, the text suggests that when he rejects the clothing of women, he not only "forsakes" the dresses on offer on the table before him, he also forsakes the woman's clothing on his back by literally stripping off the dress which he is wearing to expose in public his manhood beneath. "Thei knowen thanne which he was" (5.3177), the narrator drily comments. The outer gear of masculinity to which he changes then is not just another superficial public identity. The helm, sword, hauberk, and shield represent Achilles' true inner private identity also: Troy, glory, death. While young and compliant to his mother's wishes (5.2964, 2986–87, 3000, 3009, 3012, 3017, 3020, 3030, 3035), he might have been content to demonstrate a feminine form, but that is a mistake because it constitutes a denial of his identity and of his prophesied destiny.

However, Achilles' time spent in women's dress, as potentially deflating and embarrassing to his martial persona as it may be, is pivotal to understanding the "Achilles and Deidamia" episode as a text concerned with transformation and identity. The boy is first transformed into a woman through the agency of a powerful female figure, Thetis. The "woman" in turn is transformed into a man through the agency of a powerful male figure, the wily Ulysses. The moment Achilles rejects the clothing of women is the moment at which he transforms from a woman to a man, from a child unquestioningly obedient of parental instruction to an adult with choice in the company of his peers. Gower then consistently foregrounds Achilles as the manly, princely hero. With the addition of the Polyxena story to his narrative, he becomes the prototype of the romance hero whose love for a woman leads to his destruction.

Sir Gawain and the Green Knight affords another look, albeit one farther afield, at the Achilles figure in fourteenth-century English literature. The Trojan frame opens and closes the poem, and the poet takes pains to trace Gawain's own lineage back to the Trojan hero, Aeneas. Thus the guide's description of the Green Knight to Gawain needs to be considered within this Trojan framework:

> Ther wonez a wyȝe in that waste, the worst vpon erthe,
> For he is stiffe and sturne, and to strike louies,
> And more he is then any mon vpon myddelerde,
> And his body bigger then the best fowre
> That ar in Arthurez hous, Hestor, other other.
> He cheuez that chaunce at the chapel grene,
> Ther passes non bi that place so proude in his armes
> That he ne dyngez hym to dethe with dynt of his honde;
> For he is a mon methles, and mercy non vses [2098–2106].

The reference to Hestor at l. 2102 gives it away: while the weapon may have changed from a spear to an axe, the Green Knight is pictured by the guide as an Achilles-like opponent for the Trojan-descended hero. Here is an enemy fearsome in his physical prowess, a lover of violence, and a merciless killer of knights. This is the familiar fierce Achilles stripped of all noble restraint, and death for the Trojan hero once again seems certain.[10]

Yet, of course, the monstrous description is all pretend, because the guide's frightening description of the Green Knight as an Achilles figure is part of the setup designed to test Gawain's mettle.[11] In this story, Gawain's enemy is not the external threat posed by the wintry weather, or by an ancestral nemesis, or by the supernatural or even demonic entity he fears at 2185–96. Gawain's "enmy keen" (l. 2406), the Achilles who brings the Trojan hero to the brink of disaster, is none other than the Lady of the Castle:

> Thay lanced wordes gode,
> Much wele then watz therinne;
> Gret perile bitwene hem stod,
> Nif Maré of hir knyȝt mynne [1766–69].

They "lanced" literally means that they spoke, yet the word also invokes a martial image, which reminds the reader of the danger implicit in the social pleasantries going on. The Lady's lance is as potentially deadly as Achilles spear, and Gawain's supernatural patroness, the Virgin Mary, must stand ready to protect her favorite, as Venus once did the Trojan Aeneas.

It would be easy to overstate the case, given that there is no reference to Achilles outright in the text. Even so, there is a remarkable overlap between the incidents involving the Lady in *Sir Gawain and the Green Knight* and the conceits familiar to the Achilles legend as seen in Gower. The juxtaposition of the hunting scenes and the bedroom scenes suggests the Lady is a hunter too, just as Achilles was trained to be. She gains access to his bed on the false pretext that she represents no danger to him—the Lady is willing, secrecy is assured, and all she requires is a harmless kiss. And of course, the bedroom scenes have been orchestrated by a third party. As Thetis conspires to get Achilles into the bed of Deidamia, so too Bertilak to get the Lady into Gawain's. "And the wowyng of my wyf: I wroʒt hit myseluen. / I sende hir to asay the" (2361–62). "Achilles" here is literally a woman beneath the clothes, and the man plays the part of the sexual victim. Through the reversal of gender roles Gawain is reduced indeed to a position of sexual ambivalence (Aers 100; Dinshaw 216–19; Gilbert 63). If the bed is the "woman's" place, then a woman trying to get into Gawain's bed has oblique overtones of lesbianism. Certainly the gift exchanges with Bertilak have homoerotic potentiality: the Lady gives Gawain kisses and Gawain gives Bertilak kisses in turn; therefore, if the Lady were to give her body for Gawain to penetrate, then Gawain in turn would have to give his body to Bertilak for the same purpose. Gawain again would be in the "woman's" position.

The effeminization of Gawain is a clue that the reader should perhaps consider a third option for the text's Achilles figure, Gawain himself. His real enemy, after all, is not so much the fierce Green Knight or the lance wielding Lady as his own human nature. Any lapse in "lewte" on his part truly puts his life at risk, and because of that Gawain, like Achilles, could well die in the service of love if he is not careful. Moreover, it is also noteworthy that in the case of both Achilles and Gawain the cross-dressing motif is apparent:

> ʒet laft he not the lace, the ladiez gifte,
> That forgat not Gawayn for gode of hymseluen.
> Bi he hade belted the bronde vpon his balʒe haunchez,
> Thenn dressed he his drurye double hym aboute,
> Swythe swethled vmbe his swange swetely that knyʒt
> The gordel of the grene silke, that gay wel bisemed [2030–35].

Gawain is reduced to wearing feminine apparel in an effort to preserve his life, rather as Thetis tried to preserve her son. But Gawain is not the only male figure in the text so affected:

> For hit is my wede that thou werez, that ilke wouen girdel,
> My owen wyf hit the weued, I wot well for sothe [2358–59].

Certainly the Green Knight's claim of ownership over the girdle could well be taken as the idea that all property of the wife actually belongs to the husband; nevertheless, it is curious that Bertilak identifies the green and gold silk as being his girdle, as if he were in the habit of wearing it himself.[12]

The effeminizing effect of the cross-dressing is similar to that in Gower's "Achilles and Deidamia," although the *Gawain* text is more playful in its plot twists and turns, its ironic touches, and its play with gendered roles. While the two effeminized heroes, Achilles and Gawain, may be situated in embarrassing circumstances as/by women, the credibility of neither as a man is compromised. In fact, the public revelation of the hero's disgrace leads directly to his transformation and self-recognition: Achilles realizes where his heart truly lies when he adopts the armor and weaponry which proclaim his true, manly identity; Gawain discovers his sinful human nature and thereupon readjusts the public representation of his inner identity (Pearsall 358) to include the girdle in a manner which complements, not supersedes, his shield.

Chaucer's story of Troilus demonstrates how else the motifs common to Gower and the *Gawain* poet can be handled to a very different effect. Troilus too is a hunter, except that the concept is put off to Criseyde only dreaming of Troilus as such (2.925–31) or to suspect images used to describe him (3.602; 3.1191–92). A third party again orchestrates the one's gaining of the other's bed, literally so in the case of Pandarus, who after much deceitful manipulation (Warren 4–6) has to heave Troilus into Criseyde's bed. The armor of Troilus is indeed key to understanding him, yet evidently not equivalent to his identity in the way Achilles' armor is of him. Troilus's armor is like Gawain's shield instead, a partial representation of his true self, his Princely aspect. Chaucer meticulously negotiates a fine line in his portrayal of Troilus to balance the heroic Prince and the star-crossed Lover. On the one hand he is "Hectour the second" but he swoons like a woman. He kills more than a thousand Greeks out on the battlefield (5.1802) but at home in Troy is passive like a woman:

> And whan he fil in any slomberynges,
> Anon bygynne he sholde for to grone,
> And dremen of the dredefulleste thynges
> That myghte ben; as, mete he were allone
> In place horrible makyng ay his mone,
> Or meten that he was amonges alle
> His enemys, and in hire hondes falle [5.246–52].

Troilus and Criseyde lacks the cross-dressing scene which effeminizes Gawain and Gower's Achilles. However, Troilus's first dream in Book 5 achieves the same effect. It occurs the night immediately after Criseyde has been handed over to the Greeks and its elements of fear and isolation remind the reader of her plight. Troilus in effect is dreaming he is Criseyde, and he reacts at 5.253–56 with her accustomed emotion, fear. Like Achilles and Gawain, he has become the woman. However, for Gower and the *Gawain* poet, a positive transformation of the hero occurs through his experience with the feminine. Gower transforms Achilles into a man through his rejection of the woman's dress he has been wearing. The *Gawain* poet masculinizes the feminine object his hero has been wearing, turning it first into the Green Knight's possession and then further transforming it into the "bauderyk" worn by all the Knights of the Round Table (2516). Far from undermining their virility, their effeminization demonstrates what it means to be a man. Troilus, on the other hand, experiences no such positive masculine transformation. At best, his dream allows him a temporary abatement of his childish self-absorption so that for the first and only time in the text he might at least subconsciously empathize with Criseyde's point of view. Otherwise significant transformation and self-recognition in Troilus occurs only after his death.[13]

When one turns to consider how knowledge of Achilles' treatment by Gower and the *Gawain* poet might inform consideration of Chaucer's *Troilus and Criseyde*, it is evident that Chaucer expects his readers to recognize in Achilles the mirror image of Troilus—the parallels are too many and too consistent to ignore. However, it is an inverse reflection. The manly, silent Achilles of Gower whose feminized aspects are submerged is opposed to the effeminate, wordy Troilus whose masculinized aspects are submerged. Chaucer uses the same strategy as Gower in backgrounding one aspect, and foregrounding the other, but in reverse. In Chaucer, the reader hears mention of Prince Troilus as the great hero on the battlefield, but it is the sick, passive Lover which the text shows the reader in elaborate detail. Achilles is the straightforward example of the romance hero who dies for love. He thus acts as the unironic counterpoint to Chaucer's and the *Gawain* poet's ironic exposé of courtly love and courtly lovers.

The Achilles connection also stirs sympathy for Criseyde, but the Lady in *Sir Gawain and the Green Knight* is in a position of power. While she may well be pressured by her husband to participate in the plot against Gawain, it is her free choice to cooperate. After all, she could have chosen to betray her husband's plot or, like Phaedra, to have lied: no witnesses are present to contradict her. But she chooses instead, like Achilles, to take up her lance against her Trojan foe and in so doing to expose her body to potential harm (Pearsall 359). Criseyde, in contrast, has little power over the situation, and she reacts accordingly: as Polyxena is destroyed by Achilles' love for her, as Briseis is abandoned through Achilles' silence and inaction, so too Criseyde. She is manipulated into an unwanted love affair which results in the ruination of her name. Her lover remains silent when he should have spoken against her exchange for Antenor and allows himself to be counseled against any plan of action to prevent or even delay her handover. And, finally, perhaps the presence of Achilles also confirms that there is some poetic justice behind Troilus's manner of death after all. Achilles, so the medieval story goes, the honorable, straight romance hero, intended from the start to marry Polyxena. In Chaucer's ironic version, the subject of marriage is never far below the surface of the story, but not in relation to the marriage of Troilus and Criseyde. On their last night together, Troilus laments,

> Ye shal ek sen, youre fader shal yow glose
> To ben a wif; and as he kan wel preche,
> He shal som Grek so preyse and wel alose
> That ravysshen he shal yow with his speche,
> Or do yow don by force as he shal teche;
> And Troilus, of whom ye nyl han routhe,
> Shal causeles so sterven in his trouthe! [4.1471–77].

If Criseyde does not act as a truthful Penelope or a good Alceste to Troilus, neither is she ever his intended, honored bride. Troilus's death at the hands of Achilles, as per his own words, indeed suggests (unlike Gawain) some divine recognition of his culpability in the betrayal of Criseyde.

Notes

1. For as he drough a kyng by th'aventaille,
    Unwar of this, Achilles thorugh the maille
    And thorugh the body gan hym for to ryve;
    And thus this worthi knyght was brought of lyve. [5.1558–61].
2. But—weilawey, save only Goddes wille,
    Despitously hym slough the fierse Achille. [5.1805–6]
3. In much Trojan material of the Middle Ages Troilus is indeed a second Hector, as can be seen, for example, in Joseph of Exeter (69). Chaucer, however, presents an ambivalent portrait of his hero (Gasse 430–34).
4. Troilus's reference to "my faire suster Polixene" (3.409) is thus another reminder of Achilles's presence. Plus, Pandarus's advice to Criseyde, "Beth rather to [Troilus] cause of flat than egge" (4.927) is arguably yet another Achilles reference, if taken as an allusion to Achilles's sword, which had the power to cure any wound it inflicted. Chaucer mentions this story in the "Squire's Tale" (236–40).
5. "My going might have been deferred; a stay of my pain would have eased my heart" (Loeb translation).
6. "For as soon as Eurybates and Talthybius came to ask for me, to Eurybates was

I given over, and to Talthybius, to go with them. Each, casting eyes into the face of the other, inquired in silence where now was the love between us" (Loeb translation). Homer's Achilles, of course, protests very loudly indeed in the council at the start of the *Iliad*, and Ovid's Briseis speaks only from her limited personal knowledge of the situation.

   7. For Troilus the idea can be traced back to Servius's commentary on *Aeneid* 2.13. For Achilles, the tradition extends as far back as the *Iliad*.

   8. As Macaulay and Peck have both pointed out in their notes to these lines, Gower's source is not Horace but Juvenal's *Satire* 8.269–71. Gower's interpretation is a rather loose adaptation of Juvenal's text, which concentrates on the unimportance of noble lineage.

   9. Gower's literary merit is not often recognized, yet the "Telaphus and Teucer" episode is noteworthy for its structural balance and ironic polarities. Achilles' mercy to Teucer in the past was rewarded with "distance / amonges ous" (2695–96); Telaphus's mercy to Teucer in the present is rewarded with closeness when Telaphus becomes Teucer's nominal son and heir (3.2708–9). Achilles rescues Teucer in a quarrel so that Teucer keeps his estates (3.2693–94); Telaphus rescues Teucer in a quarrel so that Teucer loses his estates (3.2709–10). Gower misidentifies Telaphus as Achilles' son.

   10. The guide's strategy in building up Gawain's fear of the Green Knight is comparable to that of the Sibyl in Vergil's *Aeneid* (6.83–97). She alludes outright to an "alius ... Achilles" ("another Achilles") awaiting Aeneas in Italy (6.89).

   11. It is tantalizing to speculate that the guide is actually the shape-shifting Bertilak in yet another disguise; however, the text offers no definitive evidence either for or against the possibility. Both sides have been argued by scholars. See, for example, Benson 228–30; Delaney 250–55.

   12. The Lady calls the object "my girdle" (1829); the narrative voice refers to it as "the ladiez gifte" (2030); and speaking to Bertilak, Gawain calls it "your gordel" (2429). Bertilak gives Gawain possession of the girdle at 2395.

   13. The debate over the degree of Troilus's self-absorption is ongoing. For two recent points of view, see Moore 43–59 and Warren 5.

Works Cited

Aers, D. "Christianity for Courtly Subjects: Reflections on the *Gawain* poet." *A Companion to the Gawain poet*. Ed. D. Brewer and J. Gibson. Arthurian Studies 38. Woodbridge, Suffolk and Rochester, New York: D. S. Brewer, 1997. 91–101.
Benson, L. D. *Art and Tradition in Sir Gawain and the Green Knight*. New Brunswick: Rutgers UP, 1965.
Chaucer, G. *The Riverside Chaucer*. Ed. L. D. Benson. 3rd ed. Boston: Houghton Mifflin, 1987.
Delaney, P. "The Role of the Guide in *Sir Gawain and the Green Knight*." *Neophilogus* 49 (1965): 250–55.
Dinshaw, C. "A Kiss Is Just a Kiss: Heterosexuality and Its Consolations in *Sir Gawain and the Green Knight*." *Diacritics* 24 (1994): 204–26.
Euripides. *Hecuba*. Ed. Michael Tierney. Bristol: Bristol Classical Press, 1946.
Frazier, R. M., ed. and trans. *The Trojan War: The Chronicles of Dictys of Crete and Dares the Phrygian*. Bloomington: Indiana UP, 1966.
Gasse, R. "Deiphebus, Hector and Troilus in Chaucer's *Troilus and Criseyde*." *Chaucer Review* 32 (1998): 423–39.
Gilbert, J. "Gender and Sexual Transgression." *A Companion to the Gawain poet*. Ed. D. Brewer and J. Gibson. Arthurian Studies 38. Woodbridge, Suffolk and Rochester, New York: D. S. Brewer, 1997. 53–69.

Gower, J. *Confessio Amantis*. Ed. R. Peck. 1968. MART 9. Toronto, Buffalo, London: U of Toronto P, 1980.
Gower, J. *The English Works of John Gower*. 2 vols. Ed. G. M. Macaulay. EETS O.S. 81/82. Oxford: Oxford UP, 1900/1901.
Homer. *Iliad. Books I–XII*. Vol. 1. Ed. and trans. William Wyatt and A. T. Murray. Loeb 170. Cambridge and London: Harvard UP, 1924.
Joseph of Exeter. *The Iliad of Dares Phrygius*. Ed. and trans. Gildas Roberts. Capetown: A. A. Balkina, 1970.
Juvenal. *Juvenal and Persius*. Ed. and trans. G. G. Ramsay. Loeb 091. Cambridge and London: Harvard UP, 1918.
Moore, M. R. "Who's Solipsistic Now? The Character of Chaucer's Troilus." *Chaucer Review* 33 (1998): 43–59.
Ovid. *Heroides and Amores*. Vol. 1. Ed. and trans. G. Showerman. Loeb 041. Cambridge and London: Harvard UP, 1963.
Ovid. *Metamorphoses Books IX–XV*. Vol. 4. Ed. and trans. F. J. Miller. Loeb 042. Cambridge and London: Harvard UP, 1916.
Patterson, L. *Chaucer and the Subject of History*. Madison: U of Wisconsin P, 1991.
Pearsall, D. "Courtesy and Chivalry in *Sir Gawain and the Green Knight*: The Order of Shame and the Invention of Embarrassment." *A Companion to the Gawain Poet*. Ed. D. Brewer and J. Gibson. Arthurian Studies 38. Woodbridge, Suffolk and Rochester, New York: D. S. Brewer, 1997. 351–62.
Seneca. *Tragedies: Hercules Furens. Troades. Medea, Hippolytus or Phaedra, Oedipus*. Vol. 8. Ed. and trans. F. J. Miller. Loeb 450. Cambridge and London: Harvard UP, 1917.
Sir Gawain and the Green Knight. Ed. J. R. R. Tolkien and E. V. Gordon. 1925. Rev. 2d ed. by Norman Davis. Oxford: Oxford UP, 1967.
Statius. *Thebaid. Books V–XII, Achilleid*. Vol. 2. Ed. and trans. J. H. Mozley. Loeb 207. Cambridge and London: Harvard UP, 1928.
Vergil. *Aeneidos Liber Sextus*. Ed. R. G. Austin. Oxford: Oxford UP, 1977.
Warren, V. "(Mis)Reading the 'Text' of Criseyde: Context and Identity in Chaucer's *Troilus and Criseyde*." *Chaucer Review* 36 (2001): 1–15.
Windeatt, B. *Oxford Guide to Chaucer: Troilus and Criseyde*. Oxford: Oxford UP, 1992.

Classical Analogues—Eastern and Western—of Sir Gawain

Zacharias P. Thundy

NORTHERN MICHIGAN UNIVERSITY AND
THE UNIVERSITY OF NOTRE DAME

Scholars and critics of *Sir Gawain and the Green Knight* agree that the romance is overtly Celtic in sources and analogues as well as Christian in inspiration and meaning.[1] While wholeheartedly concurring with this view, I argue that the multidimensional poem is covertly very classical—Latin, Greek, Arabic in details of the story and plot—that is, the *Gawain* poem has borrowed several motifs not only from classical sources like Vergil's *Aeneid*, Ovid's *Metamorphoses*, and Homer's *Odyssey* but also from the Arabic *1,001 Nights* and the Arabic art form known as the *Arabesque*.[2]

There are four parts to this essay: (1) *Gawain* and the Western Classics, (2) *Gawain* and the Matter of Araby, (3) The Pentangle and the Arabesque, (4) *Gawain*'s Sin/Non-sin and Medieval Moral Theology.

Gawain and the Western Classics

The Gawain-story and Source-Critics

Though the plot of *Gawain* is well known to students of medieval English literature, let me recapitulate it for the benefit of others, the non-specialists, who may not have read it for a while.

There are two adventures in the story. The first, the Green Knight's challenge and the ensuing beheading match, occupies the first and fourth divisions of the poem. Gawain cuts off the head of the Green Knight after accepting the condition that a year later he himself would submit to the same fate at the hands of the Green Knight on New Year's Day at the Green Chapel.

Gawain keeps his tryst with destiny by seeking out the perilous place of the Green Knight in the valley of tears at land's end. Gawain, believing that he is protected by heaven's grace and the magic charm of the green sash, meets his opponent in the Green Chapel. The Green Knight, instead of chopping off Gawain's head, nicks the knight's bare neck with his axe-blade and forgives Gawain's failure in keeping his promise to the fullest: "But here yow lakked a lyttel, sir, and lewte yow wonted" [There was something missing in you, sir: you lacked fidelity] (2366).[3]

The second adventure occupies the second and third divisions of the poem. It is the temptation of Gawain by the Lady of the castle of Bertilak de Hautdesert; while the Lady tests Gawain's chastity three times, the host tests Gawain's truthfulness through the device of the Exchange of Winnings. Gawain's failure to fulfill the contract of exchange in the case of the green and gold girdle is matched in the fourth division with the "nirt in the neck" [slight cut in the neck] (2498).

This particular *Gawain* romance is not totally based on any previous French or other European romances; however, the two adventures, in some details, are found in other earlier Irish romances. The beheading match has a very clear analogue in the Middle Irish prose narrative of *Fled Bricrend* (*ca.* 1100): the great Celtic hero, Cuchulainn, accepts the beheading match and fulfills his word to come back and receive the blow; the champion is unharmed after three strokes of the axe. This Celtic motif of beheading was taken up in French romances dealing with the matter of Britain, like *Le Livre de Caradoc, Perlesvaus, La mule sans frein, Hunbaut,* and others. The theme of the temptation of a knight by a lady, though perhaps of very remote Celtic origins, is found only in the Continental Arthurian romances like the Swiss *Lanzelet,* the French *Ider, Lancelot du Lac, Le Chevalier à l'Epée,* and *Hunbaut.* For instance, in *Ider,* a queen, at the instigation of her husband, tests Ider's virtue by making advances to him in the hall while he is asleep; Ider crudely rejects her with a kick in her stomach to the amusement of the courtiers who are present.

What is remarkable about the Celtic and French sources of the poem is that the combined plot of *Gawain* is not found in any single extant romance. Though Kittredge believed that the immediate source of the English romance was a French romance now lost (Kittredge 128–29, 137), he gives no evidence to support his theory. Tolkien, Gordon, and Davis write: "That he knew French romances intimately is beyond question, from his language as well as his story; but his use of French terms and even idioms does not mean that he took them from a particular model" (xx).

It is equally undeniable that the *Gawain* romance is medievally Christian or traditionally Catholic in its religious and moral teachings. There are prayers in the poem to the Virgin Mary, frequent going to mass, and confession. There is emphasis in the poem on the need to avoid the sins of pride and lust and on the Christian duty to practice humility and chastity. Perceptive critics since the time of W. P. Ker (1912) have pointed out, as Bloomfield succinctly puts it, "The poem is fairly and squarely Christian."[4] The success of the poem, however, does not fundamentally arise, according to Kane, "from the concepts of conduct upon which the characters act.... The exceptional success of this romance comes from other sources than the principles of behaviour upon which its action is based."[5]

Though Kane finds the source of the success of the poem in its acute visualization of action and setting (73–76), other critics have sought the key to the poem's success in its folkloric and mythic elements. As early as 1897, Jessie Weston had suggested that Gawain was originally a sun hero and was related to the Irish hero Cuchulainn.[6] The greenness of the Knight inspired Chambers to suggest in 1903 that the Green Man of the peasant lore is the challenger in *Gawain* (*Medieval Stage*, I: 117, 185–86). Nitze thinks that the vegetation myth and ritual, which is best preserved in the *Perlesvaus* analogue, underlie the poem (351). Krappe argues that Gawain's journey to the Green Chapel is a re-creation of the myth of the hero's journey to the realm of the dead for the purpose of defeating death (206–15). Speirs, the most prominent proponent of the mythological theory, tells us that the Green Man is the descendent of the vegetation god whose death and resurrection symbolize the annual death and rebirth of nature (Speirs 274–300; Bloomfield 37–43).

Gawain and Motif Sources

Undoubtedly, Celtic, French, Christian, and mythological sources contribute immensely to the enduring popularity of *Gawain*. However, they do not account for several striking features of the poem such as the motif of the Lady's life-saving girdle, "the color of the Green Knight and his horse and the strange conception of the Green Chapel" (Tolkien, Gordon, and Davis 130). That is why we should argue that they are not the only sources of the poem. Though perhaps the greenness of the knight and the redness of his eyes are ultimately drawn from popular belief in a "green man," their immediate literary source is Vergil's *Aeneid* and Ovid's *Metamorphoses* as well as the Arabian *1,001 Nights* (to be developed in the next part of this paper). Further, Gawain's *nirt*, the girdle motif, and the tests have some fascinating analogues (sources?) in the *Odyssey*. Also, there are other important elements in the poem that ultimately go back to the matter of Araby, as I shall point out later in this article. Incidentally, no one has pointed out these classical and Arabic parallels for *Sir Gawain and the Green Knight*.[7]

Gawain and the *Aeneid*

The Green Knight as tempter is obviously a demonic figure having close associations with the underworld; he is closely related to Morgan le Fay (Morgne the goddess) who is well versed in the occult and black magic (2447) of the underworld. The association of the green color with the devil, the fairies, and the dead is quite medieval, as Burrow (14), Wimberly (175–78, 240–43) and Robertson (470–72) have pointed out; Gawain, like the typical classical hero, has to descend into hell, the realm of the "demonic" Green Knight. His abode is at the bottom of the broad valley ("the bothem of the brem valay" [2145], where he has lived a very long time ["He hath wonyd here ful yore" (2114)]. The Green Chapel turns out to be a green mound beside a brimming creek:

> a balw berw bi a bonke the brymme bysyde,
> Bi a fors of a flode that ferked thare;
> the borne blubred therinne as hit boyled hade [2172–74].
> [a round mound beside a stream, next to
> cascades of water which flowed there, foaming
> and frothing feverishly.]

This picture of the netherworld is evocative of Vergil's description of hell:

> ...facilis descensus Averno:
> sed revocare gradum superasque evadere ad auras.
> hoc opus, hic labor est...
> ...tenent media omnia silvae,
> Cocytosque sinu labens circumvenit atro [*Aeneid*. 6.126–32].

Further, the poet alludes to the demonic nature of the place: "Here myght aboute midnyght / the dele his matynnes telle" [Here the Devil might be saying his matins at about midnight (2187–88)]. Gawain says to himself:

> ..."Wysty is here;
> This oritore is vgly, with erbes ouergrowen;
> Wel bisemes the wyye wruxled in grene
> Dele here his devocioun on the develes wyse.
> Now I fele hit is the fende, in my fyve wyttes,
> That hath stoken me this steuen to strye me here" [2189–94].

[This place is deserted; it is an ugly oratory, all overgrown, suitable for the gentleman garbed in green to recite his prayers in the Devil's fashion. Now I feel it in my senses that the Devil himself led me to this place to destroy me.]

Now the Green Knight comes out of his cave and vaults across the river on his axe by using it as a pole like a ferryman: "When he wan to the watter, / ther he wade nolde, / He hypped ouer on hys ax" (2231-32).

All the foregoing references to hell, river, pole, and guardian have their source in the *Aeneid*: the Green Knight is hardy and green like Charon, the ferryman, on the banks of Acheron. Since this creature is like Charon, he is supernatural or immortal—he cannot die even though his head has been chopped off—he is demonic, he is old, and he is green. Vergil is cunningly clear on this point: Charon is "iam senior, sed cruda deo viridisque senectus" (6.304). The following Vergilian passage seems to have been in the mind of the *Gawain* poet in his description of the Green Knight and his abode:

> hinc via Tartarei quae fert Acherontis ad undas.
> turbidus hic caeno vastaque voragine gurges
> aestuat atque omnem Cocyto eructat harenam.
> portitor has horrendus aquas et flumina servat
> terribili squalore Charon, cui plurima mento
> canities inculta iacet, stant lumina flamma,
> sordidus ex umeris nodo dependet amictus.
> ipse ratem conto subigit, velisque ministrat
> et ferruginea subvectat corpora cumba,
> iam senior sed cruda deo viridisque senectus [6.295-304].

The above description of Charon by Vergil is very similar to the *Gawain poet*'s description of the Green Knight:

> Wel gay watz this gnome gered in grene,
> And the here of his hed of his hors swete.
> Fayre fannand fax vmbefoldes his schuldres;
> A much herd as a busk ouer his brest henges,
> That wyth his highlich here that of his hed reches
> Was euesed al vmbetorne abof his elbowes,
> That half his armes ther-vnder were halched in the wyse
> Of a kynges capados that closes his swyre [179-186].

[This charming knight was clothed in green. His hair, like his horse's mane, hung loose, clustering in curls like a cloak round his shoulders. His bushy beard flowed down his breast. His noble hair that hung loose from his head was cut above his elbows, shorn right round, so that half his arms were under the encircling hair, covered as by a king's cape, that closes at the neck.]

This Vergilian passage also accounts not only for the green color of the knight but also for the knight's loose cloak, beard, and especially red eyes ("rede yyen he reled aboute" [304]) vis-á-vis "stant Lumina flamma" (*Aeneid*. 6.300); only Vergil supplies the source for the red eyes of the Green Knight. Indeed, as White testifies, "the Green Knight's red eyes ... do not appear in the various sources and analogues proposed for this poem (224)."

There is another very striking verbal parallel, besides the word *green*, in the description of the Green Knight: it is the word *old* in the phrase *the olde lorde* (1124). Also, Vergil's golden bough, I suspect, is perhaps the inspiration behind the Green Knight's holly branch *(holyn bobbe*, 206).

Gawain and Ovid's Metamorphoses

On the other hand, Ovid, not Vergil, is most likely the source for the *Gawain poet*'s association of *green* with envy in the romance. It is Morgan— she envies Queen Guinevere's good fortune at Arthur's court and furious about her own expulsion from the court engineered by the queen (Tolkien, Gordon, and Davis 130)—who transforms Bertilak into the Green Knight and sends him to Arthur's court (2456–62). Of course, it is possible that "green with envy" was already a commonplace expression, though not recorded in written English, in the spoken English language in the fourteenth century. However, the first literary illustration for the phrase dates from the middle of the fifteenth century. As far as I can ascertain from Classical sources, the earliest literary reference to envy's association with *green* is found in Ovid's *Metamorphoses,* where Ovid's Envy *(Invidia)* is sleepless ("nec fruitur somno," 2.779) and greenish in hue: "pectora felle virent, lingua est suffusa veneno" (2.777). Here the parallel is not perfect in the sense that Morgan is green like Invidia; rather Morgan's instrument of jealousy—Lord Bertilak, the personification of jealousy—is green. Is it not also more than coincidental that the color of the Lady's girdle is green, that she is somewhat sleepless (1733–35), that she is tempting Gawain to sin with her mouth and tongue, and that Morgan resembles Ovid's *Invidia* in her ancient looks?

Gawain and the Odyssey

In the romance there are, in addition, three other motifs which can be accounted for by the *Odyssey*; these associations would make Gawain more like the wily Odysseus than the noble Aeneas of the Greek poem.

First, there is Gawain's *nirt* or wound by which he has acquired a new identity and which he displays at the court of Arthur ("The nirt in the nek he naked hem shewed" [2499]). This wound of Gawain is like the scar of Odysseus—the Homeric hero received it during a boar hunt. Though there is also a boar hunt in *Gawain,* the boar does not inflict any wound on Gawain.[8] That Gawain's *nirt* is a probable reference to Odysseus's scar is supported by the following two remaining parallels. In the *Odyssey* there are three tests that Penelope subjects Odysseus to: the stringing of the bow, the shooting of the arrow through the twelve axe eyes, and the feigned placing of Odysseus's bed outside the couple's bedroom. The tests are similar not in content but only in the fact that there are three tests. It is to be mentioned here that, as a reluctant lover, Gawain is like Odysseus. Odysseus spent seven years with Calypso on the island of Ogygia and shared her bed unwillingly. When Calypso offered him immortality, he spurned it; he wished rather to be with his wife and son. Gawain, too, is a reluctant lover in his behavior with Bertilak's wife: when she offers herself to Gawain, the hero turns her down. However, when she offers him the green girdle or putative immortality or temporary protection from harm's way, the Green Knight's axe, he accepts it. Odysseus also accepted Calypso's aid in equipping his raft even though he had rejected her earlier.

The green girdle of Gawain also has a counterpart in the *Odyssey.* When Odysseus's raft was in danger of sinking in the sea on account of the wrath of Poseidon and the jealousy of Calypso, the sea-nymph Ino, the daughter of Cadmus, took pity on the woebegone Odysseus. She offered him her veil, which he fastened around his waist to protect himself from death while he was being tossed about in the sea (5.37 ff.).

Like Odysseus, Gawain also is saved by a similar veil, the Lady's green girdle. The Lady assures Gawain: "For quat gome so is gorde with this grene lace, / While he hit hade hemely halched aboute, / Ther is no hathel vnder heuen tohewe hym that might" (For no man under heaven is capable of killing the man that binds his body with this green belt as long as it is fastened closely about his person (1851-53. Probably the exigency of the plot requires that the green girdle save Gawain; however, more than likely, from the Christian perspective of the author, it is the Virgin Mary to whom Gawain has prayed (645-48, 736-39, 754-60) who saves him from temporal and eternal damnation. Odysseus, too, is saved from death on the island of the Phaeacians by Virgin Nausicaa whom he has invoked for protection (*Odyssey,* Book 6). Both Odysseus and Gawain accept the gifts; both are saved from imminent death; both return the gifts, after their ordeals, to the rightful owners. But while Odysseus does not get to keep his life-saving talisman, Gawain receives permission to keep his charm, which he wears as a baldric (2506). In passing, it is worthwhile to mention that the wraith of Heracles wears a baldric in the *Odyssey* as a sign of his courage (11.609-25), whereas

Gawain's baldric seems to be a symbol of cowardice (2508). Of course, in this connection it is impossible to overlook Ovid's reference to Proserpine's girdle (*Met.* 5.470), which is clearly associated with the underworld.

We also notice a parallel between the word-portrait of Gawain's pentangled shield and Vergil's elaborate description of the etchings on Aeneas's shield in Book 8 of the *Aeneid*. Needless to say, Aeneas's to Italy and Odysseuss's voyages from Troy presage Gawain's northward travel, especially since hell lies north in medieval conception.

The Poet's Use of Classics

It is appropriate that the *Gawain poet*, in his appraisal of the flawed, but allegedly all-perfect, heroic man, makes use of the imperfect heroes associated with Britain, especially Aeneas, whose grandson Brutus is the legendary founder of Britain. On the Gawain-Aeneas connection, Johnson writes:

> Aeneas' journey from Troy to Italy may lie behind Gawain's journey to the north and his experiences there. Gawain, like Aeneas, is forced to leave his own city and finds himself lost in unfamiliar territory.... Both men are tempted in conjunction with hunting and give in to temptation.... Both poems contain a female who manipulates the action. Morgan, like Juno, stands behind Gawain's ordeal, for she wishes to destroy Camelot as Juno wishes to halt the founding of Rome.... For the Middle Ages, Aeneas was a hero, despite his reputation as a traitor [71].

Indeed, it is quite appropriate to pattern the story of Brutus after that of Aeneas, the story of Gawain after that of Aeneas, and the story of Aeneas after that of Odysseus; it is also appropriate that the poet present Gawain's adventures after those of Odysseus. The poet himself shows the suitability of this approach by means of rhetorical *insinuationes* which he has inserted into the historical introduction and conclusion and which connect the story to the authoritative matter of Troy (1–19; 2524–30; Silverstein 189–206).

There is no doubt that Vergil and the *Aeneid* were well known in the Middle Ages and probably to the *Gawain poet*. In fact, the poet mentions the name of Aeneas, who is the great-grandfather of Brutus, the legendary founder of Britain (1–7). However, one wonders why the poet refrains from mentioning Odysseus's name, probably because of the common British prejudice against him as the destroyer of Troy and because the British rulers have claimed descent from Trojan princes. However, church fathers on the whole accepted Odysseus as a morally commendable pagan hero, as "the wise Ithacan," *sapiens ithacus*. About Ino's girdle and Odysseus's landing in Ithaca, St. Basil writes:

Thus by his story of Odysseus among the Phaeacians ... the poet seeks to say aloud to mankind, "Ye men must strive after virtue which swims to land alongside the shipwrecked mariner and makes him who has been washed naked ashore more worthy of honor than the frivolous Phaeacians" [Stanford and Luce 178].

Clement of Alexandria and the Latin Father Ambrose also offered similar praise. But during and after the bitter theological controversies between the Greek-speaking Eastern Christians and the Troy-loving Western Christians, Western thinking cultivated the anti–Ulyssean attitude of Vergil's *Aeneid* and Dares' *Troiae Historia* (sixth century). In Benoit's *Roman de Troie* of 1160, Ulysses is an inveterate liar and unrivaled trickster; nonetheless, when he describes Ulysses' adventures, Dares shows him more respect than Dictys did in his *Ephemeris Belli Troiani* (fourth century). He is loved by Penelope and his people; he has a grandson born to Telemachus and Nausicaa. Benoit's Ulysses is found in the subsequent accounts of the tales of Troy such as Joseph of Exeter's *De Bello Troiano* (1188), Guido delle Colonne's *Historia Destructionis Troiae* (1287), *The Gest Hystoriale of the Destruction of Troy* (1287), *The Seege or Batayle of Troie* (early fourteenth century), Gower's *Confessio Amantis* (1393), Lydgate's *Troy Book* (1420), and Caxton's *Recuyell of Historyes of Troy* (ca. 1474). Ulysses' popularity in the Middle Ages can be gleaned also from manuscript illuminations found in England, France, Spain, Switzerland, and Germany.[9]

Conclusion

The purpose of this brief reference to the Ulysses theme in the Middle Ages has been to show that stories about Odysseus were accessible to the *Gawain* poet. What I suggest is simply that the poet had every reason and opportunity to consult his classical sources as well, the *Aeneid* and the Ulysses tradition, besides his Celtic and French sources. The classical elements of the romance add to the artistic embellishment of the story: the story takes place in a faraway land, *in illo tempore*, not just among ordinary people but also among supernatural beings. Gawain and the Green Knight are as historical and as mythical as Aeneas, Odysseus, and Charon are. In accepting the girdle of the Lady in cowardice, Gawain, like Odysseus, admits that he too is vulnerable and vincible; unlike Odysseus, Gawain performs an act of humility. Further, Gawain implies that, even though Grace may save his soul, it will not necessarily save his neck, that confession is good for the soul but bad for the body, and that Odyssean wile, like the snakelike cunning recommended by Jesus, is necessary for survival. That is why Gawain dilly-dallies with the Lady of the castle and obtains the life-saving "grace" of the girdle by using courtly tact and serpentine cunning, without committing a mortal sin according to his conscience and in the eyes of the church and the court. All the same, when his "venial" sins of cowardice and treachery are discovered ("But here yow lakked a lyttel, sir, and lewte yow wonted" [There was something missing in you, sir: you lacked fidelity, 2366], Gawain makes a virtue out of necessity by making the brand of shame into a badge of courage as he wears the baldric, a sign of imperfection, alongside his pentangle, the symbol of the golden mean of virtue, which always stands in the middle by avoiding the extremes.

Indeed, it is time that we paid closer attention to the Classics in our hermeneutics and in our explication and interpretation of all medieval literature. The English vernacular writers were much more literate than we have so far acknowledged. Of course, we say that they were well schooled in their Christian theology, but I would add that they also knew the Classical tradition better than we give them credit for.

Gawain *and the Matter of Araby*

So far I have argued that the Middle English romance *Sir Gawain and the Green Knight* contains quite a few classical allusions and references, particularly in its portrait of the Green Knight. Now by suggesting Arabic influences on the romance, I am not offering a retraction of my previous view; rather, I want to add a new dimension to the resourcefulness of the *Gawain* poet while reaffirming my conviction about the classical sources of the poem. *Sir Gawain and the Green Knight* also accesses Oriental and/or Arabic in its resources, which the poet effectively used in the composition of the colorful romance.

Apologia pro Oriente

The rationale for this eclectic view is based on the principle not that any no one view is the only truth, but that the whole truth is found in many rather than in one viewpoint. According to the ancient Indian Jain literary theory of *Anekantavada* (Principle of Uncertainty), a complete view of reality includes many perspectives. Consider the ancient Indian parable of the four blind men touching the elephant and coming up with four partially correct statements on what the elephant is, depending on which anatomical part of the animal each one touched—a broom (according to the man who touched the elephant's tail), a fan (according to the one who touched the elephant's ear), a wall (according to the person who touched the elephant's torso), and a pillar (according to the man who examined the elephant's trunk); the arbiter of the dispute judged that in reality the elephant is a combination of all four correct responses.[10] In other words, acceptance of contrary beliefs is essential to the understanding of reality. The text of *Sir Gawain and the Green Knight* is a composite reality derived from Celtic, classical, Christian, mythical, French, Oriental, and other sources.

The first serious critic who called attention to the Oriental dimension of the poem was Ananda K. Coomaraswamy, during the heyday of myth criticism when critical emphasis was on the mythical meaning of the elements in the sources in *Gawain*. Coomaraswamy was one of several major myth critics of the time, like William Nitze, A. H. Krappe, Heinrich Zimmer, John Speirs, and Jessie Weston (Bloomfield 7–19; Coomaraswamy 104–25). To the surprise of Western critics, Coomaraswamy provided a new analogue to the beheading episode of the *Gawain*-poem from Indian mythology—from the Vedic story of Indra and Namuci, in which we have the image of a dynamic disembodied head speaking. According to the later Puranic version, the story is as follows.

In one of the great battles between the gods and the asuras, Indra, the king of the gods, was unable to overcome Namuci, who hid himself in a ray of light, thus shielding the sun from the earth. Indra discovered Namuci, who agreed to come out of hiding on condition that Indra not slay him with anything dry or wet, during night or day. The battle continued. One evening Namuci went to the beach. At twilight, which is neither day nor night, Indra killed him on the seashore with the foam of the sea, which is supposedly neither dry nor wet. The separated head of Namuci followed Indra, accusing him of amicide and Brahmicide, wherever Indra went. The gift of the foam as a weapon was made to Indra by the Asvins and Sarasvati, to whom Indra promised Soma which was being drained away almost completely by Namuci. The significance of Namuci's death is that it released waters which were melted by the rays of the sun as well as the liberation of the sun from darkness. In other words, the Indra-Namuci story is a myth version of the rise of life from death for the salvation of the world. The myth's relevance to the *Gawain*-story consists primarily in the motif of the speaking head of Namuci, which kept following Indra and calling him, "O, wicked slayer of thy friend" (see Coomaraswamy).

Kittredge also has called critics' attention to the motif of the speaking head found in the *Arabian Nights* story of "The King and the Physician" (Kittredge 186). Like Coomaraswamy and other critics, Kittredge also looks at the story of the speaking head as an archetypical folklore motif. Nitze finds the source of Gawain's journey in the vegetation myth, whereas Krappe finds the root in a journey to hell for the purpose of defeating death. Zimmer also finds the vegetation myth appealing in the sense that

Gawain's journey to the underworld is a conquest of death. John Speirs, another influential critic, calls *Sir Gawain and the Green Knight* "a midwinter festival poem" and finds the Green Knight related to the Green Man—the Jack in the Green or the Wild Man of the village festivals of England and Europe, who is a descendant of the Vegetation or Nature god ... whose death and resurrection are the myth-and-ritual counterpart of the annual death and rebirth of nature" (Speirs 274–300). Among all the myth critics, Coomaraswamy stands out in the sense that he gives new analogues to the beheading episode.

Islamic Green Man

The Knight's greenishness intrigued Alice Lasater as she carefully looked at the romance from an Oriental perspective. In fact, she traces the Knight's greenishness to the East, to the matter of Arabia. Though I myself have attributed the poet's detailed portrait of the Green Knight's green color, red eyes, loose cloak, and flowing beard to Vergil's portrait of Charon in the *Aeneid*, I agree without hesitation also with Lasater's suggestion that the figure of the Green Knight can be traced back to al-Khadir, "the Green One" of Persian and Arabic lore. In my view the *Gawain* poet classicized the Khadir of the Islamic East and provided the symbolic meaning of greenness as envy from Ovid (Thundy 169ff.).

Al-Khadir, a pre–Islamic figure, appears in the Qur'an (sura XVII, sections 9 and 10), where he is a traveling companion of Musa (Moses) and a messenger of God. In *Gawain* also the Green Knight is a traveling demonic figure, nonetheless a messenger (*angelos* in Greek), whom God uses for his purposes. Whether bad demon or good angel or both, the Green One or al–Khadir is a messenger. Lasater argues that it is in Sufi writings that al-Khadir "develops into a forerunner of the Green Knight" (192), as in the writings of the Persian Farid ud-din Attar, who tells this story.

Ibrahim ibn Adham (d. 782), king of Balkh, was one day having a general audience. "Suddenly a man with aweful mien entered the chamber, so terrible to look upon that none of the royal retinue and servants dared ask him his name; the tongues of all clove to their throats." He approaches Ibrahim's throne, and when asked what he wants, replies that he has just alighted "at this caravanserai." Ibrahim replies that it is not a caravanserai. The stranger asks who possessed the throne before him and Ibrahim replies, "My father." "And before him?" "My grandfather." And so on, until the stranger remarks that it is a caravanserai, since as soon as one man leaves, another enters, and he too leaves for another. Ibrahim is shaken. He gives up his kingdom and wealth and becomes a pilgrim. On his way to Mecca, he calls on God, and Khadir then comes and explains to him the visit of the stranger and identifies himself, Khadir, as that stranger (Attar 62–67).

Remarkably, the figure of the Khadir is found also in the *1,001 Nights*: He is green in color; as he appears at the royal court unexpectedly, he bedazzles the courtiers who fall silent at the apparition; he does not give away his identity or the purpose of his presence in the royal court; only later would he reveal his identity. For example, the Khadir is a character in "The Tale of Abu Muhammad Called Lazybones"—he, the supernatural agent, is dressed in green and challenges the hero. In "The Tale of Taj al-Muluk and the princess Dunya," a reference is made to Moses's encounter with the Khadir. In "The Adventures of Bulukiya" (within "the Tale of the Queen of Serpents"), the Khadir comes to the rescue of Bulukiya of the children of Israel when he is stranded on one of the islands. In "The City of Brass," Musa Ibn-Nusayr meets a tribe of black Muslims in Africa; Musa inquires how they became Muslims without the help of the Prophets, and they respond that the Khadir (Abu al-Abbas al-Khadir) taught them Islam. The Khadir turns the unbelieving people, except the princess, who becomes a believer, into stone in "The Tale of Abdallah Ibn Fadil and His Brothers." The Khadir instructs the princess in the faith and continues to visit her every Friday after rescuing her from the jealousy of the brothers of Abdallah (Lasater 117–19, 193).

It is useful to note that the Khadir also appears in "The Friar's Tale" found in Chaucer's *Canterbury Tales*, where he is the devil as in *Sir Gawain and the Green Knight*:

> And so bifel that ones on a day
> This somnour, evere waityng on his pray
> Rod for to somne an old wydwe, a ribibe,
> Feynynge a cause, for he wolde brybe.
> And happed that he saugh before hym ryde
> A gay yeman, under a forest syde.
> A bowe he bar, and arwes brighte and kene;
> He hadde upon a courtepy of grene,
> An hat upon his heed with frenges blake [D: 1375–83].

The strong probability that Chaucer was familiar with the matter of Araby certainly finds support in "The Squire's Tale," which has parallels in the *1,001 Nights* in Princess Dunya's dream of the fowler and the pigeons, the story of the flying horse, the Canacee and falcon episode, and the incest motif.[11] One other instance in the *Canterbury Tales*, which critics have not yet noted, is Chaucer's use of "The Tale of Taj al-Muluk and the Princess Dunya" in the opening of "The Merchant's Tale, where January seeks the advice of Justinus and Placebo on his desire to get married. Chaucer's Merchant is partly patterned after the old king Sulayman Shah, who waxes eloquent on the glories of marriage in his discussion with his trusted Vizier. Lasater concludes:

> Khadir as he appears in the *Arabian Nights* stories is tall and powerful, he is an agent of the supernatural, he appears in courts to hurl challenges, and he is green—all peculiarly similar to the green knight of the Middle-English *Sir Gawain and the Green Knight*. They could be related. The *Arabian Nights* was known in Spain, but its exact relationship to medieval European tales has not been determined. And it may never be determined because it is a complex relationship involving an interchange of materials and stories, most of which were transmitted orally [119].

Sir Gawain and the Arabian 1001 *Nights*

The well-known collection of the tales known as *Arabian Nights* is called *Alf Layla wa Layla* (*1001 Nights*) in Arabic. I am using the arabic numerals in the title for very good reasons; it looks like the *Gawain* poet himself does structurally pattern both *The Pearl* and *Sir Gawain* after the Arabian work, for both English poems contain exactly 101 stanzas and the duration of the English story is "a twelmonyth and a day" (297). The rest of the article will bear out that the English poet's use of these numbers is more than coincidental.

My original contribution to this ongoing discussion of the matter of Araby in *Sir Gawain and the Green Knight* deals in particular with sections in the opening, middle, and ending of the romance to suggest that the Arabic influence is pervasive without making the tall claim that the English story is a paraphrase or retelling of an Oriental tale. Of course, the English story is much more than that but with many motifs from the Arabian *1,001 Nights* cleverly incorporated in it.

The Green Knight appears at Arthur's court on New Year's Day and challenges any knight to cut off his head upon condition that he shall submit to the same forfeit exactly one year later. At that time the Green Knight spares the life of Gawain by declining to behead him because he has kept his promise and bargains. Further, the English poet's use of the matter of Araby extends to the motifs of metamorphoses, the exchange of gifts, and the speaking head as well.

The opening stories of the *1,001 Nights* address the specter of beheading in two ways. Shah Zaman, king of Samarkand and brother of Shahryar, beheads his wife and her black lover with a single stroke of his sword during their tryst in his supposed absence. At Shahryar's palace, during the king's hunting expedition, Shah Zaman witnesses the debauchery of the queen, his sister-in-law, with a black slave and of the bevy of beautiful women with white slaves. Disappointed by the infidelity of these women, both princes leave the palace and go wandering to find another man whose misfortune is greater than theirs. Presently they come upon a giant genie sleeping in the lap of a beautiful woman whom the evil Ifrit has abducted on her wedding night and whom he keeps alive in a casket secured by seven padlocks. The lady discovers the princes perched on the tree above and beckons them to come down and forces them to make love to her under pain of death at the hands of the genie. Out of fear of the genie, they do as they are commanded by the lady, who lets them have their freedom after they have done what they are bidden to do. When the princes return to the palace, Shahryar orders that his queen and concubines be beheaded along with their lovers, arguing that there is not even a single chaste woman anywhere on earth. After Shah Zaman leaves for his country, Shahryar starts the custom of sleeping with a new beautiful maiden every night and having her beheaded on the following day, saying, "There never was nor is there one chaste woman upon the face of the earth." Finally, the Vizier's intelligent and resourceful daughter Shahrazad, after making a secret alliance with her sister Dunyazad, overcomes King Shahryar's loathing of womankind by telling him enchanting, suspenseful stories designed to last longer than one night in the telling, forcing the king to put off execution for one thousand and one nights. In the meantime, according to tradition, Shahrazad bears the king three children and wins pardon from him.[12]

On the very first night, Shahrazad, with the permission of King Shahryar, tells the story of the Merchant and the genie to his sister and the king. Briefly, the story is as follows:

A rich merchant happens to eat a few dried dates and spit the stones out with such force that they kill a genie's son on whose head the stones fall. The angry genie appears to the merchant in a hurry and threatens to slay him. The unlucky man pleads for mercy and delay of his execution because he has debts to pay and accounts to settle. He promises to return on New Year's Day to meet with the genie. The man keeps his word and returns to the garden to keep his tryst with destiny. While the merchant is waiting for the genie and wailing over his impending doom, three old sheikhs—one with a chained gazelle, the second with two dogs in tow, and the third with a she-mule—approach the merchant and promise to help him. As the angry genie appears with a drawn sword, the sheikhs approach him one by one and beg him to spare one-third of the merchant's blood if each one would tell a marvelous tale.[13]

The first sheikh tells an incredibly charming tale of enchantment.

According to him, the gazelle is his own childless jealous wife who has transformed the sheikh's concubine and fifteen-year-old son into a cow and calf. The wife then has the cow slaughtered as well as the calf. The merchant's daughter, who is herself an enchantress like Morgan le Fay, identifies the true nature of the calf and transforms it back to human form and then turns the sheikh's wife into a gazelle. Then she marries the son of the sheikh.

The two dogs of the second sheikh happen to be his traitorous brothers who have tried to kill him and his wife in their sleep in order to inherit the sheikh's wealth. The sheikh's wife, who transforms the brothers into dogs for a period of ten years, is a genie. The sheikh found her years ago in tatters and in terrible straits. He accepted her offer to be his wife and loved her. In her turn, she saves his life at sea and punishes the sheikh's wicked brothers.[14]

The third sheikh's companion, the she-mule, turns out to be his unfaithful wife who had earlier transformed her husband into a dog. However, a butcher's daughter, an enchantress, restores him to his original form and helps him change his wicked wife into a mule.

After the third sheikh has told a tale more marvelous than the other two to the genie, the genie is pleased and lets the merchant have his life and liberty.

The following similarities between these Arabian tales and *Sir Gawain and the Green Knight* are striking:

1. Both works stress marvelous elements: King Arthur would not eat his meal until and unless he had seen a marvel; the genie, like King Shahryar, wants to hear wondrous tales.

2. The idea of covenant is important in both tales; in *Sir Gawain and the Green Knight*, Gawain promises to return a year later to receive a stroke from the Green Knight just as the merchant agrees to return to the genie after a year.

3. The most important similarity between the two works seems to be that the final encounter takes place on New Year's Day.

4. In both tales the lives of the heroes are spared in the end because the protagonists keep their promises.

5. There are three bargains in both stories: In *Sir Gawain and the Green Knight*, Gawain and Bertilak make to each other three promises and keep them, albeit with some reservations; in the *Arabian Nights*, the genie and the sheikhs make three promises and keep them.

6. Animals are central to both stories, especially the gazelle and dogs.

7. Both stories make several references to unfaithful women: In *Sir*

Gawain and the Green Knight, besides Gawain's references to the unfaithful women, there is the portrait of Bertilak's wife who tries to seduce Gawain; the *1,001 Nights* begins with the stories of the infidelities of the wives of Shahryar and his brother.

8. The literary device of misogyny is a central element in both works. As for *Sir Gawain and the Green Knight*, Gawain's tirade against women found toward the end of the poem (2414–29) makes good sense perhaps only in the context of the misogyny of the *1,001 Nights*, if the English poet was inspired by the Arabian stories of the wiles of jealous and unfaithful women. However, we must say that the poet's view of misogyny seems to be different from Gawain's, just as the Shahryar's hatred for womankind is not shared by the *1,001 Nights*. In the Arabic work Shahrazad reeducates and reindoctrinates King Shahryar and saves womankind from doom. In *Gawain* it is Bertilak's wife who reeducates Gawain and saves his life with her green lace, at least in the sense that Gawain's life was spared while he wore the love-lace of the Lady who is a benign tester under the guise of being a temptress; in fact, she shows concern for Gawain (1286–87). The English poet's views on women, therefore, are not identical with the views of the poem's protagonist, Gawain.

9. Both tales sport ambiguously good and ambiguously evil "genii."[15] The figure of the genie in the *1,001 Nights* is similar to the figure of Bertilak; they are quasi-demonic figures. In *Sir Gawain and the Green Knight*, Bertilak is a figure from Hell, an "aghlich mayster" (136) and "half etayn" (140), but in the end is benevolent (2364–65) and a cheerful host; he is also God's angel who teaches Gawain and Arthur's court a good lesson in humility.[16] It seems that the author of the English poem has combined the benevolent figure of the green al-Khadir with the not-totally-malevolent figure of the genie in the case of the Green Knight.

10. The Bertilak of the English poem and the genie of the Arabic work are both shape-shifters.[17]

Courtesy and Keeping Promises

In the tale of "The Porter and the Three Ladies," we find two motifs that are central to *Gawain* and *Pearl*: the importance of courtesy/courteous speech and the dilemma of keeping one's word.

As for courtesy in *Gawain*, most readers recognize the courtly manners of Arthur and his court at the beginning of the poem, as the Green Knight acknowledges it (257–78). At the castle of Sir Bertilak, Gawain converses courteously about the court he represents (903), and behaves with utmost courtesy with the ladies of the castle (970–80). In the bedroom scene Gawain and the wife of Sir Bertilak engage in courteous conversation and clasp each other courteously on three occasions and exchange kisses; though the Lady is ready and willing, Gawain courteously refrains from making love to her.

The *Pearl* poem abounds in courteous speech with the word "cortayse" repeated many times in lines 421–80. If Gawain is rebuked by the Lady for not fully yielding to her sexual advances, in *Pearl* it is the young maiden who rebukes the dreamer for his failure to understand the full meaning of her speech. Indeed, in a dream-vision, like in the Biblical book of Revelation, the heavenly lady, like Dante's Beatrice, rebukes, comforts, enlightens, and leads the visionary within sight of the heavenly court with its exquisite beauty and courtly manners. Though otherworldly the poem is, the word "courtesy" places the poem in the world of courtly romance, where a lover seeks his beloved and finds her to the extent they are one in the Mystical Body of Jesus Christ, as St. Paul would put it in I Cor. 12: 21–26, according to the heavenly maiden (476). While cheerfully recognizing the mystical character of the work like those of the spiritual romances of the Arthurian cycle and the story of the Holy Grail, we cannot afford to overlook the covert sexual symbols as in *Roman de la Rose*, especially in the other poem by the *Gawain* poet *Pearl*, where the pearl is lost in the grassy plot of a garden (10) and has rolled away from a mound (41). The overt mystical meaning of the poem is easily admitted here while we recognize the covert mystical sense in the many stories of *Alf Layla*, including the story of "The Porter and the Three Ladies," where the ladies stand for heavenly Houris like the celestial maiden in *Pearl*. If this reading of *Pearl* is tenable, it can be suggested that *Pearl* covertly, on the superficial level, has sexual undertones whereas *Gawain* overtly has sexual overtones. *Alf Layla wa Layla* also has allegorical meanings, which Arabic rhetoricians call *al-manah* (recognition of implications) (Naddaff, 24).

The motifs of courtesy and sexuality found in *Gawain* and *Pearl* seem to be derived from the tales of "The Porter and the Three Ladies" found in *1,001 Nights*. The Oriental work also, like the English poems, operates on a metaphoric level. The beautiful maiden whom the Porter encounters has teeth like pearls or daisies or hail and her forelock is like the night. The Arabic poet here talks about metaphoric transference, *isti'arah*, which Al-Jurjani in *Dala'il al-Ijaz* describes as follows:

> We know that you do not say: "I saw a lion" [when describing a man] unless you have the purpose of attributing to the man the same status of the lion, in his courage, daring, the power of his attack, and his unhesitant nature as well as attributing to him the quality of never feeling fear and never being in a state of terror. One also knows that if the hearer understands this meaning, he

does not understand it from the word "lion" itself but by understanding its meaning [Naddaff, 24].

As for the graphic details found in *1,001 Nights*, we have to compare these sensuous details as a prefiguration of heavenly pleasures.

The frame of the Arabian story is as follows. A beautiful damsel hires a handsome bachelor porter in Baghdad to help her carry her purchases from the market to her mansion, where the porter meets two of the girl's sisters, who more than equal her in beauty and charm. When the damsel offers his wages in dinars, the porter refuses the money and offers his company, the company of a courteous man of smart wits and common sense; the women accept his offer on condition that he not ask any questions as to what concerns him on pain of being flogged. He agrees and forthwith enters a dream realm, where he drinks wine and dallies in the company of the beautiful ladies "in the paradise of pleasure as though he were sitting in the seventh sphere among the Houris of heaven" (Burton II: 341). The tale continues:

> They carried on until they got drunk and the wine turned their heads. When the wine got the better of them, the doorkeeper went to the pool, took off her clothes, and stood stark naked ... [and] went into the pool.... Then she washed herself under her breasts, between her thighs, and inside her navel. Then she rushed out of the pool, sat naked in the porter's lap and, pointing to her slit, asked, "My lord and my love, what is this?" "Your womb," said he, and she replied, "Pooh, pooh, you have no shame," and slapped him on the neck. "Your vulva," said he, and other sister pinched him, shouting, "Bah, this is an ugly word." "Your cunt," said he, and the third sister boxed him on the chest and knocked him over, saying, "Fie, have some shame." "Your clitoris," said he, and again the naked girl slapped him, saying, "No." "Your pudenda, your pussy, your sex tool," said he, and she kept replying, "No, no." He kept giving various other names, but every time he uttered a name, one of the girls hit him and asked, "What do you call this?" And they went on, this one boxing him, that one slapping him, another hitting him. At last, he turned to them and asked, "All right, what is its name?" The naked girl replied, "The basil of the bridges." The porter cried, "The basil of the bridges! You should have told me this from the beginning, oh, oh!" Then they passed the cup around and went on drinking for a while. [The second sister, the shopper, continued the game, going through the same questions and receiving the same answers from the porter. Finally, one of the girls said, "The husked sesame," as the porter moaned with sore neck and shoulders. Next the eldest entered the quiz game. Even his use of

basil of the bridges and husked sesame did not satisfy her. She said, "Why don't you say the Inn of Abu Masrur?" The linguistic game continued when the porter turned the tables on the giggling girls.]

Then the porter stood up, took off his clothes, and, revealing something dangling between his legs, he leapt and plunged into the middle of the pool ... then he rushed out of the pool, planted himself in the lap of the fairest girl, put his arms on the lap of the doorkeeper, rested his legs in the lap of the shopper and, pointing to his penis, asked, "Ladies, what is this?" They were pleased with his antics and laughed, for his disposition agreed with theirs, and they found him entertaining. One of them said, "Your cock," and he replied, "You have no shame; this is an ugly word." The other said, "Your penis," and he replied, "You should be ashamed; may God put you to shame." The third said, "Your dick," and he replied, "No." Another said, "Your stick," and he replied, "No." Another said, "Your thing, your testicles, your prick," and he kept saying, "No, no, no." At last they asked, "Friend, what is its name?" The porter replied, "Don't you know its name? It is smashing mule." They asked, "What is the meaning of the name of the smashing mule?" He replied, "It is the one who grazes in the basil of the bridges, eats the husked sesame, and gallops in the Inn [khan] of Abu Masrur." Again they laughed until they fell on their backs and almost fainted with laughter.[18]

This long citation is not all that irrelevant; it indicates the playful nature of courteous speech and points perhaps to the figurative nature of Gawain's horse Gringolet in the poem, provided the *Gawain* poet is deliberately alluding to his use of the Porter's Tale from the *1,001 Nights*.

To keep or not to keep the promises made is the dilemma faced by Gawain in the poem. It turns out to be a catch-22 proposition for the protagonist: either it would put Gawain's life or the Lady's life in jeopardy. Gawain chooses to put his life in jeopardy rather than the Lady's. A similar situation is found in the Porter's Tale. All those who stayed in the ladies' mansion are to abide by the rule of the house written in the letters of gold over the door: "Speak not of that which concerns you not or you will hear that which shall please you not." All the guests—the porter, the three kalandars, the Khalifah Harun-al-Rashid, the wazir Jafar al-Barmaki, and Masrur the sword-bearer (the last three disguised as merchants)—agree to abide by the house rule of keeping mum about that which concerns them not. The situation is the same as that of Gawain, who promises to give the lord of the castle whatever he receives on the day of the hunt. However, in the course of the day both the Muslim Khalifah, along with his fellow guests with the exception of Jafar, and the Christian knight Gawain find it impossible to stick to their promises. Seeing the marks of whips and rods on the body of the two sisters, the porter asks for an explanation, at which the mistress gets angry and orders them all bound together until each one has finished his story. Finally, she pardons them all and sends them on their way home. The next day the Khalifah summons the three sisters to his court, where he orders the sisters to tell their stories, after which each one is rewarded by the king, who himself marries Fahimah, the youngest of the sisters. Like the Khalifah, Gawain also breaks his promise to protect the life of the wife of the lord of the castle, but in the end he also is forgiven.

Further, as in *Gawain* where we have the sorceress Morgan, the Porter's Tale also has a female sorceress, a supernatural Ifritah, who changed her sisters into bitches. The association of the Gawain poem with *1,001 Nights* is probably is a good explanation for the English poet's reference to Morgan as a supernatural being or a goddess (2452, *Morgne the goddess*; Tolkien-Gordon, 129). Most importantly, the Porter's Tale refers to "the sacred symbol of the Seal of Sulaiman [Solomon]" (Mardrus 110), which is most likely the pentangle, referred to in *Gawain* (625).

The Speaking Head

My argument for the *Gawain* poet's use of the *Arabian Nights* finds additional support in the motif of the speaking head of the *Arabian Nights*, which the English poet seems to have used. The story of "The King and the Physician" narrated by Shahrazad on the sixteenth night is as follows:

The sage Dooban heals King Yoonan of leprosy. The king, however, has the suspicion that Dooban may kill him and usurp his throne. After giving Dooban a day to settle his accounts, the king orders Dooban's head cut off. The sage requests that the king place his severed head in a tray of powder and read from a book and ask the head any questions, which it would answer truthfully. As the king flips the stuck-together pages of the book with his saliva-moistened thumbs, he finds nothing written on the first few pages. The head orders: "Turn over more leaves." The king continues to put his finger in his mouth and turn the pages. The poison with which the book was laced penetrates the king's digestive system, and in a short while the king lies down dead.

The feasibility of the English poet's use of the motif of the speaking head in combination with the other motifs mentioned above also finds additional support in the Islamic arabesque artwork, which seems to be the prototype of the endless knot of Gawain's famous pentangle. The non-representational arabesque art, which is complex, linear decoration based on flowing lines and which is fully exploited in Moorish art, seems to have inspired the English author's conception of Gawain's pentangle[19]—more about the arabesque in the next section.

The author of the Middle English poem was probably familiar with the stories of *1,001 Nights,* just like his contemporary Chaucer, who used several episodes from the Arabic work. The influence factor seems to have been mutual. Just as Oriental material appears in Chaucer, Boccaccio, Dante, Froissart, and the Arthurian romances, European tales and romances appear in *1001 Nights*—the *Book of Sindibad,* for example, contains motifs from the *Odyssey* (the cyclops, for example) and from the *Journeys of St. Brendan* (the whale story, for instance) (Palacios 207–13). The popular medieval collections of exemplary stories like the *Gesta Romanorum,* the *Directorium Humanae Vitae* (the Latin version of the Arabic *Kalilah wa Dimnah* from the Sanskrit original of the *Panchatantra*), the *Book of the Seven Sages of Rome,* and Pedro Alfonso's *Disciplina Clericalis* contain numerous Oriental stories. In other words, medieval European literature was extensively influenced and inspired by Oriental oral stories and literary resources ever since the period of the crusades. Oral communication seems to have been the main route for the transmission of the tales, as Chaucer puts it in his prologue to "The Man of Law's Tale" (the tale of Constance): "I were right now of tales desolaat,/ Nere that a marchant, goon is many a yeere, / Me taughte a tale, which that ye shal heere" (B: 131–33).

The *1,001 Nights,* which we know today as *Arabian Nights,* is a cumulative Arabic work which received its present form between the twelfth and the fourteenth centuries. It is, however, based on a Persian work called *Hazar Afsan* ("One Thousand Tales") with a frame story involving a king and the vizier's daughter Shirazad and her slave girl Duniazad. Historian al-Masudi (d. 956) mentions *Hazar Afsan* as one of the works translated from Pahlavi to Arabic under al-Mansur (754–55) (Lasater 113). Ibn al-Nadim, the author of *Fihrist* (ca. 988), also mentions *Hazar Afsan.* From the evidence of these two historians, it can be presumed that the *Nights* was formed before the tenth century with its nucleus being *Hazar Afsan*: "I have seen it in complete form a number of times" (2: 713). As for the presence of the *Nights* in Europe, a Spanish poet of Granada, Ibn-Said (1218–86), mentions the work; he is in turn cited by another historian, al-Makkari (Lasater 114). As these literary references indicate, the *Nights* was known in Europe not only in its oral versions but also in its literary form in the thirteenth century. Kathryn L. Lynch believes that even "Chaucer knew the *Thousand and One Nights*" (532). She observes that "when Dorigen in the Franklin's Tale offers '[m]o than a thousand stories' (line 1412) as a gambit to delay her own death, Chaucer may be self-consciously casting her as a native Shahrazad" (534). Fascinating. Lynch continues:

> One can easily imagine that within the next four hundred years [1000–1400] the stories would be told and retold, traveling beyond the Middle East to Europe as trade routes opened and other sorts of learning made their way west. In fact, there are good reasons to believe that the *Thousand and One Nights* was primarily known during the Middle Ages in oral rather than written versions.... Like the Canterbury tales, these narratives are imagined as tales shared among travelers, merchants, and pilgrims; and their far-flung origins—Arabic, Indian, Persian, Egyptian—bear invisible witness to their passage as stories from one hearer to another [533].[20]

Indeed, this section on the *Gawain* poet's use of the matter of Araby is only one more instance in the ongoing literary studies that indicate conclusively the contribution of the Arabic literary world toward the development of medieval Western literary tradition. Studies in intertextuality like mine should not be construed merely as a case of source-hunting but as detective work that throws light on the meaning and context of medieval literary tradition. Much more work remains to be done in this currently rather neglected area of literary scholarship, which will contribute significantly to multicultural understanding and to the respect we owe to the contributions of the Eastern tradition toward the foundation of the Western world—medieval and modern. Now we move on to further explore the Arabic dimension of the English poem.

The Pentangle and the Arabesque

It may come as a surprise that the icon of the pentangle stands as the symbol of perfection in the poem. The mystery of the pentangle solves itself in the Arabic context of the Fibonacci numbers, and some other features of the poem receive significant clarification in the context of the arabesque art form.

The Pentangle: A Puzzle

According to Henry Savage,

> One of the most mystifying puzzles of the poem is the import and significance of the pentangle, or Endless Knot, as the English call it. Why should the poet have spent so much time describing the figure and assuring us that it was particularly appropriate to Gawain's character and personality? For myself, I may say frankly that I can see no reason for his having done so [Savage 158].

Savage goes on to suggest that the pentangle refers to the Order of the Star (*Ordre d'Etoile*), established in 1351 by Jean le Bon of France. It is quite possible that there may exist a connection between the poem and the French Order of the Star, especially in view of the poem's association with theFrench Order of the Garter and the poet's French quotation.

Gawain's pentangle also intrigued Alice Lasater as she carefully looked at the romance from an Oriental perspective. She writes:

> The pentangle, though R. S. Loomis has attempted to derive it from a wheel in order to show a Celtic origin for it is neither Celtic nor Christian in origin, and the only European literature in which it appears prior to Sir Gawain are books of magic and necromancy associated with Solomon; Dante's *Convivio*, where it is used to illustrate man's natural perfection; and the *Geometria speculativa* of Thomas Bradwardine (c. 1344), where it is described as a geometric figure. It was, however, almost exclusively a figure of magical significance and one with Semitic connotations.[21]

Also, as Margaret Williams suggests, "The pentangle on Gawain's shield can be traced back through Jewish legends from Spain to Byzantium, and from there back to the East where it is found on Babylonian pottery" (60). The poem describes Gawain's pentangle as follows:

> Then thay schewed hym the schelde, that was of schyr goulez
> Wyth the pentangel depaynt of pure golde hwez.
> He braydez hit by the bauderyk, aboute the hals kestes,
> That bisemed the segge semlyly fayre...
> Hit is a syngne that Salamon set sumquyle
> In bytoknyng of trawthe, by tytle that hit habbez,
> For hit is a figure that haldez fyue poyntez,
> And uche lyne umbelappez and loukez in other,
> And ayquere hit is endelez; and Englych hit callen
> Oueral, as I here, the endeles knot.
> Forthy hit acordez to this knight and to his cler armez,
> For ay faithful in fyue and sere fyue sythez,
> Gawan watz for gode knawen, and as golde pured,
> Voyded of vch vylany, with vertuez ennourned
> In mote;
> Forthy the pentangle new
> He ber in schelde and cote,
> As tulke of tale most trwe
> And gentylest knight of lote.
> Fyrst he watz funden fautlez in his fyue wyttez,
> And efte fayled neuer the freke in his fyue fyngres,
> And all his afaunce vpon folde watz in the fyue woundez
> That Cryst kaght on the croys, as the crede tellez [619–44].

> [Then they displayed the bright red shield
> With its pentangle inlaid in pure gold.
> It suited him...
> It is a sign that King Solomon used once
> To signify fidelity by title.
> This figure has five points;
> Each line overlaps and locks in the others
> Passing over one and under another.
> It's called in English "the endless knot."
> In five ways the knight was fivefold faithful.
> Sir Gawain was as good as pure gold unblemished
> Devoid of any villainy.
> He bore that pentangle on shield and coat.
> He was the truest man
> And the gentlest knight ever known.
> He was without fault in his five senses;
> He placed his faith in the five wounds of Christ.]

Poem and Pentangle: Symmetry and Contrast

There are two issues built into the image of this endless knot: one, perfection signified by the word "endless"; two, imperfection connoted by the word "knot," which of course mars the smooth perfection of a string or line. In other words, is some imperfection compatible with an otherwise perfect finite human being? The poet seems to answer this question affirmatively especially in view of the slight imperfection of the otherwise perfect knightly courage and moral rectitude of Gawain. I shall show later in this essay the nature of Gawain's moral rectitude or "imperfect" perfection, since no finite creature is capable of absolute human perfection except for the two human beings referred to constantly in the poem, Jesus Christ and the Virgin Mary; however, the poet implies that Gawain is as nearly perfect, in spite of inherent human weaknesses, as any human can be.

It is noteworthy that the poem, in general, is preoccupied with the symmetry of numbers and proportional contrast: there are two contrasting New Year's Days (January 1, not March 25), two contrasting beheading scenes, two contrasting courts, two protective devices (Gawain's shield and the Lady's girdle), two confessions (one to the priest and the other to the Green Knight), three temptations to match three hunts, three kisses to match the winnings of the three hunts, two ineffective strokes of the axe to correspond to the first two days' perfect exchange of gifts, one stroke with a nick on the neck to correspond to the minor violation of trust on the third day, five points of the pentangle to correspond to the five senses and the five wounds of Christ and the five sets of five mentioned in lines

640–45 (Howard 425–33). On the other hand, reference to intersecting lines creating unevenly long but perfectly proportioned angles on the pentangle bespeaks of proportion or perfection, geometric and moral. The geometrically pleasing pentangle is the symbol of perfection on account of its golden points where the lines intersect and create the golden mean; in other words, the poet introduces a motif, the adaptation of the pentangle, which "seems to be wholly original," according to Richard Hamilton Green.[22] The pentangle/pentagram is yet another Arabic or Oriental motif borrowed from the golden mean of the Fibonacci numbers inherent in the construction of the pentangle.

Fibonacci Numbers and the Golden Mean

In our perception, beauty manifests itself everywhere in the universe: in trees, flowers, animals, architecture, art, and the human body. All these beautiful physical objects have one thing in common: proportion based on the Fibonacci numbers. Medieval philosophers like Aquinas remind us that beauty consists in proportion; that is, there is a direct relationship between beauty and mathematics since proportion in physical objects is mathematically measurable.

Fibonacci, Filius Bonacci or Leonardo of Pisa, grew up in the North African city of Bugia, where his father was a customs official. He received his mathematical education from Muslim scholars, who taught him the Arabic numeral system. He published in 1202 *Liber Abaci*, a comprehensive mathematical treatise, which contains all the advanced arithmetical and algebraic—*algebra* is itself an Arabic word—knowledge of that time.[23] The book survives in its second version from 1228. It was from this work that Europeans learned the Hindu (Arabic) numerals. Later in 1220 he continued the work with its geometrical applications in *Practica Geometriae*.

Fibonacci cites an experiment conducted by someone who placed a pair of rabbits in a walled enclosure to find out how many offspring this pair would produce in the course of a year if each pair of rabbits gave birth to a new pair each month starting the second month of its life. The results for a year would be the following number of pairs: 1, 2, 3, 5, 8, 13, 21, 34, 55, 89, 144, 233, and 377. Fibonacci writes in *Liber Abaci*:

> We see how we arrive at it: we add to the first number the second one; that is, 1 and 2; the second one to the third; the third to the fourth; the fourth to the fifth; and in this way, one after another, until we add together the tenth and eleventh numbers (144 and 233) and obtain the total number of rabbits (377); and it is possible to do this in this order for an infinite number of months [284].

As we examine the numbers 1, 2, 3, 5, 8, 13, 21, 34, 55, 89, 144, 233, and 337, we are struck by the numerical sequence in which each number equals the sum of two preceding numbers, giving us *recurrent sequences* and the equation called *recurrent relation* in mathematics. We can make up any number of different numerical sequences by satisfying the condition equaling the sum of two previous numbers for creating the third one; for example, 2, 5, 7, 12, 31, etc., or 1, 3, 4, 7, 11, 18, 29, etc. The only stipulation is that we must know the first two terms of the sequence in order to define it. Now even if the second number of the series is 1, the sequential condition mentioned above will help us calculate the terms of this series as follows: 1, 1, 2, 3, 5, 8, 13, 21, 34, 55, 89, 144, 233, 377. Now if each member in the series is divided by its preceding value (for example, 13 by 8), the result is a ratio that moves to 1:0.618 (designated by the Greek letter phi). Luca Pacioli (1502) reportedly called this ratio "divine proportion." Currently, we call it the "golden section" and the "golden mean," after the Greeks; Kepler called the discovery "one of the jewels in geometry."

It is the most important mathematical description of natural phenomena ever discovered in architecture and geometry, though apparently it had been in use for millennia even before the time of Fibonacci. For example, the Pyramid of Giza was designed according to the golden ratio; one edge of the pyramid is 783.3 feet and the height is 484.4 feet; the length divided by the height leads to the ratio of 1 : 0 .618. The same phenomenon is also found in the Mexican pyramids. The Parthenon of Athens also fits perfectly into a golden rectangle based upon the proportions of 1: 0.618034, the magic number, since the Greeks apparently based much of their art and architecture upon the 1: 0.618034 ratio, which they called the "golden mean." The golden mean is defined as the point that divides a line into two parts in such a manner that the smaller part is in proportion to the larger part as the larger part is to the entire line. According to the Greeks, this proportion, whether they knew the mathematic basis for the golden mean or not, simply pleases the eye.

Let us now look at a regular pentagram or the pentangle:

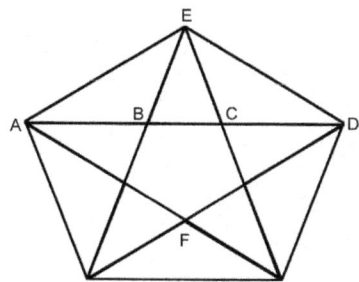

The angle AFD is 108 degrees and the angle ADF is 36 degrees. Point C divides the segment AD according to the golden ratio.

We may set AD = ∝ (the golden ratio), then observe the following.

AF = AC

$\dfrac{AC}{CD} = \propto$

$\dfrac{AC}{AB} = \dfrac{AB}{BC} = \propto$

Thus each of the segments BC, AB, AC, and AD is (times as large as the one preceding it.

Also, $\dfrac{AD}{AE} = \propto$

In fact, our sense of the aestheticism of physical perfection is based on Fibonacci numbers; for example, tests indicate that people prefer rectangles that approximate the golden mean; artists, like Greek sculptors, select the navel as the golden mean of the human body; the golden mean also underlies the aesthetic perception of the size of the eyes, nose, forehead, and ears. Indeed, Fibonacci himself discusses some of the proportional properties of the pentagram in his *Practica Geometriae* (82–83; 214).[24]

The poet explicitly refers to some of the properties of the pentangle, especially to its underlying principle of proportion ("each line overlaps and locks") and to perfection ("endless") when he says that

> This figure has five points;
> Each line overlaps and locks in the others
> Passing over one and under another.
> It's called in English "the endless knot."
> In five ways the knight was fivefold faithful [627–31].

When the *Gawain* poet chose the golden pentangle as Gawain's distinctive sign and token ("Why the Pentangle suited that noble prince" [623]), he also added to it the connotation of moral perfection by calling the reader's attention to the emblem's aesthetic function in the moral universe ("forever faithful in five ways" [632]). By referring explicitly to gold in Gawain's pentangle and to holiness in Gawain himself and by alluding to the golden ratio inherent in the structure of the pentangle, the poet implicitly alludes to the presence of the golden mean in Gawain's moral/spiritual life.[25] As we make the aforementioned justified leap from aesthetics to ethics, let me point out another aspect of Arab aesthetics, the arabesque art form that informs the English poem.

The *Gawain* Poem and the Arabesque Art Form

In general, the highly abstract art of the Near East during the Middle Ages is known as the *arabesque*. More precisely, it is the "stylized form of tendril ornament, based on the acanthus tendril of late antique or early Byzantine and Sassanian Persian art, which developed in the Islamic regions from the ninth century A.D., onward" (Riegel 397).[26] In the arabesque denaturalized tendril, the individual motifs vary only slightly and then repeat continuously and yet not monotonously in a symmetric pattern. Riegel calls this constant repetition infinite rapport (*unendliche Rapport*) (401).

There is a spiritual dimension to this form of art either in its visual form or in its narrative form:

> The most common interpretation of the arabesque reads it as reflecting a concern for the infinite and eternal over and above the transience of earthly existence, as drawing the eye of the viewer away from the things of this world toward the perception of a design that potentially repeats itself into the realm of the divine. Such an interpretation results from the fundamental presence of repetition, of, specifically, the repetition of a denaturalized, nonrepresentational vegetal pattern that itself speaks of the insignificance of the material realm [Naddaff 113].

Though examples of figural representation can be found in monuments built during the Shiite rule of the Fatimids of Egypt, in general Sunni Islamic *hadiths* (traditions) forbid the realistic figural representation of living beings, especially of human beings, which would be an abominable idol, the invention of infidels; one *hadith* says that "the maker of images or pictures will be punished at the last judgment by the decree of Allah who will inflict upon them the impossible task of breathing life into their works" (Naddaff 114). Such a judgment is based on the premise that human image-makers equate themselves with Allah, the supreme image-maker (*musawwir*), and commit the sin of blasphemy, which is punished by the death in the Sharia legal system, as is evident in the *fatwa* of death sentence pronounced on Salman Rushdie for blaspheming against the Prophet. Artists got around this prohibition by making their figures look unreal—inanimate and abstract—as is also true in the case of Rushdie, whose literary figures are surreal. Caliph Omar reportedly told a complaining artist "to continue to paint portraits but make them resemble flowers that feature a line drawn across the necks of the individuals portrayed" (Naddaff 115).

The Byzantine iconoclastic emperors in the ninth century followed the example of the Caliph of Damascus, and, basing their iconoclastic arguments that all images are abominable idols on the Bible (Exodus 20:4, 5, Deut. 5:8, John 4:24, and Rom. 1: 23–25), they went on a rampage by destroying images. Out went the ancient Greek realism in art and in came the Byzantine abstract icons known for their stiffness and formality. This Byzantine tradition continued to exert its influence in Western European iconography up to the twelfth century. Meantime, the Benedictine School and particularly the Franciscan School—St. Francis has been called with some justification the father of Italian art—created the *giottesco* style (after Giotto di Bondone), the *dolce stil nuovo*, which charmed Italy and the rest of Europe during the fourteenth century. However, the illuminator of the *Gawain* manuscript in the fourteenth century apparently refused to follow the mainline tradition in his sketches and instead embraced the arabesque.

The arabesque is, indeed, very Eastern and Islamic in aesthetics. It is non-figural and anti-mimetic in its denatured threads of the leaf pattern that spins a potentially infinite design. There is no external phenomenon that is its representational source, which implies that the design's own unfolding is its meaning.

It is the arabesque art form that informs the classical Arabian work of *1,001 Nights* with its endless repetition of tales and its non-representational, anti-mimetic motifs of magic, fantastic spaces, genies, metamorphosed creatures, and heroes/villains that defy all sense of realism. It is the realm of the fantastic and marvelous, where the ordinary laws of nature are inoperative as in the myths of traditional religions. Indeed, the arabesque avoids pictorially the natural leaf and depicts a universe that has only a faint resemblance to the world in which the reader moves as in the medieval world of Harun al-Rashid (Naddaff 117–18).

It is this kind of arabesque narrative universe that we find in many medieval romances, particularly in the tales of the Arthurian cycle with its infinitively repetitive tales, transformed ladies, fantastic weapons, fairylands, and non-representational characters that bear only a faint resemblance to the real world of King Arthur, just as in *1,001 Nights*—a potentially rewarding project for a future dissertation and further research, with the interesting suggestion that the notoriously elusive motif of Tristan sleeping with a drawn sword between him and Isolde is from the Aladdin cycle of *1,001 Nights*. Chaucer's *Canterbury Tales* also imitates *1,001 Nights*, as Katherine Gittes has already convincingly demonstrated.[27]

On a smaller scale, though not in its labyrinthine dimensions, *Gawain* also shares the features of the arabesque art form in its repetitive symmetry, as was already discussed, its rejection of realistic figural representation, and its depiction of the arabesque tendril motif, which is the hallmark of the classical arabesque.

There are four illustrations to *Gawain*: (1) Gawain taking the axe from King Arthur, (2) the beheading of the Green Knight, (3) the Lady's visit to Gawain, and (4) Gawain on horseback at the Green Chapel, with the Green Knight holding the axe. Reproduced here is the illustration in which Gawain beheads the Green Knight (Folio 94b) along with Folio 95 with its tendril ornamentation, where the text of *Gawain* starts. The stiff and formal figures may appear crude to most viewers, but in the poem's Arabic context these figures are abstract, non-representational ones in conformity with the injunction against realistic portrayals found in the Islamic tradition. In Folio 94 one of the knights holds an Oriental scimitar, which seems to give away the illustrator's intention that the poem is about matters Eastern. Additional support for the arabesqueness of the poem comes from the tendril ornamentation found in the margin of Folio 95. Further, the spiritual dimension of the Arabesque is clearly manifest in Gawain's fervent piety and in his devotion to the blessed Virgin. Someday an art historian may be able to throw more light on the Arabic dimension of the twelve illustrations found in the manuscript as well as on all four poems.

The Golden Mean in Ethics

The leap from aesthetic to moral/spiritual is warranted in critical discourse because it has been warranted in the *Gawain* poet's discourse; for instance, the poet says that Gawain "was without fault in his five senses; / He placed his faith in the five wounds of Christ," where the number five refers to the five angles of the pentangle. Now, in the moral world, the golden mean stands for moderation or prudence or the avoidance of both extremes (maximum and minimum; neither too much nor too little) in the practice of moral virtues (justice, fortitude, prudence, and temperance) but not in the practice of the theological virtues (faith, hope, and charity). In other words, as virtue stands in the middle, Gawain follows the middle road by avoiding both extremes. He is only humanly perfect in the sense that he manages to avoid serious offenses but not minor offenses, which are not incompatible with Christian perfection since even the Biblical just person falls several times a day. Indeed, being human, Gawain is not totally sinless like Jesus Christ and the Virgin Mary of the medieval Catholic tradition. If, therefore, Gawain is not totally sinless, what moral failure is Gawain guilty of? Can the terrible sin of sacrilegious confession be attributed to him?

Certainly, Gawain is not sinless, but his sins do not amount to "mortal sins" during his pursuit of the golden mean of moral perfection, which is the focus of the following section.

Gawain's Sin/Non-sin and
Medieval Moral Theology

Most critics see that Gawain's failure to return the green girdle is his real sin. "Gawain's retention of the green girdle amounts to a failure of loyalty towards his host in the exchange of winnings game which was occasioned by his fear of death (2366–68)" (Newhauser 465); however, Gawain blames himself for cowardice, covetousness, and untruth (2507–09)—interestingly, only in hindsight; that is, only after he is accused by Bertilak of untruth. As I read it, the poet suggests that Gawain's failure to return the girdle is perhaps at best only a venial sin; Gawain himself sees the failure to return the green girdle as a sin only after his second encounter with Bertilak. In this unorthodox interpretation of Gawain's failure to return the green girdle as a venial sin, I shall use the principles of moral theology used by priests in the confessional in assessing the existence, nature, and gravity of sins committed and confessed. Also, it is not correct to accuse Gawain of the awful sin of sacrilegious confession, which would seriously detract from his perfection symbolized by the golden pentangle.

To clarify the issue more satisfactorily, let me suggest that there are two Gawains in the poem: Gawain I, the Gawain before the ordeal in the Green Chapel, and Gawain II, the Gawain after the ordeal in the Green Chapel.

The Sin of Gawain or Gawain I

Gawain's sin is similar to Job's. He thinks he trusts totally in God but does not—a case of invincible ignorance, which will later be unmasked by Bertilak. His trust in God is not total; he relies too much on his own resources; that is, he places his trust in the putative power of the green girdle rather than in God in the moment of truth. Everyone, including Gawain, seems to think that

> All his trust on earth was in the five wounds,
> Which came to Christ on the cross, as the Creed tells.
> His prowess all depended on the five pure joys
> That the holy Queen of Heaven had of her child [642–47].

Britton J. Harwood points this out clearly: "If all Gawain's faith had been in the Passion, he would have refused the belt patiently, in the theological sense, rather than accepted it patiently.... If all his happiness came vicariously through the Virgin, he would never have accepted a possibly unlawful help ... at the cost of breaking his word" (489). However, Gawain's lack of trust in God exhibited in his acceptance of the girdle is not deserving of hell, because Gawain's lack of trust in God is not a mortal sin but a case of invincible ignorance and action under duress, both of which mitigate the gravity of sin. It is only a venial sin (Harwood 495). The objective correlative of the moral state of the soul of Gawain can be clearly seen in the fact that Gawain is punished for this sin only with a minor cut on the neck rather than with a mortal stroke. Bertilak's words seem to confirm this inference: "You have confessed your faults fully with fair acknowledgment / And plainly done penance at the point of my axe" (2391–92).

This reading of the poem does not seem to agree with what Gawain says of his sin and with what some critics who concur with Gawain say. However, I am glad to point out that my reading is in agreement with the general assessment of Gawain's sin by Tolkien, who says:

> Of the ... charge: disloyalty, troth-breach, treachery, all the hard things that he calls it, Gawain was guilty only in so far as he had broken the rules of an absurd game imposed on him by his host (after he had rashly promised to do anything his host asked); and even that was at the request of a lady, made (we may note) after he had accepted her gift, and so was in a cleft stick. Certainly this is an imperfection upon some plane; but on how high a plane, and of what importance? The laughter of the Court of Camelot—and to what higher court in matters of honour could one go?—is probably sufficient answer [16].

It is Gawain II—not Gawain I—who thinks that he has committed the sins of cowardice, covetousness, and untruth:

> Curses on both cowardice and covetousness!
> Their vice and villainy are virtue's undoing.
> Connived with covetousness to corrupt my nature
> And the liberality and loyalty belonging to chivalry.
> Now I am faulty and false and found fearful always
> In the train of treachery and untruth go misery and woe [2374–83].

Thus, Gawain the convert or the apprehended thief—in Britton Harwood's words, "His [Gawain's] retention of the belt is a theft ("hit is my wede that thou werez," the Green Knight will say [2358]) (489)—accuses himself of cowardice in committing the sin of covetousness, which is his desire to possess the girdle (excessive love of self and life) and of the sin of breaking his compact with Bertilak. But Bertilak discounts these expostfacto sins and says that Gawain I, the renowned knight, lacked something else: he was found wanting in faith in and loyalty toward God.

> But here your faith failed you, you flagged somewhat, sir;
> Yet it was not for a well-wrought thing [covetousness],

nor for wooing either [lust],
But for love of your life, which is less blameworthy [2366–68].

It is interesting to note that Gawain II seems to agree with his second "confessor" with regard to the latter's assessment of his sin:

Not for glorious gold shall I gladly wear it [the lace],
But as a sign of my transgression, I shall see it often,
So when pride shall prick me for my prowess in arms,
One look at this love-lace shall make me humble again [2430–38].

The obvious conclusion seems to be that the real sin of Gawain I, though only a venial one, is lack of complete trust in the Creator or excessive trust in the "power" of the girdle. In this sense, Gawain sins against the First Commandment: "I am the Lord thy God; thou shalt not have other gods beside me."[28] The medieval church also taught that not all sins, even against the First Commandment, are mortal sins deserving of hell.

Gawain II's Sins

We cannot totally disagree with Gawain II, who claims to have committed the sins of cowardice and covetousness and untruth. The first two are material sins; the third is not even a material sin except in the eyes of Bertilak. When Gawain flinched as the axe came down, he failed in fortitude, which is cowardice. The flinching, however, was not premeditated cowardice; it was only a reflex reaction which was not controlled by the will—hence there cannot be a formal sin, which requires knowledge and consent. In the same way, Gawain's act of coveting or desiring the green girdle was the result of excessive fear for his own life, fear which beclouded his intellect invincibly (*ignorantia invincibilis antecedens*); hence, in this case also there cannot be a formal sin.

Gawain II's alleged act of untruth—not keeping the terms of the contract with his host—is neither a material sin nor a formal sin in the case of Gawain I. Of course, Bertilak could conceive of it both as a material sin and as a formal sin; that is how he views it, but he forgives it as a venial sin at best and makes Gawain do penance for it; the venial nature of Gawain's sin is clear from the lightness of his punishment or penance. Also Bertilak seems to recognize for a fact that Gawain considered his sin only as a venial sin and that Gawain has done penance for the venial sin with a scratch on the neck:

"From your failure at the third [test]
The tap you took arose" [2356–57].

> You have confessed your faults fully with fair acknowledgment
> And plainly done penance at the point of my axe" [2391–92].

When confronted by Bertilak's announcement that Gawain is wearing the girdle that is his (Bertilak's), Gawain II seems to agree with his accuser; it is only then that Gawain accuses himself of untruth and then returns the girdle to Bertilak. Obviously Gawain has no choice but return the girdle.

That is, however, not the case with Gawain I at the time he kept the lace and departed to meet the Green Knight in the Green Chapel. At that time Gawain I had no reason to think that he had committed a formal sin or even a material sin. Rather, there was no sin at all in the "casuist Catholic" Gawain's understanding of sin when he decided to keep the girdle and refused to surrender it to the lord of the castle and when he confessed it to the priest.

These two points—the issue of Gawain's sin and the nature of confession—merit further exploration.

Did Gawain I Break His Promise?

In traditional Catholic catechism, medieval and modern, sin is a willful transgression of the law. Sin is either venial or mortal. Full knowledge, full consent, and gravity of matter are required conditions for a mortal sin to exist. If one of the three elements is lacking, then the sin is only a venial sin. A formal sin is one which is recognized as such by the sinner who is able to explain its nature. A material sin exists in fact when there is transgression of the divine law even though the sinner is not aware of the transgression. Traditional Catholics know the distinctions between mortal sins, venial sins, and imperfections so that they would know which ones they should confess and which ones they don't have to confess to the priest, who passes final judgment in the internal forum in matters of conscience. Once the priest has handled the matter of sin in the tribunal of the confessional, the matter is settled once and for all, even in the case of the sins of murder—except in cases of certain crimes whose absolution is reserved for the ordinary (bishop) or the Pope; in the case of murder, confession to the priest is necessary, but not before the civil tribunal except when restitution and unjust accusations are involved. The penitent has the right to remain silent—the historical basis for the Fifth Amendment in the American judicial system.

Did Gawain I Make a False Confession?

Many of us think that Gawain I's sin is his refusal to honor the terms of the contract with the host of the castle when Gawain I failed to surrender the girdle to the host, when he committed the sin of dishonesty, and when he even made a sacrilegious confession by deliberately withholding from the priest confessor the declaration of the sin of breaking the promise made to his host; as a result, we think that Gawain I committed not only a material sin, but also a formal sin.

Such a reading of the flaw or sins of Gawain does not seem to be quite in accordance with the poetic text, which reads:

> He laid aside the love-lace the lady had given him
> Secreted it carefully where he could discover it later,
> Then he went at once to the chapel,
> Privily approached a priest and prayed him there
> To uplift him in his life and enlighten him
> On how he might have salvation in the hereafter.
> Then confessing his faults, he completely shrove himself,
> Begging mercy for both mortal and venial sins.
> He asked the holy man for absolution
> And [the priest] absolved him without hesitation and sent him out pure
> That Doomsday should have been declared the day after [1874–84].

J. A. Burrow, the influential critic, echoes the sentiments of most critics when he objects that "Gawain's confession (always supposing it to relate somehow to the business of the girdle) must be seen as invalid—not a remedy, but a symptom of his fall from grace" (109).[29]

My response to this objection is simply that there is no false confession here; on the contrary there is full absolution here. Of course, one might suggest that the poet is being ironic in this passage. Not so. He means what he says here if he is a Catholic who believes that whatever the priest in the internal forum of the confessional binds is bound in heaven and whatever he looses on earth is loosed in heaven.

In the confessional Gawain presents his case to himself and to the priest as a dilemma. He has made two promises, both of which he cannot keep at the same time. He had promised to give the host his winnings (*chek*) of the day, which we know are the green lace and the Lady's kisses. That is not necessarily the way Gawain has to interpret the terms of his covenant. According to the text, the host says, "'Whatsoever I win in the woods shall be yours, and you exchange what gain you achieve with me'" (1106–7). Strictly speaking, Gawain does not promise to give everything he wins; in other words, Gawain promises to give his winnings but not all his winnings; this is like saying that Gawain would tell the truth but not the whole truth. If Gawain had sexual intercourse with the lady of the castle, it would naturally be immoral on his part to engage in sexual intercourse with the lord of the castle. That would be committing another sin to keep a silly promise. No one would be bound to keep that kind of a promise in the medieval Christian universe of Gawain. The other horn of the dilemma is that Gawain has promised the Lady that he would conceal the green lace from the host. Larry Benson reads the text to mean that the promise made to the Lady is not quite serious enough to be binding and that the Lady told Gawain that she would give him the lace if he would conceal it from the host: "The lady offers Gawain yet another bargain, though it is less formally expressed; she will give him the green lace if he agrees to conceal it from her husband. He does so, and he is thus guilty of betraying his host" (228). However, that is not what the text says:

> She pressed the belt upon him with potent words
> And gladly gave it to him when he agreed to accept it,
> Beseeching him for her sake to conceal it always,
> And hide it from her husband with all diligence.
> That never should another know of it; the noble one agreed [1860–64].

Obviously, Gawain cannot keep both promises. Since the Lady is already gone, he cannot give it back to her. But he has to set his conscience aright; he has to consult the priest to make sure that he is not doing anything wrong, because the next day could be the day that he would meet his Maker and Judge and could be damned in hell for an unforgiven mortal sin if he had committed one.

Gawain is faced with a moral choice involving sin, which he wants to eschew. He has made two promises; the breaking of either of them could be a sin. He has to make a choice between two evils; he does not have direct certainty as to which course is right; he needs counsel to choose the lesser evil. That is precisely why the poet seems to use the words "lern hym better" ("enlighten him") in line 1878. He would need at least indirect certainty, which does not exclude the probability that the opposite is not wrong. Since he promised the Lady that no one else should know about it, he has to be discreet about revealing the real nature of the lace even to the priest; the fact that he was not wearing it during his confession prevented the priest from proffering to return the lace to the lord of the castle by some indirect means, which could very well compromise the secrecy of the confession anyway. Gawain could not reveal the nature of the object even to the priest since doing so would reveal the identity of the lady in confession, which would be another sin. Nonetheless Gawain could tell the priest his dilemma in vague language and secure his approval in favor of liberty with the assurance that one is not committing a formal sin. How would he go about resolving the dilemma?

Gawain or the priest could put Gawain's predicament in the following rational syllogism and come up with an answer:

Major: Given two probable propositions or courses of action, one is free to follow the more probable proposition.

Minor: In Gawain's case, the act of not giving the green lace and keeping the promise made to the Lady is probably more correct than the act of keeping the promise to give *all* the winnings of the day to the lord of the castle.

Conclusion: Therefore, Gawain may keep the promise made to the Lady with one of the double effects or side effects being that the promise made to the lord of the castle not be kept. The analogy in this case is that of saving the life of the mother when that process would result in the death of the baby in a tubal pregnancy; in this case, the death of the baby is not intended; it is only permitted; it happens only as a side effect.

As for the Major, *lex dubia non obligat* ("a doubtful law does not oblige"); that is, doubts are raised about the interpretations and applications of the law of restitution or commutative justice; for example, Gawain did not promise in unequivocal terms that he would give *all* his winnings to the lord of the castle. Further, *in dubio melior est condicio possidentis* ("in doubt, presumption is in favor of the possessor," or in modern paraphrase, "nine-tenths of possession is law"). It is called the principle of possession. Pope Alexander III was asked once whether a certain church was bound to give tithes to another church which claimed the tithes as its own. The Pope responded that the first church was not bound to do so because *de jure divino et humano melior est condicio possidentis* (Prümmer 220). Therefore, in a doubtful situation the presumption is in favor of the one who possesses the object. The application of this principle in confession is as follows: Penitents who doubt whether they have committed a mortal sin or the sins they have committed are mortal are not bound, strictly speaking, to declare these in confession. Penitents have the freedom to confess or not; Gawain had the freedom even not to tell the priest about the green girdle in good conscience; Gawain also had the freedom not to give the girdle to the lord of the castle because Gawain was in possession of the girdle, which was freely given to him by the Lady, and Gawain was not told that the girdle belonged to the husband of the Lady. Further, Gawain was bound to give the girdle to the host until the second obligation of keeping the girdle is imposed on him by the Lady and accepted by him. In this case, unless the first obligation is absolutely certain, Gawain remains free as to its fulfillment.

As for the minor premise, it is more probably a case that Gawain should keep his promise to the Lady than to Bertilak. If Gawain were to give the girdle to the lord, untold harm could be brought upon the Lady, who could be accused of adultery and executed or exiled for a crime she had never committed; further, Gawain could bring death and disgrace upon himself and Arthur's court and would not be able to keep the first promise he made to the Green Knight that he would keep his tryst with him on New Year's Day. The principle of double effect could easily be applied in this case.

Gawain could also appeal to the principle of penal law in his keeping of the girdle even if he knew that it belonged to the lord of the castle. The penal law is a law which is not quite just and, therefore, does not oblige us in conscience, but if caught or convicted we are bound in conscience to pay the price; many kinds of indirect taxes imposed on us arbitrarily by governments, like poll taxes and luxury taxes, fall into this category but not income tax laws. One typical example of penal law is the law against speeding. Many of us all the time "break" that law while keeping up with the flow of traffic, especially on the highways, for very good reasons and don't think we are committing any crime or sin; but, if caught speeding, we know that we have to pay the fine, and we do. Gawain, when caught by Bertilak with the girdle, returns it and accepts his punishment at the hands of Bertilak, and he does not complain.

What Gawain is following in the confessional is the line of reasoning or the moral system known as Probabiliorism, which needs further clarification.

In the quest for moral certainty, a person faces five choices or five moral systems, which are rules of prudence that deal with hesitations of conscience when faced with a good action not prescribed by the law and an action whose legal obligation is doubtful. Doubts can arise about the law itself: is it still in force? Does it really bind? How far does its scope extend? Or the doubt may concern facts: Does the obligation actually apply in a given instance? The following moral systems have to be briefly identified for the purpose of this short paper.

1. **Rigorism.** According to this view one must always choose the safer opinion, which is the law even if the opinion favoring freedom is the most probable one. For example, public law takes precedence over private promises. According to this view Gawain must keep his public promise to the lord to follow the rule of William of Auxerre that if anyone doubts whether something is a mortal sin and does it, he/she sins mortally.

2. **Tutiorism.** Given the choice of following the less safe opinion versus the certain formulation of the law, one may follow the former provided it is the most probable view. Both Rigorism and Tutiorism seem to require strict certainty rather than moral certainty for moral actions.

3. Probabilism. When there are divergent views as to the lawfulness of an action, for each of which there are solid arguments, then we are free to adopt either course. In the eyes of probabilists, the probable opinion can be followed even if its opposite is more probable. The opinion of one author or of a confessor is adequate enough to establish the probability of a certain position. This view was advanced by the Dominican Bartholomew Medina (1577). He writes: "It seems to me that if there is a probable opinion, it is lawful to follow it, even though the opposite is more probable" (*Commentarium in Ia, 2ae* ST 19.6). The Jesuits in the seventeenth century popularized it. Pascal and the Jansenists tried to refute it. The probabilist position bases itself on the principle that a doubtful law does not impose any obligation. Probabilists often resort to the following line of argumentation given by St. Thomas Aquinas:

> If the error arise from ignorance of some circumstance, and without negligence, so that it cause the act to be involuntary, then that error of reason or conscience excuses the will that abides by that erring reason, from being evil. For instance, if erring reason tell a man that he should go to another man's wife, the will that abides by that erring reason is evil; since this error arises from ignorance of the Divine Law, which he is bound to know. But if a man's reason errs in mistaking another for his wife, and if he wish to give her right when she asks for it, his will is excused from being evil, because this error arises from ignorance of a circumstance, which ignorance excuses, and causes the act to be involuntary [Ia IIae, W. 19. 6].[30]

4. Probabiliorism. The less safe opinion which favors freedom may be followed to the detriment of the safe opinion which favors the law when the former is more probable than the latter although it is not quite certain; that is, when there are confessors and good authorities favoring the less safe opinion, we may follow them. As noted earlier, Gawain seems to have followed the moral system of probabiliorism when he made his decision to keep the girdle. In such a case the confessor had no right to tell the penitent that he was guilty of sin in not following the rigorous view which always favors the law or the tutiorist view which insists on the following of the most probable opinion.

5. Equiprobabilism (attributed to the Redemptorist Alphonsus Liguori, of the eighteenth century). The less safe opinion which favors freedom can be followed on condition that it is as probable as the safe opinion which favors the law.

Which of these five moral positions were held in the Middle Ages by church theologians and confessors? Often they used tutiorism or the safer way to solve moral dilemmas as we do today in public cases which affect common good. According to Dominic Prümmer, early and medieval theologians like Lactantius, Basilius, Gregory Nazianzen, Augustine, Antoninus, Joannes Nider and others by and large favored probabiliorism, according to which the opinion favoring freedom can be followed if it is clearly more probable than the opinion favoring the law (230).[31] Penitentials and confessorial practices seem to indicate that many confessors even followed probabilism in actual pastoral contexts. Incidentally, probabilists argue that medieval theologians favored probabilism![32]

Conclusion

The sin of Gawain I is lack of loyalty or trust in God and excessive trust in the power of a talisman or in self or in created things. Gawain I had no real reason to think that he had broken his promise to Bertilak or that he was a thief because he was in possession of the green girdle; as a good moral theologian, he could argue, like his priest confessor, that presumption is in favor of the possessor. He had more than probable reason to think that the girdle belonged to the lady of the castle who was wearing it and who gave it to him. There is no evidence in the poetic text to show that Gawain committed a false confession. When Gawain I was caught, he changed his colors and became Gawain II, who "realized" that the girdle really belonged to the lord of the castle; therefore, he gave it back to the rightful owner and blamed the ladies when he found out that they were in collusion with Bertilak; he no longer had any reason to protect the ladies. Gawain II then accused himself unfairly of serious transgressions against the virtues of fortitude, temperance, and loyalty—cowardice, covetousness, and untruth. Bertilak assured Gawain II that the sins of Gawain I, though only venial, were still serious. Gawain learned the lesson of humility well and realized the need to fight against the temptation of pride. The poem does not show that the court of Arthur learned the same lessons that Gawain learned.[33]

General Conclusion

As this study shows, in order to account for the resourcefulness of the *Gawain* poet, we have to go beyond the well-known boundaries of medieval romances into the realms of Greek and Latin classics, the matter of Araby, the arabesque art form, and medieval moral theology. I hope that future scholars will correct, clarify, and improve upon what I have proposed in this study.

Notes

1. G. L. Kittredge has fully discussed the Celtic and French sources and analogues of the English romance in *A Study of Gawain and the Green Knight* (Cambridge: Harvard UP, 1916). Mabel Day in the introduction to Gollancz's edition of *Sir Gawain and the Green Knight* (EETS 210 [1910], Laura Hibbard Loomis in ch. 39 of *Arthurian Literature in the Middle Ages* (Oxford: Clarendon P, 1959), and Maureen Fries ("Teaching *Sir Gawain and the Green Knight* in the Context of Arthurian and Other Romance Traditions," in *Approaches to Teaching: Sir Gawain and the Green Knight*, ed. Miriam Youngerman Miller and Jane Chance [New York: MLA, 1986] have also treated the issue, albeit briefly.

2. Support for the Oriental dimensions of *Gawain* comes from another beautiful poem attributed to the same poetic genius, *The Pearl*, which is equally erudite as the romance with the poet's clever use of Persian sources and the Eastern Christian theology of the Syrian Ephrem. Space considerations prompt me to postpone discussion of *The Pearl* for another monograph.

3. *Sir Gawain & the Green Knight*, ed. J. R. R. Tolkien, E. V. Gordon, and Norman Davis (Oxford Oxford UP, 1967). All references to the poem are from this edition, though I have taken the liberty to modernize spelling; translations are mine.

4. Morton W. Bloomfield, *Sir Gawain and the Green Knight*: An Appraisal, PMLA 76 (1961):7–19; reprinted in Donald R. Howard and Christian K. Zacher. eds., *Critical Studies of Sir Gawain and the Green Knight* (Notre Dame: U of Notre Dame Pr, 1968), 24–55 (the quote is from p. 45); see 44–46 for a bibliography of the Christian interpretation of the poem.

5. George Kane, *Middle English Literature: A Critical Study of the Romances, the Religious Lyrics*, Piers Plowman (London: Methuen, 1957),. 76. The second and third part of this essay will clarify this issue.

6. Jessie Weston, *The Legend of Sir Gawain: Studies upon Its Original Scope and Significance* (London: D. Nutt, 1897); Bloomfield 37.

7. For some interesting observations on the non-classical sources of the poem, see Kittredge 139–41.

8. It may be added here that Aeneas also received a wound from an arrow during his battle against the Latins in Italy. The wound was miraculously healed through the intervention of Venus. Also, in *Gawain* the green girdle is the occasion of the wound of Gawain. It is interesting to note here that in the *Aeneid* (12.940–52) Pallas's baldric and belt, which Turnus was wearing, caused his death at the hands of the enraged Aeneas, who avenged Pallas's death on Turnus.

9. Perhaps the most remarkable of the medieval literary portraits of Ulysses is found in the 26th canto of Dante's *Inferno* where Dante is being consumed in an eternal flame. According to Dante—the Dantean version is not found in any literary works before his time—the romantically heroic and heroically curious Ulysses and his companions, now old and slow, make a last voyage beyond the Pillars of Hercules, the limit of legitimate exploration, in quest of forbidden adventures. They sail southward. A mysterious mountain appears beyond the Pillars of Hercules. The sailors are happy. Suddenly, however, a storm arises and sinks the ship (26.100–142).

10. According to the Indian epistemological theory of *Syatvada* (principle of skepticism), the following seven statements can be made: (1) Maybe it is. (2) Maybe it is not. (3) Maybe it is and it is not. (4) Maybe it is not describable. (5) Maybe it is but is not describable. (6) Maybe it is not and is not describable. (7) Maybe it is and it is not and is not describable. The following example illustrates the relativity of the truth value of

our statements: Mahavira is on the fourth floor of a building; his mother is on the seventh floor, and his father on the first floor. Father says, "Mahavira is upstairs"; mother says, "Mahavira is downstairs"; the conclusion is that since any viewpoint as the only viewpoint may be flawed, it must be preceded by "maybe." What my argument amounts to is simply that maybe the romance *Sir Gawain and the Green Knight* is also Oriental in inspiration and execution just as maybe the poem is also Celtic, classical, and French in its literary antecedents. Epistemologically speaking it is outrageous to outlaw the theory of the Oriental subtextuality of the *Gawain* poem out of hand.

11. See H. S. V. Jones's three articles: "Some Observations upon the Squire's Tale," *PMLA*, n.s. 13 (1905): 346–59; "The Cléomadès, the Méliacin, and the Arabian Tale of the "Enchanted Horse," *JEGP* 6 (1907): 221–43; and "The Cléomadès and Related Folk-Tales," *PMLA*, n.s. 16 (1908): 557–98. See also Lasater, pp. 127–36.

12. For the history of the *Arabian Nights*, see Philip Hitti, *History of the Arabs* (London, 1949), p. 404; Reynold Nicholson, *A Literary History of the Arabs* (Cambridge UP, 1969), 456–58; Richard Burton, *The Book of the Thousand Nights and a Night*, 6 vols., 1886, (rpt. New York, 1934); Joseph Campbell, ed., *The Portable Arabian Nights* (New York: Viking, 1952), 5–6. It is unfair to brand the *Arabian Nights* as an anti-feminist work; we find anti-feminist and pro-feminist views throughout the book. As for the names of the heroines of the prologue, Shahrazad and Dunyazad, the meaning of the former is "deliverer of the city," and the latter means "deliverer of the world."

13. See R. A. Shoaf, *The Poem as Green Girdle: Commercium in Sir Gawain and the Green Knight* (Gainesville: UP of Florida, 1984) for a good discussion on the role of mercantilism or covenant in the poem.

14. This story is similar to "The Wife of Bath's Tale" in Chaucer's *Canterbury Tales*.

15. The Arabic *jinniyah* (feminine singular) is related to the Latin *genius* and French *genie*. He is related to the Greek *daimon*, a family divided into two categories: the good (agatho-daemons) and the bad (kako-daemons). The Muslims have made him into a supernatural anthropos-like being, created from fire (Qur'an 15:27 and 55:14).

16. See Zacharias P. Thundy, "Green and Red: More on Classical Influences in *Sir Gawain and the Green Knight*," *Classical and Modern Languages* 12 (1992): 169ff.

17. The name *Bertilak* is a crux. No known Celtic or French knight appears by this name in any other Arthurian romances. I suggest that Bertilak, who has obvious demonic associations in the romance, is possibly an Oriental word in origin: *ber* (son) + *tilak* (killer) means "son of the killer" in Aramaic; *ktl* in Aramaic means "kill"; it is possible that the English poet metathesized *ktl* into *tilak*. The devil in the Bible is a murderer; Bertilak as a demonic figure would mean, then, "son of the devil." This onomastic derivation may not sound far-fetched if we are willing to give some credit to the linguistic erudition and skills of the medieval ancestors. We find clear evidence of much linguistic erudition in Wolfram's *Parzival*.

18. The translation is from Sandra Naddaff, *Arabesque* (Evanston: Northwestern UP, 1991), 16–28. The ladies in the dialogue are asking the porter for a metaphoric name for the body part; he is punished for lacking in courtesy only in sexual discourse when he has entered the universe of female discourse.

19. The *Gawain* poet describes the pentangle of Gawain's virtues as follows: "Now all those five groups, in truth, were fastened upon this knight, and each one joined to another so that none had an end; and they were fixed upon five points that were never wanting; nor did they come together on any side, or come apart either, without end at any corner that I find anywhere, wherever the tracing began or came to an end" (656–61).

20. See also D. B. McDonald, "The Earlier History of the Arabian Nights," *Journal of the Royal Asiatic Society* (1924): 362–66; David Pinault, *Story-Telling Techniques in the Arabian Nights* (Leiden: E. J. Brill, 1992), 1–12.

21. Alice Lasater, *Spain to England: A Comparative Study of Arabic, European, and English Literature of the Middle Ages* (Jackson, 1974), p. 184; R. S. Loomis, "More Celtic Elements in *Gawain and the Green Knight*," *Journal of English and Germanic Philology* 42 (1943): 168–69; Norman Davis, ed., *Sir Gawain and the Green Knight* (Oxford: Clarendon, 1967), 93.

22. Richard Hamilton Green, "Gawain's Shield and the Quest for Perfection," *ELH* 19 (1962): 121–39.

23. *Liber Abaci di Leonardo Pisano*, ed. Baldassarre Boncompagni (Rome: Tipografia delle Scienze Matematiche e Fisiche, 1885), 283–84.

24. To learn more about the important properties of the Fibonacci numbers, see N. N. Vorob'ev, *Fibonacci Numbers* (New York and London: Blaisdell, 1961), a work I have consulted and borrowed from in the preparation of this study. I would add that the poet seems to be quite aware of the Fibonacci numbers involved in the rabbit experiment since we find that the poet himself has used several of the numbers like 1, 3, 5, 55, etc., in the date January 1, three temptations, three kisses, the five points of the pentangle, the five fives referred to in lines 640–47, and the circle drawn around the pentangle in Fibonacci (*Practica Geometriae*, 214), as in lines 615–16. Such an analysis is beyond the scope of this paper.

25. In the case of a believer the moral as purely human becomes spiritual or colored by the faith of the believer, since faith and baptism transform the natural human being and the purely moral perfection into spiritual or Christian perfection and since, according to traditional medieval Christian theology, antelapsarian *homo naturalis* as such does not exist in the post–Christ dispensation. In other words, pure moral virtues and moral perfection become Christian virtues and Christian perfection. Above all one may recall here the classical adage that virtue stands in the middle.

26. Most of the information on the Arabesque contained in this section is heavily dependent on Alois Riegel, *Problems of Style* (Princeton: Princeton UP, 1992) and Sandra Naddaff, *arabesque: Narrative Structure and the Aesthetics of Repetition in 1001 Nights* (Evanston Northwestern, UP, 1991).

27. Katherine S. Gittes, *The Framing of the Canterbury Tales* (New York: Greenwood, 1991); see also Carol F. Heffernan, "The Medieval Tale of Florence and the East," *South Asian Review* 16 (1995): 1–10.

28. I have stirred up a hornets' nest here by calling those two statements the First Commandment; Catholics call it the First Commandment, but Protestants who are very serious about the Bible break it into two commandments, so that Catholics' Sixth Commandment is "Thou shalt not commit adultery" and in the Protestant version it is "Thou shalt not kill." The point that is of some interest here is that gambling and bingo are forbidden for serious Christians on the basis of this commandment; interestingly, Catholics don't consider bingo a sin; that is why Catholics hold bingo in their church halls.

29. Several critics, like Stevens (76), Field (260–69), Christmas (239–47), Leyerle (58), and Trask (2) think that Gawain's intention to keep the girdle would constitute only a venial sin.

30. Doesn't this passage remind us Chaucer's "Reeve's Tale"? Obviously, Chaucer knew his Aquinas well enough to play games with his readers.

31. Prümmer, 230: "Joannes Nider O. Pr. in suo optimo libro, cui titulus est "Consolatorium timoratae conscientiae" (P.3, c.1) expresse adoptat opinionem B. Alberti et nititur eisdem verbis ac S. Antoninus, qui certe favet Probabiliorismo...."Sed agendo contra tale [*leve*] dubium non peccatur, dum adhaeret opinioni alicuius doctoris et *habet rationes probabibiliores pro ipsa magis quam pro opposita opinione*" (S. Theol. P. i, tit. 3, c. 10, § 10).

32. T. Deman, "Probabilisme," *Dictionnaire de théologie catholique, passim.*
33. A shorter version of this paper was presented at the 29th International Medieval Conference, Kalamazoo, Michigan, May 7, 1994.

Works Cited

Al-Nadim, Ibn. *The Fihrist of al-Nadim: A Tenth-Century Survey of Muslim Culture.* Trans. Bayard Dodge. 2 vols. New York: Columbia UP, 1970.
Aquinas, Thomas, St. *Summa Theologica.* Ed. De Rubeis, Billuart, et al. Turino: Marietti, 1937.
Attar, Farid ud-Din. *Muslim Saints and Mystics.* Trans. A. J. Arberry. Chicago: U of Chicago P, 1966.
Benson, Larry D. *Art and Tradition in Sir Gawain and the Green Knight.* New Brunswick: Rutgers UP, 1965.
Bloomfield, Morton. "*Sir Gawain and the Green Knight*: An Appraisal." *PMLA* 76 (1961): 7–19.
Burrow, J. A. *A Reading of Sir Gawain and the Green Knight.* London: Routledge, 1965.
Burton, Richard. *The Book of the Thousand Nights and a Night.* 6 vols. 1886, rpt. New York: Heritage, 1934.
Campbell, Joseph, ed. *The Portable Arabian Nights.* New York: Viking, 1952.
Chambers, E. K. *Medieval Stage.* Oxford: Clarendon P, 1903.
Christmas, Peter. "A Reading of *Sir Gawain and the Green Knight.*" *Neophilologus* 58 (1974): 238–47.
Coomaraswamy, Ananda K. "*Sir Gawain and the Green Knight*: India and Namuci." *Speculum* 19 (1944): 104–25.
Deman, T. "Probabilisme." *Dictionnaire de Théologie catholique.* Paris: Librairie Tetouzey et Ané, 1933.
Fibonaci. *Liber Abaci di Leonardo Pisano.* Ed. Baldassarre Boncompagni. Rome: Tipografia delle Scienze Matematiche e fisiche, 1885.
Field, P. J. C. "A Reading of *Sir Gawain and the Green Knight.*" *Studies in Philology* 68 (1971): 255–69.
Gittes, Katherine S. *The Framing of the Canterbury Tales.* New York: Greenwood, 1991.
Gollancz, Israel. *Sir Gawain and the Green Knight.* EETS 210. London: Oxford UP, 1910.
Goltra, Robert. "The Confession in the Green Chapel: Gawain's True Absolution." *Emporia State Research Studies* 32 (1984): 5–14.
Green, Richard Hamilton. "Gawain's Shield and the Quest for Perfection" *ELH* 19 (1962): 121–39.
Harwood, Britton J. "*Gawain* and the Gift." *PMLA* 106 (1991): 483–99.
Heffernan, Carol F. "The Medieval Tale of Florence and the East." *South Asian Review* 16 (1995): 1–10.
Hitti, Philip. *History of the Arabs.* LondonL Macmillian, 1949.
Howard, Donald R. "Structure and Symmetry in *Sir Gawain.*" *Speculum* 39 (1964): 425–33.
Howard, Donald R., and Christian K. Zacher, eds. *Critical Studies of* Sir Gawain and the Green Knight. Notre Dame: U of Notre Dame P, 1968.
Johnson, Lynn Staley. *The Voice of the Gawain poet.* Madison: U of Wisconsin P, 1984.
Jones, H. S. V. "Some Observations upon the Squire's Tale." *PMLA*, n.s. 13 (1905): 346–59.
———." The *Cléomadès*, the *Méliacin*, and the Arabian Tale of the 'Enchanted Horse,'" *JEGP* 6 (1907): 221–43.
———."The *Cléomadès* and Related Folk-Tales." *PMLA*, n.s. 16 (1908): 557–98.

Kane, George. *Middle English Literature: A Critical Study of the Romances, the Religious Lyrics, Piers Plowman.* London: Methuen, 1957.
Ker, W.P. *English LiteratureL Medieval.* New York: Holt, 1932.
Kittredge, G. L. *A Study of Gawain and the Green Knight.* Cambridge: Harvard UP, 1916.
Krappe, A. H. "Who Was the Green Knight?" *Speculum* 13 (1938): 206–15.
Lasater, Alice. *Spain to England: A Comparative Study of Arabic, European, and English Literature of the Middle Ages.* Jackson: U of Mississippi P., 1974.
Leyerle, John. "The Game and Play of Hero." In *Concepts of the Hero in the Middle Ages and the Renaissance.* Ed. Norman Burns and Christopher Reagan. Albany: State U of New York P, 1975. 49–82.
Loomis, R. S. *Arthurian Literature in the Middle Ages.* Oxford: Clarendon P, 1959.
_____. "More Celtic Elements in *Gawain and the Green Knight.*" *Journal of English and Germanic Philology* 42 (1943): 168–69.
Lynch, Kathryn L. "East Meets West in Chaucer's Squire's and Franklin's Tales." *Speculum* 70 (1995): 532ff.
Mardrus, Joseph Charles. *The Book of the Thousand Nights and One Night.* Four volumes. New York: St. Martin's Press, 1972.
McDonald, D. B. "The Earlier History of the Arabian Nights." *Journal of the Royal Asiatic Society* (1924): 362–66.
Miller, M. Y., and Chance, Jane. *Approaches to Teaching Sir Gawain and the Green Knight.* New York: MLA, 1986.
Naddaff, Sandra. *Arabesque: Narrative Structure and the Aesthetics of Repetition in 1,001 Nights.* Evanston: Northwestern UP, 1991.
Newhauser, Richard. "Court Festivities in *Sir Gawain and the Green Knight*: Paradigm and Transformation." In *Feste und Feiern im Mittelalter.* Ed. Detlef Altenburg et al. Sigmaringen: Jan Thorbecke, 1991. 461–68.
Nicholson, Reynold. *A Literary History of the Arabs.* Cambridge: Cambridge UP, 1969.
Nitze, William A. "Is the Green Knight Story a Vegetation Myth?" *MP* 33 (1935–1936): 351–66.
Nuis, Hermine J. van. "Sir Gawain's Excesses: The Tension Between His Real and Apparent Self." *Concerning Poetry* 17 (1984): 13–25.
Palacios, Miguel Asín. *Islam and the Divine Comedy.* Trans. Harold Sunderland. London: Longman, 1926.
Pinault, David. *Story-Telling Techniques in the Arabian Nights.* Leiden: E. J. Brill, 1992.
Prümmer, Dominic. *Manuale Theologiae Moralis* I. Barcelona: Herder, 1946.
Riegel, Alois. *Problems of Style* Princeton: UP, 1992.
Robertson, D. W. "Why the Devil Wears Green." *MLN* 69 (1954): 470–72.
Savage, Henry. *The Gawain poet: Studies in His Personality and Background.* Chapel Hill: U of North Carolina P, 1956.
Shedd, Gordon M. "Knight in Tarnished Armour: The Meaning of *Sir Gawain and the Green Knight.*" *Modern Language Review* 62 (1971): 255–69.
Shoaf, R. A. *The Poem as Green Girdle: Commercium in* Sir Gawain and the Green Knight. Gainesville: U of Florida P., 1984.
Silverstein, Theodore. "*Sir Gawain*, Dear Brutus, and Britain's Fortunate Founding: A Study in Comedy and Convention." *MP* 62 (1965): 189–206.
Speirs, John. "Sir Gawain and the Green Knight." *SCR* 16 (1949): 274–300.
Stanford, W. B., and J. V. Luce. *The Quest for Ulysses.* New York: Praeger, 1974.
Stevens, Martin. "Laughter and Game in *Sir Gawain and the Green Knight.*" *Speculum* 47 (1972): 65–78.
Thundy, Zacharias P. "Green and Red: More Classical Influences in *Sir Gawain and the Green Knight.*" *Classical and Modern Literature* 12 (1992): 169–178.

Tolkien, J. R. R. *Sir Gawain and the Green Knight, Pearl, and Si Orfeo*. Boston: Houghton Mifflin, 1975.
Tolkien, J. R. R. and Gordon, E. V., eds. *Sir Gawain and the Green Knight*. Oxford: Clarendon, 1965.
Vorob'ev, N. N. *Fibonacci Numbers*. New York and London: Blaisdell, 1961.
Weston, Jessie. *The Legend of Sir Gawain: Studies upon Its Original Scope and Significance*. London: D. Nutt, 1897.
White, Robert B., Jr. "A Note on the Green Knight's Red Eyes." *ELN* 2 (1965): 250–52.
Williams, Margaret. *The Pearl poet: His Complete Works*. New York: Random House, 1967.
Wimberly, L. C. *Folklore in the English & Scottish Ballads*. Chicago: U of Chicago P, 1928.
Zimmer, Heinrich Robert. *The King and the Corpse: Tales of Soul's Conquest of Evil*. Princeton: Princeton UP, 1956.

Sir Gawain and the Green Knight: *Classical Magic and Its Function in Medieval Romance*

Mickey Sweeney

DOMINICAN UNIVERSITY

Perhaps the greatest compliment offered to a text in the halls of modern academe is debate; if critics must return again and again to a text to argue intention and meaning, the author has achieved an uncommon level of respect. The poet of *Sir Gawain and the Green Knight* is such an author; so provocative is this work that scholars have yet to decide definitively even something as basic as tone—is it a black comedy as Benson suggests (209) or the tragic downfall of an unsuspecting hero?[1]

In coming to terms with the source of the magic so integral to the poem, we find the further complications of generic considerations and cultural expectations. Knowing more about the poet might resolve such issues more readily; if we were certain of social status or occupation and training we could, perhaps, dismiss certain interpretive strains, or the work of applying the appropriate framework to his poetry might be facilitated.[2] Without any such information we can only reconstruct a plausible interpretative structure, plausibility, of course, being the perfect realm in which to entertain debate and re-evaluation.

The *Gawain* poet's use of magic is one of the elements which have provided critics with much to debate.[3] In the poem magic embraces the interests of the secular world and those of the spiritual one. In occupying the nebulous spaces between miracle, superstition, imagination, and the demonic, magic represents a curious and perhaps unique tool by which an author can captivate an audience across socio-political and economic divides.[4] Its place amidst classical and Christian religious systems also allows an author to layer one motif with several complex and diverse meanings based upon the several different traditions in which it has symbolic weight.[5]

Despite the active and significant place of magic in both the classical and medieval worlds, historically critics such John Matthews, Anne Wilson, and John Speirs have argued primarily for an anthropological approach to SGGK, suggesting interpretive strategies that vary from the supernatural elements in romance originating in earth magic, with roots going back to pagan midwinter festivals, to links between the beheading game and the Goddess of Britain and the Fisher King myths. Sheila Fisher's "Taken Men and Token Women" and Geraldine Heng's "Feminine Knots and the Other in *Sir Gawain and the Green Knight*" argue from contrasting ends of the "feminist principle" spectrum; Fisher suggests that the progression of the poem demonstrates the denial of power to women while Heng sees the erosion of the "all-powerful masculine narrative" (72; 509 n.3).[6] Ivo Kamps argues:

> Round Table society maintains its order and integrity by displacing its own social impulses onto scapegoat characters like Morgan le Fay, Morgawse, and Merlin—characters who are excluded from society, but whose subversive force reappears.... Gawain's virtue, skill, and success or failure become less significant, while efforts of "minor" figures like Arthur and Morgan le Fay (usually treated only marginally by the critics), in fact prove absolutely central in the formation and maintenance of Camelot society [314].

When addressing magic at all, as Kamps notes, we still commonly to discuss only Morgan's seemingly minor status and her impact on the court (318–22). In *Art and Tradition* Benson argues that Morgan's role "seems imposed upon the fabric of the poem" (312). More recently Dennis Moore provides a more sympathetic reading when he suggests that Morgan's position in the poem is a part of a "deliberate stratagem" (221), but not many others seem to have taken up this line of interpretation. If one would speculate about the reason, it might be owing to the most influential of all "Celtic critics," R. S. Loomis, who was one of the first to define the supernatural in the poem by its connection to Morgan. Given his exhaustive study of magic and its relationship to Celtic origins, it is not surprising that more contemporary scholars appropriate that base upon which to build their assessments of magic in romance. His research and the work of his colleagues clearly demonstrate the need to appreciate the Celtic roots of many of the poem's elements, but I would argue that it is equally fruitful to assess the nature of magic in the poem by two different but essentialcriteria: first, the alternative functions of magic in romance literature, and second, the role of magic in the intellectual history of the Middle Ages.

These diverse perspectives demonstrate that magic functioned not only to engage, a claim often used to judge its place in the romances, but also as a legitimate means of introducing philosophical and cultural debate. Magic in *Sir Gawain and the Green Knight* provides the backbone for the plot, thus the need for giving it primary consideration. However, it is important to evaluate its function in wider terms than simple plot facilitation, for magic also opens the door to the dimension of Gawain's thoughts and his struggles with his faith and moral code—prime sources of interest in the tale. Such realms of investigation are not particularly promoted by the relationship of magic to the Celtic world; they are, however, integral to the function of magic in classical texts and the way the medieval world interpreted both those historical works and the place of magic in its own culture.

The Meaning of Magic

Dating from even before the Classical period, magic holds a nebulous, yet potent, position in society as a prospective means of manmade power, philosophical investigation, and religious controversy. It has from its very conception confused the boundaries between our limitations and the power of God(s). It is impractical in this format to argue for belief in magic in either the classical or medieval periods, but it is important to note, as Georg Luck does, that

> Ancient magic may have been based on "primitive" ideas, but the form in which it was handed down to us was by no means primitive. On the contrary: magic in this sense existed only within the highly developed cultures and formed an important part of them. Not only the lower classes, the ignorant and uneducated, believed in it, but the "intellectuals" down to the end of antiquity were convinced that dangerous supernatural powers operated around them and that these powers could be controlled by certain means [*Arcana Mundi* 9].

The term magic is derived from the word *magoi*, which first appears in Herodotus's *Histories*, where he tells us that they were a Median tribe or caste recognized in ancient Iran as specialists in ritual and religious knowledge (1.172–73). The three most famous Greek magicians (shamans) between Homer and the Hellenistic period were Orpheus, Pythagoras, and Empedocles (Dodds 140). In *Arcana Mundi*, Luck argues that "The similarities between these three spectacular figures suggest the existence, in Greek Civilization, of a type of miracle-worker who was also an original thinker and a great teacher, someone who offered a philosophical theory to explain the universe and the human soul ... and who may also have been a poet" (11). Such origins mark the medieval idea of magic as a phenomenon which had influence in both secular and religious realms, as well as introducing the formula which subsequent historians, philosophers, writers, theologians, and political analysts would find so irresistible. Although medieval exposure to Greek literature was primarily through Latin sources, the respect which both the Romans and the medieval world had for Hellenistic culture meant that its influence was keenly felt throughout the ages. Germination in such classical roots created a concept of magic that was used by romance writers to explore the ramifications of such provocative issues as the role of an individual man in the hierarchical structure (*Tristan, Cligés*) and/or the moral fitness of a man in terms of his society and his faith (Arthur, Perceval, and Gawain stories). The role of magic in a historical text, much like that of a miracle in a religious work, acts as a means to establish the power of an individual. Given magic's versatility and curious ambiguity as real, sinful, and yet potentially imaginary, the list of symbolic and metaphoric uses could be, and indeed is, long and varied.

Magic is most often linked to an exploration of our place in the universe, free will, and our relationship to God(s) and our fellow creatures. That it was real, if only in the sense that people believed, can be demonstrated by the impact of such stories/histories offered concerning the powers attributed to magicians; for example, tales abound which pit the powers of the gods against one another or against the atrocities committed by a magician in court. It may seem a game of semantics, but the distinction between, for example, Moses as prophet and miracle worker versus the Pharaoh's wizards and magicians in the book of *Exodus* became crucial as the Christian church constructed a theology which interpreted some forms of magic to be demonically inspired temptation.

Such complicated approaches to magic are not limited to the ancient world, as can be demonstrated by endless accusations of witchcraft in various medieval royal courts or the impact of the witch trials across Europe in both the Middle Ages and the early modern period. Pollack and Maitland's transcription of the "Statute of Treason" provides a historical source from which the modern reader can derive a sense of the seriousness with which the medieval audience would have considered, for example, Gawain's breach of *trowth* and use of magic:

> In England, The Great Statute of Treasons of 1352, distinguished high treason as any crime against the king's person and regality.... The codes express condemnation of these and other forms of treason which struck at the roots of the social order—[such as] counterfeiting the ruler's coinage, falsifying his seal, spreading heresy, [and] practising sorcery—in moral as well as legal terms. The moral failing inherent in his breach of troth put the traitor beyond reach of mercy or compassion: "He should perish in torments to which hellfire will seem a relief" [503].

This mix between moral, legal, and religious boundaries illuminates ways in which magic and religion coexist not only within romance, but also in medieval life. Philip IV of France's trial of the Templars also demonstrates that magic was a powerful force at all levels of medieval society. Jeffrey Burton Russell depicts a history of the political manipulation of the idea of magic that reached even the highest strata of sophisticated and educated society:

> It continued into the reign of his [Louis X's] brother Charles IV (1322–1328), who tried the Countess Matilda of Artois for magically poisoning his predecessor.... Edward II used his French cousin's methods in 1324 when over twenty persons were tried for having attempted to bring about the death of the English King and his favourites by magic [172–73].

It is virtually impossible for the modern reader to gauge whether political opportunism was simply disguised as belief in magic, but it is clear that the concept of magic could be used outside the literary context to deadly effect. The ambiguities involved alert the modern audience to the fragile relationship between Christianity and magic, two powers which rest upon the need of a community to believe in their existence. It is clear that magic attracted the interests of both medieval intellectuals and theologians; Jean Delumeau completes this picture by arguing that "the peasantry of late medieval Europe were in fact polytheistic and deeply magical, making use of pagan rites and deflecting christian sacraments to this-worldly ends" (as cited in Duffy 277). The place of magic in the medieval world of politics was made possible by its acceptance, and as Valerie Flint argues in *The Rise of Magic in Early Medieval Europe*, its perpetuation by the early church as it struggled for mastery over the gods of Rome.

Flint's research demonstrates that church fathers did not argue for the non-existence of magic; instead, they redefined pagan claims to miracles as magic and relegated them to the world of evil and sin. Saint Augustine reasons, for example, that good Christians perform miracles from a state of righteous goodness, while magicians act through private agreement with demons for selfish gain. The church was on the one hand confirming that a man's greatness is assessed by relationship to miracles, while fighting a rear-guard action to define miracles against the cultural understanding of magic. In *Religion and the Decline of Magic*, Keith Thomas reasons that this struggle continues into the Middle Ages:

> The medieval Church thus found itself saddled with the tradition that the working of miracles was the most efficacious means of demonstrating its monopoly of the truth. By the twelfth and thirteenth centuries the *Lives* of the Saints had assumed a stereotyped pattern. They related the miraculous achievements of holy men, and stressed how they could prophesy the future, control the weather, provide protection against fire and flood, magically transport heavy objects, and bring relief to the sick ... the Church did not as an institution claim the power to work miracles. But it reaped prestige from the doings of those of its members to whom God was deemed to have extended miraculous gifts [26].

Such powers could be used to describe many of Merlin's functions in Geoffrey of Monmouth's *Historia* or many of the feats of magicians in the ancient world. The church did struggle to establish clear-cut definitions of what constituted magic, but terminology often became muddied by the regular exchanging of such sensitive vocabulary as *magia*, *miracula*, *astrologia*, *mirabilia*, and *malefici* and certainly by the fourteenth century use of such terms as *magyk natureel*, *illusioun*, and *merveille* by historians, writers, and even theologians themselves. By the time the *Gawain* poet incorporated magic into his text, he had a long and fruitful classical tradition of magic, the historical conventions of early medieval writers, such as Geoffrey of Monmouth, Henry of Huntingdon, or Wace, and the Celtic, as well as romance traditions upon which to draw in formulating his conception of magic's function and symbolic value in the text.

Tracing the Roots of Magic in Medieval Intellectual History

Eugene Tavenner's *Studies in Magic from Latin Literature* provides a very detailed account of the evolution of the Greek word *magoi* from priest to that of trickster with consideration for the development of both the positive and negative attributions. He makes clear that the Latin *magus* is the sister to the Greek in both its usage and meaning; *magus* translates as *magician*, *magia* and *magicus* being the nominal and adjectival forms, respectively, for magic as we now understand it—our attempt to control nature or his fellow human beings with supra-natural powers.[7] Even when cynical, classical authors are rarely altogether dismissive of magic. Apuleius's *Apologia* suggests that a magician's power is the result of communication between himself and the gods, established by means of magic spells whereby the magician gets whatever he wants (Tavenner 6; Luck, *Ancient Pathways* 220).[8] He points to the use of *magus* in creditable terms:

> If what I read in a large number of authors be true, namely that magician is the Persian word for priest, what is there criminal in being a priest and having due knowledge, science and skill in all ceremonial law, sacrificial duties and the binding rules of religion? [trans. Butler 55].

Philostratus writes concerning the *Life of Apollonius of Tyana* (4.44) that his subject practiced such a "philosophy" "in order to know the gods and to understand human beings, because it was more difficult to know someone else than to know one's self" (as trans. in Luck, *Arcana Mundi* 105). As Luck suggests, this magician philosopher is particularly fascinating as he has been discussed as the "pagan imitator of Christ" (*Ancient Pathways* 219). The connections between the world of the ancients and that of the fourteenth century are such that the idea and even term of *philosopher-magician* still hold much weight. The most famous example is Chaucer's philosopher-magician, the Clerk d'Orliens of "The Franklin's Tale," a character (in)famous for employing *magyk natureel* in order to facilitate the selfish demands of Aurelius's love for Dorigen.

Not to stretch too far, but it is interesting that these magic-philosophers serve similar functions: they provoke audiences into examination of the self and the characters under discussion. To trace the evolution of the magician-philosopher would require more space than is available here, but much has already been made of the Clerk d'Orliens' workmanlike or scientific approach to magic, and the same could be said for predecessors to such figures, such as Chrétien de Troyes' Thessala or Geoffrey of Monmouth's Merlin. Thessala is the medieval equivalent to a modern-day alternative pharmacist: a pinch of this, a tap of that. There is no mention by Chaucer or Chrétien of any devilry or *maleficium*. And it is of no surprise that the reputation of Thessaly for powerful witches reached the medieval world, made famous as it was by such accounts as can be found in Lucan's *Civil War*. Equally, Merlin is often described as an accomplished "magical engineer." Indeed, if anything, both medieval and classical applications seem determined to downplay the sinister aspects of magical power and underscore, especially in the Clerk d'Orliens case, the status of a *philosopher* who is conversant with magic (Chaucer ll. 1561, 1585, 1607). The Clerk does not conjure demons, so we may clear him of any charges of "necromancy" (Luengo 3-4). It is interesting that such a situation would strengthen the Clerk's relationship to the actual status of magic in the fourteenth century; Luengo argues that

> More often than not, magic was associated in the medieval mind with astrology and hence shared the praise and censure directed at astrology at different times by various medieval thinkers.... Augustine condemned astrology outright, while Roger Bacon and Thomas Aquinas accepted it for scientific purposes [meteorology and medicine, for example]. Both Bacon and Aquinas were careful to distinguish between legitimate scientific astrology (or "magyk natureel") and astrology put to illegitimate use: judicial astrology or divination ... necromancy or black magic [Luengo 2].[9]

It is foolhardy to try to trace direct connections to the use of this terminology by Chaucer, but clearly the idea of magic as a way of connecting to the gods or dealing with human fate was still strong, and indeed would stay strong, as is evidenced by the popularity of the early modern playwright Marlowe's magician-philosopher Doctor Faustus.

As we come to terms with the history of magic, it is clear that classical authors were conversant with, or indeed, contributed to, magic's nebulous place in the secular, imaginative, and religious worlds of their own cultures. When defending himself against the accusation of witchcraft, Apuleius for example, in his *Apology*, details some of the confusion regarding the relationship between magic and philosophers:

> But it is a fairly common misunderstanding by which the uneducated accuse philosophers. Some of them think that those who investigate the simple causes and elements of matter are antireligious, and that they deny the very existence of the gods, as for instance, Anaxagoras, Leucippus, Democritus, Epicurus, and other leading scientists. Others, commonly called "magi," spend great care in the exploration of the workings of providence in the world and worship the gods with great devotion, as if they actually knew how to make the things happen that they know do happen. This was the case with Epimenides, Orpheus, Pythagoras, and Ostanes [as trans. in Luck, *Arcana Mundi* 112–13].

Luck translates Apuleius's use of Plato's *Alcibiades* and *Charmides* as his strategy to "demonstrate how highly the Persians regarded 'magic' and the 'magi': magic formed part of the education that the royal princes received; hence it must have been a religion, a philosophy, rather than some kind of witchcraft" (*Arcana Mundi* 110). Pliny the Elder in *Natural History* states that magic "is a very deceptive, and yet very powerful art, compounded of elements drawn from medicine, religion, and astrology" (301–2).[10] Pliny details an enormous range of medicinal and magical potions, while taking magicians with a grain of salt (25.59, 29.30, 37.75); he does not, however, altogether discount them, but suggests instead that a wise man is a careful one (28.4). He states:

> I shall include several of the magicians' remedies, and in the first place the amulets they recommend: the dust in which a hawk has rolled himself tied in a linen cloth by a red thread, or the longest tooth of a black dog [trans. Jones, *Pliny* 8.340–43].

Flint argues, in examining the many ambivalent attitudes seen in the Roman world, that it has penetrated, in short, "that no-man's–land between magic, science, and religion in which all three can come together and in which much magic might be salvaged and valued." Furthermore, she suggests that Pliny's ambivalence toward magic is so instructive "partly because his account of magic is so extensive, partly because of the eagerness with which his work ... was seized upon in medieval Europe, and partly because, denouncer of magic as he can be, he cannot, in the last resort, wholly make up his mind about it." Hence it became possible for other rational and religious persons to believe "that magic, of a kind, had a Christian place" (27).

If we examine, even briefly, Tufts' *Perseus* collection, a discussion of *magicus* can be found in such diverse texts as Ovidius Naso's *Metamorphoses*, Cornelius Tacitus's *Annals*, and the Latin Vulgate (Saint Jerome, chap. 8 etc.).[11] Thus it is possible to contend that the cultured Roman would have had to come to terms with some understanding of magic, so widespread was its presence; it could even be argued, as Tavenner does, that magic could have been understood by an educated Roman as "an art based on medicine, astrology, and religion, whereby man attempts to control the gods and thereby to control natural phenomena in accordance to his selfish desires" (7). Such a definition, endorsed by some of the most popular writers of the classical period, lays the groundwork for medieval appreciation of magic as a concept, if not a reality, which had its foundation in both cultural and religious traditions. In one of the seminal works on magic and intellectual history, Lynn Thorndike reinforces this line of thinking by arguing, as Flint did, that Pliny's work is of special interest because of its impact not only on his own period, but on that of the Middle Ages as well:

> Indeed not only is the *Natural History* just the sort of work that delighted the Middle Ages, but Pliny seems to have exerted a considerable direct influence on writers down through the sixteenth century. Isidore of Seville practically copied his unfavorable comments on the magi and his discussion of the powers of stones. Bede

seems to have owed a great deal to him. Alcuin openly praised that "most devoted investigator of nature." Roger Bacon quoted him; the *Natural History* was a mine whence Agrippa dug much of the material for his *Occult Philosophy* and to which Porta seems equally indebted in his *Natural Magic* [41].[12]

If we look to Isidore of Seville, Henry Huntingdon, William Malmesbury, Chrétien de Troyes, Michael Scot, Roger Bacon, Aquinas, Dante, and Chaucer to name only a few, we find that some of the greatest minds of the medieval period, as well as that of the classical, dealt with magic in terms of literature, history, theology, and cultural practice. Equally, astrology, so often intertwined with discussion of magic, was a popular subject at medieval universities and thought essential to mathematics and medicine, not to mention its undisputed influence on the developing sciences. Our interest here is primarily literary, so at a minimum it is crucial to explore the relationships between romance, philosophy, history, the classical world, and religion to see what functions magic might have fulfilled for the *Gawain* author. Insights garnered from the intellectual history of magic and the development of romance arguably offer a wider interpretive base upon which to explore the *Gawain* poet's controversial use of magic as both a secular and spiritual means of controlling Gawain and the world of Arthur's court.

As we look to see what type of influence the classical and historical ideas of magic could have had upon the late medieval author of the *Gawain* poem, it is striking to note that the controversial relationship between the use of magic and religion in the work finds resonance in a classical reading of magic's power and influence. I would argue that both Morgan and Gawain use magic to achieve their own ends; Morgan's desire to humiliate Arthur and frighten Guenore to death and Gawain's desire to insure against his own death at the hands of the Green Knight are both attempts by humans to use magic for personal gain. Such applications speak to the heart of the controversy surrounding magic from the classical period to its place in the medieval world: the core of magic's theoretical influence comes from its use as a "power" which enabled an individual to affect his own fate or the fate of others, or, indeed, mediate a god's power over an individual. It is, of course, not helpful to reduce classical approaches to magic to simplistic formulas, but it is perhaps of some small value to outline basic differences, as one could argue that medieval authors readily merged traditions in an attempt to find the most powerful arsenal of vocabulary, metaphors, and symbols for their texts.

In that light it is of particular interest that Morgan is described as a goddess, which arguably brings to the fore classical/pre–Christian associations, but equally, as Loomis points out, it speaks to the tradition in which many medieval authors referred to Morgan le Fay as "'dea quaedam phantastica' [and] spoke of Gawain and Lunete as the sun and the moon, and testified that the common folk in old times regarded Merlin as a god" (4, 136). Is this figure only a Celtic god or could it be argued that the classical gods blended into a tradition of all pre–Christian influences? In tandem with the "Troy" introduction to the poem, it seems reasonable to suggest that the *Gawain* poet is constructing on one level a historical/classical framework for his characters.[13] Indeed, even Loomis considers "the vast literature of the Round Table cycle as mainly springing from the imagination of French authors of the twelfth and thirteenth centuries," in other words, not solely from the fountainhead of Celtic myths, but from the already heavily classically influenced sources of Geoffrey of Monmouth's and Wace's histories—long accepted resources for Chrétien's Arthurian romances. In tracing how the romance authors mediated or translated their raw materials into *bel conjointures*, we must examine what influences came together in the twelfth and thirteenth centuries; how would these scholars and entertainers have best employed their knowledge and skills? On an even more basic level, it would be important to consider what functions literature served in the minds of its authors and audience in as much as we can determine such things and how such considerations would have affected the *Gawain* poet.

The History of Magical Romance

Chrétien de Troyes used marvelous and magical methods to test his heroes; for example, Lancelot in *Le Chevalier de la Charrette* suffers from an illicit love for his queen. This love symbolizes both an avenue to personal happiness and the path to complete chaos, the destruction of the feudal system's method of functioning. Lancelot's moral virtue is tried by the infamous ride in the cart; his weakness is demonstrated by his burns from the flaming bed and wounds from the sword bridge—both magical/marvelous tests. If Lancelot's spiritual perfection had matched his fighting skills, he would survive these trials unscathed. The use of magic and the marvelous create ways to judge this character which allow for the exploration of the pros and cons of certain stances on dangerous social issues; without such a realm for discussion, Christian rules or strict social mores would automatically have condemned a situation comprising morally grey areas.

Chrétien's *Perceval* and its continuations serve as an even more persuasive example of a ready history of magic having an important role in romance; see, for example, Elisabeth Brewer's argument that the *Gawain* poet must have been familiar with Chrétien's text. In *Sir Gawain and the Green Knight: Sources and Analogues*, she details the relationship between the Gawain figure of that romance and *SGGK*, noting similarities between the "spiritual" quests, the sorrow surrounding the two departures, scenes in which both Gawains engage in love-talk but strive to remain chaste; both quests are the results of binding oaths and are governed by strict time limits, and both heroes have well-established reputations for courtesy (4–5). Chrétien's Gawain is also confronted by a pair of women, one older, the other younger, at a marvelous castle that houses a bed which will be the source of much trouble. Brewer argues: "These resemblances are mostly on a small scale, only to be fully grasped in a continuous reading of *Perceval*, but in such a reading their accumulated force is irresistible as an argument for the *Gawain* Poet's knowledge of the poem" (4). When we come to terms with these similarities, it is of course reasonable to argue that Chrétien could have provided the source of the *Gawain* poet's use of Celtic magic. Douglas Kelly has long argued that Chrétien's approach to *conjointure* was actually based upon the melding of twelfth-century forms of rhetoric and Celtic traditions (13). I would argue, however, that innovations in twelfth-century historiography must also be calculated as integral to that equation and suggest that the *Gawain* poet had, thereby, a ready source of classical and historical appreciations of magic. Take into consideration the popularity of such late–twelfth-century authors as John of Salisbury and his conservative reconfiguration of classical (Pliny primarily) and Isidorean definitions of *maleficia* and *magica*. One could argue, as indeed Thorndike does, that in repeating old definitions

> he adds some current superstitions and shows that the magic arts are far from having fallen into disuse.... He shows us how vain must have been all the ecclesiastical thunders and warnings of demons and damnation, like his own, directed against magic, from the fact that not merely kings of the past like Saul and Pharaoh, but clergy of the present themselves—a priest and a deacon, a chancellor and an archbishop of England—practice or patronize such arts [*History* 170].

That the debate concerning the place of magic in the realms of religion, philosophy, and culture was ongoing is something that Michael Scott, another well-known figure in the history of the "arts," demonstrates when he repeats Hugh Saint Victor's claim that magic, or *magus*, is *not* "received in philosophy, destroys religion, and corrupts morals" but is "wise in the secrets of nature and in the prediction of the future" (as cited in Thorndike, *History* 319). If the reach of such texts into the fourteenth century is too tenuous to be convincing, consider alone, then, the influence of Wace's translation of Geoffrey of Monmouth's *Historia* and the intense interest in history and the recognition of the impact of the classical world that Chrétien acknowledges in his prologue to *Cligés*:

> Li livres est molt anciens
> Qui tesmoigne l'estoire a voire:
> Por ce fet ele meulz a croirre.
> Par les livres que nos avons
> Les faiz des anciens savons
> Et dou siecle qui fu jadis.
> Ce nos ont nostre livre apris
> Que Grece ot de chevalerie
> Le premier los et de clergie,
> Puis vint chevalerie a Rome
> Et de la clergie la somme,
> Qui or est en France venue.
> Dex doint qu'ele i soit retenue
> Tant que li leus li embelisse
> Si que ja mais de France n'isse
> L'ennors qui s'i est arrestee [44–46].

(From the books in our possession we know of the deeds of the ancients and of the world as it was in olden days. These books of ours have taught us that Greece once stood preeminent in both chivalry and learning. Then chivalry proceeded to Rome in company with the highest learning. Now they have come to France. God grant that they be sustained here and never depart.) [Staines 87].

The "father of romance" clearly demonstrates respect for classical traditions. More importantly, his awareness of such respectful attitudes in his audience thereby suggests a reason for applying a form of magic understood to be a complex blend of religion and philosophy—much as Pliny and Apuleius suggested it should be understood—to the romances. That Chrétien's work is the foundation for the romances to follow is a point that will spark little controversy.

The *Gawain* poet also used magical or marvelous encounters as a means of tackling difficult social issues and revealing a hero's moral weakness. In terms of reading the *Gawain* story from diverse perspectives, it would be interesting to explore whether a reader could be tempted to see allusions to the Paris story of the golden apple in Gawain's being tested by Mary, Morgan, and the Temptress, as well as the significance of Morgan's relationship to such other vital women as the Lady of Avalon (also interestingly enough connected to apples) or the Lady of the Lake. Could the *Gawain* poet have seen himself as the next inheritor of the classical mantle which Chrétien was so keen to claim? It is true that such classical references would be difficult to trace outside of the influences of Vergil, Dictys, Dares, and Benoit de Sainte Maure's *Roman de Troie*.[14] It would seem, however, straightforward enough that the *Gawain* poet sought to capitalize on historical traditions of magic (the tradition of magic in "written history") in making such clear references to Merlin and Morgan in those crucial passages. It would be difficult to gauge if the audience would be inspired to think of Merlin without reference to the character of Geoffrey's *Historia*, or Morgan as something apart from her well-known figure in the Arthurian cycle but, clearly, Morgan's description is deliberately provocative on several levels (Powell 146):

> Þurȝ myȝt of Morgne la Faye, þat in my hous lenges,
> And koyntyse of clergye bi craftes wel lerned,
> Þe maystrés of Merlyn mony hatz taken—
> For ho hatz dalt drwry ful dere sumtyme
> With þat conable klerk, þat knowes alle your knyȝtez
> at hame;
> Morgne þe goddes
> Þerfore hit is hir name:
> Weldeȝ non so hyȝe hawtesse
> Þat ho ne con make ful tame [2446–55].

(through the power of Morgan le Fay, who dwells in my house, and by her wiles has learned much skill in magic lore, has acquired many of the miraculous powers of Merlin—for she once had very intimate love-dealings with that accomplished wizard, as all your knights at home will know; and so Morgan the goddess is her name; there is no one so arrogantly proud whom she cannot humble utterly) [Barron 139].

Morgan's pedigree, as it were, is also provocatively introduced as one of "mixed blood," owing to her association with Merlin, known for his changeable nature and infamous as the product of the union between a princess who becomes a nun and an incubus (Thorpe 167–69), which means that once again we are returned to the convoluted history of magic and Christianity. What is of particular note is the very specific mention of Morgan's desire to humble all those who are arrogantly proud. It is clear that the poet is seeking to merge even the agendas of these powerful yet seemingly diametrically opposed women—it should be Mary, not Morgan, who seeks to humble an arrogant court, pride being one of the greatest of the deadly sins.

It is clear, however, that one of the most provocative points in the poem comes from Gawain's appeals to Mary: Hautdesert appears to Gawain when he seems at his wits' end, but the poet makes it difficult to know if it appears as the result of Mary's intervention or Morgan's subversion of his prayer. This is in many ways a crucial point to understanding the poet's agenda for the text: magic is acting as a means of communicating with the gods to achieve one's own ends, as Apuleius, cited earlier, suggested was so crucial. We can see magic being used in ways evocative of magic's function in classical *and* medieval society: to address and negotiate the gap between social codes and Christian dogma. There are problems with both, and magic in this poem is employed to reveal their inadequacies. Magic is being used to understand humanity's place in the world and to test Gawain's faith *and* moral codes. The poet has adopted Pliny's ambivalent attitude, as it were, and put to good use magic's ambiguous status as powerful in the worlds of the imagination, religious faith, and secular culture.

When Gawain takes the magic girdle, he does so to save himself from an unnatural death. His action demonstrates to the audience that he is thinking on the level of biology, perhaps reminiscent of Thessala's pharmaceutical approach: such a choice will preserve his body. The author also reveals several other levels of impact: in terms of Gawain's social status and code, it becomes clear that in betraying his host, he has tarnished his reputation; in terms of faith, Gawain betrays his beliefs by taking magical protection. By employing magic the *Gawain* poet enables the audience to see the poem at all of these different, although often interwoven, interpretive levels.

Romance: Finding Meaning as the Daughter of History

John F. Benton argues that there is an interesting movement from history to romance:

> The study of either manuscripts or authors produced a similar result, a realization that courtly audiences found in their literature, works of moral instruction and serious history with political overtones, as well as compositions which must have amused and sometimes inspired them, as they can still move and inspire us. Much courtly literature was as accurate, true-to-life, and down-to-earth as authors' skill and knowledge could make it, but some works clearly contain a generous portion of the miraculous and the fantastic [44].

It is of tremendous interest that the authors who set the stage for the movement from history to fiction are concerned with the issues of authority versus truth and the power of magic as a means to establish secular influence and educate an audience, both in terms of languages and cultures.

Wace gives popular currency to Geoffrey of Monmouth's "authoritative work" by translating it, which sets the stage for its enormous impact; from the twelfth century alone, 48 copies survive. But it is also clear that Wace was not insensitive to the issues surrounding the authority of Geoffrey's "historical" materials, demonstrated by the disquiet expressed regarding Arthur's legitimacy. In the movement from history to romance, these authors were concerned to maintain a place in the realm of valued accomplishments; they wanted their texts to have meaning and influence in their society:

> Que pur amur de sa largesce
> Que pur poür de sa prüesce,
> En cele grant pais ke jo di,
> Ne sai si vus l'avez oï,
> Furent les merveilles pruvees
> E les aventures truvees
> Ki d'Artur sunt tant recuntees
> Ke a fable sunt aturnees:
> Ne tut mençunge, ne tut veir,
> Ne tut folie ne tut saveir [Wace 9785–94].

> (In this time of great peace I speak of—I do not know if you have heard of it—the wondrous events that appeared and the adventures were sought out which, whether for love of his generosity, or for fear of his bravery, are so often told about Arthur that they have become the stuff of fiction [*fable*]: not all lies, not all truth, neither total folly nor total wisdom) [Weiss 246–47].

Wace corrects the flaws in Merlin's prophecies as presented in Geoffrey's *Historia*. In Geoffrey's work, Merlin is shown to help only the two kings who learn from the lessons of history not to go a-conquering, namely Uther and Ambrosius. Geoffrey incorporated a thematic structure into his history which demonstrated that man could have impact upon his own world, even guide his own fate, as evidenced by Uther's demand that Merlin use magic to quench his lust for Igraine. The greatest king of Britain is thereby the product of man's will and desire, unless one would want to argue that lust and magic were the tools of God.

Previous historians had interpreted fortuitous events as miraculous, and as a sign that God demonstrated his support for a hero or a country.

Carol Harding argues that Eusebius and Augustine reaffirm that God does control history; fortune and blind chance do not fit into their views. Orosius combines Augustinian and Eusebian ideas to create his own "synthesis of national history and biblical narrative with its exegetical interpretations" (46). Rodney Thompson argues that for Bede, "supernatural happenings are pregnant with theological meaning: they are signs of God's favor, they are intimately related to the spirituality and moral virtue of the performer or recipient, and they are told in order to edify" (23). Based on the methods of Gildas and Bede, Geoffrey's proclaimed predecessors, the fall of Britain had previously been interpreted through the tools of scriptural exegesis. Robert Hanning describes this endeavor, however, as "[Geoffrey reconstructing] the *rise* and *fall* of Britain—an earlier phase still of history's endlessly recurring cycle—as the ideal context within which to work out the implications of the new historiography. The traditional interpretations of Bede and Gildas exercised an honorable tyranny over the end of British history from which no later writer could hope to escape" (*Vision* 136–37). Geoffrey, however, deviates from "seeing God's footprint in history" and explores a new interpretation for the rise and fall of Britain (*Vision* 26, 36).[15]

William of Malmesbury questions the status of Geoffrey's Latin *Historia* by saying: "this is the Arthur concerning whom idle tales of the Bretons rave wildly even today, a man certainly worthy to be celebrated, [but] not in foolish dreams of deceitful fables, but in truthful histories" (trans. Thompson 11). If we try to establish what William meant by "truthful histories," it is only possible to define them by what they were not (i.e., they were neither idle tales nor fables). It is interesting that despite establishing these criteria for twelfth-century historical works, in his own *Gesta regum Anglorum* William took care to describe the occult practices of Pope Sylvester II, Gerbert the magician, the witch of Berkeley and the two clerks of Nantes, as well as a catalogue of marvels that included magicians' trips to hidden worlds.[16] Clearly, such information for him did not fall under the category of fables, which would lead one to speculate that magic itself was still considered a viable topic of conversation, not something to be dismissed out of hand.[17]

He was, however, nothing if not dismissive of the *Historia*, but that has perhaps more to do with Geoffrey's "romance" approach, in which he employs unverifiable "facts" as well as magic and the marvelous to establish authority for his rulers outside the traditional avenues of power and without preordained religious intent. Arthur is no saint; Geoffrey's characters, much like Chrétien's soon-to-follow romance knights, are not just great men: they are leaders intimately related to magical powers or events.

Hanning argues that part of the foundation for this new historical vision is the twelfth-century resurgence of interest in classical authors. This intellectual trend encouraged new areas of non–Christian study, for example the *Aeneid*.[18] Barrett Wendell references C. H. Haskins's list of twelfth-century textbooks and concludes that after learning the alphabet and reading some elementary books, students turn to "satire and history, to Statius, the divine *Aeneid* and Lucan ... Juvenal, Horace, Ovid, the *Bucolics* of Vergil, Sallust, Cicero, Martial, Petronius, Suetonius, Livy, Seneca, Aristotle, Apuleius, Quintilian, Boethius, Euclid, Hippocrates, Galen, the Code of Justinian, and almost every book in the Bible" (495). The exploration of these types of interests could have contributed to Geoffrey's vision of history through more classical eyes, or more specifically, history as seen in terms of patterns which need to be identified and interpreted. Although William was a noted classicist himself, such liberties may also have been what set William's teeth on edge when it came to Geoffrey's text. Latin and history were the domains of the religious and the truth, not the profane and the worldly.

Even William of Malmesbury, however, deemed all things Anglo-French, or simply French, cultured, and if he is an adequate guide to cultural trends, then by mixing French courtly culture with the mythic themes of once and future kings and magic, Geoffrey created what seems to have been an irresistible combination (Gillingham 57, xix).[19] It may even be that by discussing magical elements in a context normally preserved for religion, Geoffrey made plain what has always been an uncomfortably symbiotic relationship between magic and miracles, marvels and wonders. Geoffrey achieves what Hanning argues is a human-focused history quite unlike the works of his predecessors. This change in perception may also have added significantly to the types of themes secular fiction could address. Chrétien's romances, Geoffrey's descendents, are focused on a man's honor and the nature of love; they often explore free will and, particularly in Chrétien's *Perceval*, the relationship between the state of a man's soul and his social status. This combination of themes, I would argue, is owing to the classical vision of magic as an art form comprising of religious, philosophical, and secular realms of inquiry.

Winthrop Wetherbee argues that in the twelfth century "intellectuals had emerged as a social type ... possessed of the artistic skill to express its new social awareness in a range of literary forms" (x). It is clear from the fairly illustrious list of chroniclers of Arthur in the Latin tradition that the educated cleric would have been interested in producing not only history, but religious and political satires, tracts concerning political theory, and, perhaps, even a wide variety of "entertainment" genres. Gerald of

Wales, Walter Map, and Andreas Capellanus begin a list of educated men associated with the court of Henry II, who actively participated in the renaissance of the twelfth century; a list of this nature is completed by the inclusion of such literary innovators as Chrétien de Troyes and Gottfried von Strassburg, men of comparable education and interests. So, Siân Echard argues, these men and their interests in history, chronicle writing, politics, religion, and culture mark the renaissance man who was also keen on the new sciences, mathematics, astrology, and, I would suggest, often magic (2–3). In pursuing Echard's line of inquiry, we find that such noted thinkers as Walter Map and John of Salisbury both felt that "narrative, even fictional, frivolous narrative may serve the serious purposes of philosophy" (15). Echard cites John of Salisbury: "I do not promise that all the things which are written here are true, but, whether they be true or false they will be of use to the reader" (*Policraticus*, Prol., 16). Furthermore, Echard argues for Map's often underappreciated work, that he "implies there is more to his *nugae* than meets the eye. Cleverness and relaxation—what Map and John both with differing motives, call *nugae*—may simultaneously serve frivolous and serious purposes" (19).[20] What is most interesting for this reading would be the application of Echard's argument for closer study not only to Map's *nugae*, but equally to his use of the marvelous and fantastic. Gerald of Wales and Map both were well known for their interests in *mirabilia*, which Gerald defines as "vero dicimus quae nostrae cognotioni non subjacent etiam cum sint naturalia" ("we call marvels those phenomena that surpass our understanding even though they be natural"). It is clear that these educated and well-trained Latin/classical scholars were interested in a wide range of topics and able to transform their materials, even seemingly basic and unsophisticated materials, into complex and clever creations. In the complicated political world of the twelfth century, the ability to create ambiguity certainly stood in good stead the author who believed himself responsible for educating and reforming his often powerful audience. It is certainly not surprising that such a manipulation of conventional historiography as perpetrated by Geoffrey, Map, or Gerald would irritate more traditional and conservative writers. William of Newburgh, for example, claimed that Geoffrey was no historian, but simply a "story-teller," a *Fabulator*, which P.G. Walsh argues carries the implication of "romancer" (7, 20). But of what exactly would he be accusing Geoffrey? Could it be simply the telling of stories or the embellishing of facts or even the inclusion of untruths to direct the reader toward the discovery of meaning?[21] Did Geoffrey's work incur ire by a seemingly credulous attitude toward what Wace refers to as *"merveilles"*?

Henry of Huntington defines the purpose of history in terms with which William of Malmesbury, and other conservative historians, could find much with which to agree:

> Thus also in the executed deeds of all peoples and nations, things which are expressly the judgments of God, *benignity*, munificence, probity, caution, things both similar and contrary to these, not only stir up spiritual men toward the good and repel [them] from evil, but even rouse secular men toward good things and fortify [them] in evil circumstances. History therefore represents past things as if present to the sight; it marks out future things from past things by imagining [Howlett 34].

I would offer for debate that Geoffrey of Monmouth, Wace, and Chrétien de Troyes each devise texts that fulfill such a mandate through using magic and the marvelous to create situations in which people must explore their relationship to god(s), their state of sin, and their social standing in the community.[22]

Wace would feel sympathy with the point of view that the role of fiction, like that of history, is instructional. But no one addresses such complications as eloquently as Chrétien himself in his introduction of *bele conjointure* in *Erec and Enide*. Romance becomes under his influence not *l'estoire* of storytellers, but a marriage of a variety of sources that create new meaning from their unification.[23] In the introduction to *Erec and Enide*, Chrétien coins the term *conjointure* to classify his own works:

> et tret d'un conte d'aventure
> une most bele *conjointure*
> par qu'an puet prover et savoir
> que cil ne fet mie savoir
> qui s'escïence n'abandone
> tant con Dex la grasce l'an done:
> d'Erec, le fil Lac, est li contes,
> que devant rois et devant contes
> depecier et corronpre suelent
> cil qui de conter vivre vuelent.
> Des or comancerai l'estoire
> qui toz jorz mer iert an mimoire
> tant con durra chrestïantez [l.13–25].

> (and from a tale of adventure he [Chrétien] fashions a very elegant composition, giving manifest proof that there is no wisdom in not freely making one's knowledge available so far as God's grace allows. This tale which the professional storytellers habitually fragment and corrupt in the presence of kings and counts, is about

Erec, son of Lac. Now I shall begin this story, which shall henceforth always be remembered as long as Christendom endures) [Nykrog 603].

If we return to the introduction to *Cligès*, the impact of Geoffrey's privileging of ancient books and Wace's concern that his *Brut* convey truth is readily apparent, as is the privileging of the "historical" or, in Henry of Huntingdon's words, "moral" agenda for a text. Chrétien clearly is interested in acquiring the mantle of classical authority by appropriating it; he places himself and his newly polished story as the inheritor of classical knowledge and skills. It is clear that this poet wants to insert himself into a tradition which stands for learning, culture, and serious intellectual endeavor, everything which he would hope to achieve with his romances. It is also interesting for us in terms of the *Gawain* poet that Chrétien mentions the figure of Morgain, who is said to be the mistress of Guigomar, the lord of Avalon (*Erec et Enide* 2353–66). What is, of course, seminal to this argument is that he creates texts which would become famous for their use of magic and the marvelous in conjunction with their Christian and secular agendas. That Chrétien incorporates a character that first appeared in the *Vita Merlini* (ca. 1150, ll. 908–40) and the texts of Gervaise of Tilbury and Giraldus Cambrensis only adds weight to this reading (Twomey 98–103).

The demonstration of this connection is nowhere more evident than in his introduction to the *Perceval* text. He tells his audience that he writes for the greatest man in the empire of Rome, Philip Count of Flanders, whose worthiness surpasses even that of Alexander. Could it be that he is actually designating an heir to the gifts which the empire has to offer? That of course is a difficult argument to prove, but it is worth noting that Philip was officially a "Prince" of the Holy Roman Empire and clearly an important player in the politics of the day. In Chrétien's introduction we once again find this curious mixture of Christian, philosophical, magical, and pagan ideas being given value, not unlike the classical approach which has been under discussion throughout this essay; Chrétien quotes from the gospels but tells the story of the search for the Graal, whose magical powers will seemingly restore the Fisher King and his land to prosperity. It is of note that Perceval, like Gawain, begins the romance as an innocent, as symbolized by the acquisition of new armor, and he learns how to function in the world through a series of harsh experiences. The romances also explore theory of kingship, ideas of justice, and the construction of social identity and community, all of which would not be out of place in twelfth-century histories or the works of the Classical world.

So just as I would argue that Chrétien had been influenced by approaches or traditions which embody magic other than just Celtic, it is possible to argue that so too would the *Gawain* poet have been influenced, as he seemingly goes out his way to demonstrate the historical and Christian roots of his ideas by creating the pentangle shield. Like Chrétien asserting his right to be the heir of classical learning, the *Gawain* poet creates a symbol for Gawain which equally identifies him as the inheritor of a wealth of classical, Christian, pagan, and historical ideas.

Gawain—Embodiment of Classical Traditions?

Gawain is the representative of a court in its springtime, trying out for the first time this newly painted, and thus perhaps newly formalized, composition of noble, magical, and Christian codes. Gawain's shield, referred to everywhere (the poet tells us) as 'Þe endeles knot" (630), is designed with the pentangle and the Virgin's face:

> Hit is a syngne Þat Salamon set sumquyle
> In bytoknyng of trawÞe, by tytle Þat hit habbez,
> For hit is a figure Þat haldez fyue poyntez
> And vche lyne vmbelappez and loukez oÞer.
> And ayquere hit is endelez; [625–29]

(It is a symbol that Solomon devised once upon a time as a token of fidelity, appropriately, for it is a figure which contains five points, and each line overlaps and interlocks with another, and it is unbroken anywhere;)

> ForÞy Þe pentangel nwe
> He ber in schelde and cote,
> As tulk of tale most trwe
> And gentylest kny3t of lote [636–39].

(For this reason he bore the pentangle newly painted upon shield and surcoat, as being a man most true to his word and in bearing the noblest of knights.)

In his note on the pentangle, Norman Davis finds that the word "pentangle" appeared only in English and for the first time in this text:

> The figure is said to have been used by the Pythagoreans as a symbol of health, and also by the neo–Platonists and Gnostics to signify perfection; but it was also known to the Jews as well, thus coming to be called "Solomon's seal" ... [and] was eventually adopted as the symbol of Judaism (the *Magen David*, "Shield of

David'). The Pentangle was long used as a magic sign, believed to give power over evil spirits. Its use in this way was condemned by Christian writers ... but it had much earlier come to be adapted to Christian symbolism, the five points sometimes being connected with the five letters of the name of Jesus, or the five wounds.... Nothing like the symbolism attributed to it here is known anywhere else, and there is no evidence whatever for its being called "the endless knot" in spite of the poet's "oueral" (l.630) [SGGK 93].

The *Gawain* poet deliberately chose to name his configuration after a king who for all his wisdom still drifted into idolatry, a man famous for beginning in greatness, but perhaps owing to the sins of his parents (similar in some basic ways to Uther and Igraine), ends in a whirlwind of despair and corruption. The significance of these references to Solomon are alone provocative enough to merit their prominence in the text, but it should be noted that they serve as another link to the historical past which is far removed from Celtic associations. In creating a framework composed of Troy, Solomon, and the ideas of Camelot made famous by Geoffrey of Monmouth in his "pseudo" historical *Historia*, the author was, arguably, striving to place his romance in a historical/classical context. This romance is not only a product of the desire to entertain, but, much like the works of Walter Map and John of Salisbury, it also strives to educate and provoke reflection. This text is deliberately located in a framework of historical and morally significant works that sought to thrill but also educate their audiences. The *Gawain* poet's main character struggles through a moral and philosophical crisis brought on by interaction with magic. Magic reveals Gawain's weakness, and the weakness of the codes that represent the best of that society's moral guidelines, chivalry and Christianity. The *Gawain* poet may indeed be instructing his audience to mind the lessons of history, the history of Troy, or Camelot, or indeed just the fate of one of England's most famous knights.

Of course, with respect to the examples argued here as significant to a classical and historical tradition, a dozen others can be argued to have significance in the Celtic and folkloric framework, so clearly that it is important to say that these avenues of investigation provoke more questions than they answer, particularly as it is difficult to gauge how familiar the *Gawain* poet was with classical texts. As we explore an alternative avenue of authority for the poet's complex use of magic, however, it is useful and fruitful to look to the history of the romance genre itself and explore its connection to classical ideas of magic for signs of influence. Geoffrey of Monmouth, Wace, and Chrétien de Troyes are each closely linked to the twelfth-century surge of interest in historical, classical, and literary texts that so heavily influenced the romance genre that they can still be felt in the *Gawain* poet's fourteenth-century poem. Before Geoffrey there is a rich tradition of classical and theological writers who helped to create and enervate the significance of magic in their culture. The idea of a poet-philosopher-magician took root in the world of Apuleius, Pliny, and Philostratus. The significance of magic to humanity and our relationship to the gods is so old that perhaps it is inappropriate to discuss it in terms of dates and origins. Clearly magic played a significant role in the evolution of theology, politics, culture, and individual morality from the classical period through to the early modern world, which must be accounted for when one analyzes texts which incorporate magic into their method of creating meaning for audiences.

Luck argues in *Arcana Mundi* that "it is probably fair to say that Seneca created horror not for horror's sake but because, as a Stoic philosopher, he believed that shock produced by horror cleansed the soul of all of the emotions that interfere with peace of mind. As a Stoic ... some of the tenets of magic would have made sense to him, even though he may not have accepted their exaggerated claims" (31). In *Sir Gawain and the Green Knight*, the poet offers Gawain no such peace of mind from his experience of magic, and yet it is not beyond imagining that the author exposed Gawain and his audience to a powerful medium of exploration so that they could gain knowledge from Gawain's mistakes. In calling upon classical traditions the poet makes possible a discussion of our relationship to God, in that Gawain takes the magic girdle to prevent an unnatural death and control his own fate. The poet also makes possible an investigation of Gawain's, Mary's, and Morgan's power over fellow human beings: whose role is it to curb human pride? The audience is also left with a sadder, angrier, but perhaps wiser, more humane Gawain—a Perceval who has completed his journey and yet must still struggle with the consequence of sin and unknowable fate.

Notes

1. The intent of the *Gawain* poet for his romance has been determined by Benson to be in the final analysis to produce not a romance but rather an anti-romance—made so by an audience's laughter-filled response: "When Gawain returns shamefaced to Camelot from an opponent who only laughs at him, we recognize that the poem has moved from pure romance to a gently satiric anti-romance, since even the reader cannot suppress a smile at the hero's expense, and comedy is not the stuff of which romance heroes are made" (209).
2. The detailed knowledge of hunting and chivalry contained in the poem has

convinced the majority of critics that the *Gawain* poet is indeed male, but again this is built on reasonable deduction rather than hard facts.

   3. The *SOED* defines magic as: "Magic sb. I.a. The pretended art of influencing the course of events, and of producing marvellous physical phenomena, by processes supposed to owe their efficacy to their power of compelling the intervention of spiritual beings, or of bringing into operation some occult controlling principle in nature; sorcery, witchcraft.... *The magic which made use of evil or doubtful spirits was of course always regarded as sinful; but natural magic, i.e., that which did not involve spirits, was in the Middle Ages usually recognized as a legitimate department of study and practice, so long as it was not used for maleficent ends."* The *Middle English Dictionary* (MED) defines magic as: "*Magik* [O.F. *magique*] (a) The knowledge of hidden natural forces (e.g. magnetism, stellar influence), and the art of using these in calculating future events, curing disease, etc., ~natural; (b) sorcery, enchantment."

   4. The view that magic is unsophisticated and rather simplistic fatally undermines the critic's ability to see the romances in terms of their historical development toward a highly sophisticated genre. Over the period from Augustine to Aquinas, the research of Flint, Thorndike, and Thomas demonstrates that a variety of intellectuals who are not easily undermined as simply superstitious or credulous concerned themselves with magic and divination.

   5. For many scholars it is simply romance's status as popular material which undermines its credibility as serious or meaningful literature. Lee Ramsey writes that "[romance] was an ephemeral literature. When its day passed, it lost its effectiveness and came to seem dull or ridiculous.... The typical medieval romance shares characteristics common to other, later forms of popular literature. The most important of these characteristics is the emphasis on plot and action to the exclusion of everything else— rhetoric, idea, and character development included. The rhetoric of the romances is often poor, the philosophic content meager, and the characters simple and obvious. The emotional effects sought after are likewise obvious" (7, 5).

   6. For a more exhaustive exploration of current *SGGK* criticism see Michael Twomey, "Morgain la Fée in *Sir Gawain and the Green Knight*: From Troy to Camelot and Blanch and Wasserman, "The Current State of *Sir Gawain and the Green Knight* Criticism," *Chaucer Review* 27:4 (1993): 401–12.

   7. I have deliberately left this definition in its most general format. To see a more complex discussion of the difficulties in defining magic in both the medieval and classical periods, see the introduction to Flint's *The Rise of Magic*.

   8. It is important to note that Apuleius of Madaura was himself accused of witchcraft; thus his *Apologia* should be evaluated with his agenda in mind.

   9. Augustine 30. 66–68; Aquinas 40.51–55; Bacon 1.381–90.

   10. Unless otherwise noted I have employed Tavenner's translation of Pliny. See *Natural History*, especially Book 30, for a more complete appreciation of Pliny's views on magic.

   11. http://www.perseus.tufts.edu

   12. *Etymologies* XVI, Migne vol. 1, xxxii. *Alcuini Epistolae* 103 vol. VI, 431–32. *Patrol. Latina* vol. C, col. 278, letter 85.

   13. Twomey (98–108) and Patton (165n1) argue that the *Prose Lancelot* is the source for the use of "Morgain la deesse" (*SGGK* 2452) as it appears in the episode *Val sans Retour*.

   14. "The story of Troy betrayal alluded to in the opening lines of *SGGK* most likely come from the Old French *Roman de Troie* by Benoit de Sainte-Maure, written about 1160, or from Guido delle Colonne's *Historia Destructionis Troiae*, dated 1287." See Alfred David, "Gawain and Aeneas," *English Studies* 49 (1968): 402–9.

15. For a dissenting point of view see Myra Rosenhaus, *Britain Between Myth and Reality*, Dissertation, Indiana University, 1982.

16. See Gerbert the magician, "The witch of Berkeley and the two clerks of Nantes," in *Gesta* I, 194–203, 2.167ff, 294–95.

17. William believed that the role of recording miracles lay in encouragement of the simple. "For reasoned arguments encourage the faith of the perfect, but the hope and love of the simple is kindled by the telling of miracles, just as the dull fire is fuelled by pouring on oil": William's "Miracles of the Virgin" (2.2) in A.G. Rigg's *A History of Anglo-Latin Literature, 1066–1422* (Cambridge: Cambridge UP, 1992), 35.

18. For discussion of Livy as a model for Geoffrey, see Per Nykrog, "The Rise of Literary Fiction," in *Renaissance and Renewal in the Twelfth Century*, ed. R. Benson (Oxford: Clarendon P, 1982), 596. Hanning argues: "Against this near intoxication with the human greatness of national leaders [as seen in Geoffrey's text] must be set the cyclical view of history.... For, if the heroic deeds of men emphasize human control of history, the view of history as an endless series of cycles emphasizes the power of history over men. Operating through Fortune, the inexplicable and fickle force which raises man on her wheel and then throws him off, history tyrannizes over man and mocks his efforts to control his fate and that of his nation" (History 139).

19. "The French," wrote William, "are unrivalled among western nations in military skill and polished manners." WM c. 106 and pages 5–6 cf. Orderic ii, 256, as cited in Gillingham, *The English in the Twelfth Century*, 57. It is interesting to note, however, that as Gillingham argues, William of Malmesbury and Henry of Huntingdon viewed themselves as English as early as the 1120s, with only a reminiscent presence of subjugation. Geoffrey Gaimar writes the history of England, not France, *in French* in the late 1130s for the wife of a Lincolnshire landowner, *Estorie des Engleis*, thereby suggesting that the francophone secular elite could see an Anglo-Saxon past as something worth acknowledging, perhaps owing to Stephan and Matilda's civil war? See Gillingham 99.

20. Echard is citing Christopher Brooke, *The Twelfth Century Renaissance* (London: Thames and Hudson, 1969), 172. *Nugae* is defined as *frivolous* in Echard's text.

21. This idea would find support in the way in which Alanus de Insulis in *De planctu naturae* used the related terms "conjunctura" and "integumentum, involucrum, pallium and cortex." A medieval Christian poem could be like a pagan poem in that the external narrative could be a lie, invented to created a false "pictura" which would require the interpretation of "signs" on the part of the reader. To read the Bible a Christian would have to see through the "cortex" or the level of surface meaning to achieve insight into the "nucleus" of truth. For further discussion see D. W. Robertson, *Essays in Medieval Culture* (Princeton: Princeton UP, 1980), esp. 52–53.

22. Gervase of Canterbury writes that *Historia* is a mode of dramatic presentation: the author manipulates the rhetorical effects in order to sway the affective responses of the listeners or readers ("audientes vel legentes dulci sermone et eleganti demulc[et]" and as a consequence he disposes his public to heed the exemplary truths he expounds ("actus mores vitamque ipsius quam describit veraciter edoc[et]") (Stubbs, *Ingressus ad prologum*).

23. Lewis Thorpe, suggests that *historia* is a word well worth exploring for a moment— etymologically, *historia, histoire, historie,* and *estoire* are very close to our modern "story"— and semantically so far away from the modern connotations of the word *history*.

Works Cited

Apuleius of Madaura. "*Apologia.*" *The Apologia and the Florida of Apuleius of Madaura.* Ed. and trans. H. E. Butler. Oxford: Oxford UP, 1909.

Aquinas, Thomas. "Superstition and Irreverence." *Summa Theologiae*. Vol. 40. Ed. and trans. Thomas F. O'Meara, O.P. and Michael Duffy, O.P. New York: McGraw-Hill, 1968. 51–55.

Augustine. *Confessionum*, IV, 3. *Corpus Scriptorum Ecclesiasticum Latinarum*. Vol. 30 Vienna: Tempsky, 1866–. 66–68.

Bacon, Roger. *Opus Majus*. Ed. and trans. J. Bridges. Frankfurt: Minerva, 1964.

Barron, W. R. J. *Sir Gawain and the Green Knight*. Manchester: Manchester UP; New York: Barnes and Noble, 1974.

Benson, Larry D. *Art and Tradition in* Sir Gawain and the Green Knight. New Brunswick: Rutgers UP, 1965.

Benton, John F. "Collaborative Approaches to Fantasy and Reality." In *Court and Poet: Selected Proceedings of the Third Congress and of the International Courtly Literature Society*. Ed. G. Burgess. Liverpool: Francis Cairns, 1980.

Blanch, Robert, and Julian N. Wasserman. "Medieval Contracts and Covenants: The Legal Coloring of Sir Gawain and the Green Knight.: Neophilologus 68 (1984): 568–610.

Brewer, Elisabeth. Sir Gawain and the Green Knight: *Sources and Analogues*. London: Boydell and Brewer, 1973, 1992.

Chrétien de Troyes. *The Complete Romances of Chrétien de Troyes*. Ed. and trans. David Staines. Bloomington: Indiana UP, 1993.

———. "Erec and Enide." In *Les Romans de Chrétien de Troyes*. Vol. 1. Ed. Mario Roques. Paris: Librairie Ancienne Honoré Champion, 1955.

———. *Cligés*. Ed. and trans. Marie-Claire Gérard-Zai. Paris: Librarie Général Française, 1994.

David, Alfred. "Gawain and Aeneas." *English Studies* 49 (1968): 402–9.

Dodds, E. R. "The Greeks and the Irrational." In *A History of Greek Philosophy*. Ed. W. K. C. Guthrie. 6 vols. Cambridge: Cambridge UP, 1962–81.

Duffy, Eamon. *The Stripping of the Altars*. New Haven: Yale UP, 1992.

Echard, Siân. *Arthurian Narrative in the Latin Tradition*. Cambridge: Cambridge UP, 1998.

Fisher, Sheila. "Taken Men and Token Women in *Sir Gawain and the Green Knight*." In *Seeking the Women in Late Medieval and Renaissance Writing: Essays in Feminist and Contextual Criticism*. Ed. Sheila Fisher and Janet Halley. Knoxville: U of Tennessee P, 1989: 71–105.

Flint, Valerie. *The Rise of Magic in Early Medieval Europe*. Princeton: Princeton UP, 1991.

Foley, Michael. "The *Gawain* Poet: An Annotated Bibliography, 1978–1985." *The Chaucer Review* 23:3 (1989): 251–82.

Geoffrey of Monmouth. *The History of the Kings of Britain*. Ed. and trans. Lewis Thorpe. New York and London: Penguin Classics, 1966.

Gervase of Canterbury. *The Chronicle of the Reigns of Stephen, Henry II and Richard I. The Historical Works of Gervase of Canterbury*. Ed. William Stubbs. Vol. 1. London: Rolls Series, 1965.

Gervase of Tillbury. *Otia imperialia. Radulphi de Coggeshall Chronicon Anglicanum*, etc. Ed. Joseph Stevenson. Rolls Series, 66. London: Trubner, 1875. 438.

Gillingham, John. *The English in the Twelfth Century: Imperialism, National Identity and Political Values*. London: Boydell and Brewer, 2000.

Giraldus Cambrensis. *Speculum ecclesiae* (2:9). *Giraldus Cambrensis Opera*. Ed. Joseph Brewer. 8 vols. London: Longman, 1861–91.

Hanning, Robert. *The Vision of History in Early Britian from Gildas to Geoffrey of Monmouth*. New York: Columbia UP, 1966.

———. *The Individual in the Twelfth Century*. New Haven and London: Yale UP, 1977.

Harding, Carol. *Merlin and Legendary Romance.* New York: Garland Publishing, 1988.
Heng, Geraldine. "Feminine Knots and the Other in *Sir Gawain and the Green Knight.*" PMLA 106 (1991): 500–54.
Henry of Huntingdon. *Historia Anglorum—Prologue. The English Origins of Old French Literature.* Ed. and trans. D. R. Howlett. Dublin: Four Courts Press, 1996.
Herodotus. *Histories I.* In *Herodotus I.* Ed. and trans. A. G. Godley. Cambridge, MA: Loeb Classical Library, 1926.
Kamps, Ivo. "Magic, Women, and Incest: the Real Challenges in *Sir Gawain and the Green Knight.*" *Exemplaria* 1:2 (1989): 313–33.
Jackson, Rosemary. *Fantasy: The Literature of Subversion.* London: Methuen, 1981.
Jameson, Frederick. "Magical Narratives: Romance as Genre." *New Literary History* 7 (1975): 146–65.
Kelly, Douglas. *The Art of Medieval French Romance.* Madison: U of Wisconsin P, 1992.
Loomis, R. S. *Celtic Myth and Arthurian Romance.* Chicago: Academy Chicago Publishers, 1977.
Luck, Georg. *Arcana Mundi.* Baltimore and London: John Hopkins UP, 1985.
_____. *Ancient Pathways & Hidden Pursuits: Religion Morals, and Magic in the Ancient World.* Ann Arbor: U of Michigan P, 2000.
Luengo, Anthony. "Magic and Illusion in the *Franklin's Tale.*" *Journal of English and Germanic Philology* 77 (1978): 1–16.
Matthews, John. *Gawain: Knight of the Goddess—Restoring an Archetype.* London: Aquarian Thorsons, 1990.
Moore, Dennis. "Making Sense of an Ending: Morgan Le Fay in *Sir Gawain and the Green Knight.*" *Mediaevalia* 10 (1984): 213–33.
Nykrog, Per. "The Rise of Literary Fiction." In *Renaissance and Renewal in the Twelfth Century.* Ed. R. Benson. Oxford: Clarendon, 1982.
Paton, Lucy Allen. *Studies in the Fairy Mythology of Arthurian Romance.* Radcliffe College Monographs, No. 13. Boston: Ginn, 1903.
Pliny. *Natural History.* Ed. and trans. H. Rackham, et al. 10 vols. Loeb Classical Library, 1938–1954. Ed. and trans. W. H. S. Jones. Boston: Harvard UP, 1980.
Pollack, F., and F. W. Maitland. "Statute of Treason." In *The History of English Law Before the Time of Edward I.* 2nd ed., Cambridge: Cambridge UP,1968.
Powell, T. K. E. *The Celts.* London: Thames and Hudson, 1989.
Ramsey, Lee. *Chivalric Romance: Popular Literature in Medieval England.* Bloomington: Indiana UP, 1983.
Rigg, A. G. *A History of Anglo-Latin Literature, 1066–1422.* London: Cambridge UP, 1992.
Russell, Jeffrey Burton. *Witchcraft in the Middle Ages.* Ithaca: Cornell UP, 1972.
Speirs, John. "Sir Gawain and the Green Knight." *Scrutiny* 26 (1949): 270–300.
Staines, David, ed. and trans. *The Complete Romances of Chrétien de Troyes.* Bloomington: Indiana UP, 1993.
Tavenner, Eugene. *Studies in Magic from Latin Literature.* New York: Columbia UP, 1916.
Thomas, Keith. *Religion and the Decline of Magic.* New York: Scribner, 1971.
Thorndike, Lynn. *The Place of Magic in the Intellectual History of Europe.* New York: AMS Press, 1967.
_____. *History of Magic and Experimental Science.* New York: Columbia UP, 1964.
Twomey, Michael W. "Morgain la Fee in *Sir Gawain and the Green Knight*: From Troy to Camelot." *Text and Intertext in Medieval Arthurian Literature.* Ed. Norris J. Lacy. Garland, New York: 1996. 91–115.
Vita Merlini. Ed. John Jay Perry. Urbana: U of Illinois P, 1925.
Wace. *Roman de Brut: A History of the British; Text and Translation.* Ed. Judith Weiss. Exeter: U of Exeter P, 1999.

Wendell, Barrett. *The Traditions of European Literature from Homer to Dante*. London: John Murray, 1921.
Wetherbee, Winthrop, ed. and trans. *Johannes de Hauvilla: Architrenius*. Cambridge: Cambridge UP, 1994.
William of Malmesbury. *Gesta regum Anglorum* in *William of Malmesbury*. Ed. and trans. Rodney Thompson. London: Boydell Press, 1987.
William of Newburgh, the History of English Affairs. Ed. and trans. P.G. Walsh and M.J. Kennedy. London: Aris and Philips, 1988.
Wilson, Anne. *The Magical Quest: The Use of Magic in Arthurian Romance*. Manchester: Manchester UP, 1988.

About the Contributors

Randi Eldevik is associate professor of English at Oklahoma State University in Oklahoma City. She has published on a variety of topics including Old Norse literature and Spenser. Her work includes *The Matter of the North*, a translation of Torfi Tulinius's *La matiere du Nord*.

Rosanne Gasse is associate professor of English at Brandon University in Brandon, Manitoba, Canada. She has published articles on Langland, Chaucer, Middle English romances, and most recently on medicine in *Piers Plowman*.

Peter H. Goodrich is professor of English at Northern Michigan University in Marquette. He has published on medieval and modern fantasy, particularly Arthurian legend and the figure of Merlin. His works include *The Romance of Merlin* (Garland, 1990) and, with Raymond H. Thompson, *Merlin: A Casebook* (Routledge, 2003).

Stefan Thomas Hall is assistant professor of English at the University of Wisconsin, Green Bay. He publishes on a variety of topics, particularly in Scandinavian and Scottish studies, and is an accomplished player of the guitar and the lute. He is currently working on a book on trolls and folk beliefs.

Nicholas Haydock is professor of English at the University of Puerto Rico, Mayaguez, where he teaches courses on medieval and early modern literature, literary theory, film, and medievalism. His recent publications include work on Robert Henryson, William Dunbar, and movies about the Middle Ages. He is currently finishing a book manuscript entitled "The Place of Robert Henryson's *The Testament of Cresseid*."

William F. Hodapp is associate professor of English, chair of English, and Coordinator of Medieval and Renaissance Studies at the College of

St. Scholastica in Duluth, Minnesota. With interests in high to late medieval culture, he has published on Chaucer, John Lydgate, John Peckham, Richard Rolle, and medieval drama, as well as on the *Gawain* poet.

E. L. Risden is associate professor of English at St. Norbert College in De Pere, Wisconsin. He has published literary criticism, fiction, poetry, translations, and a textbook. He has also recently served as co-editor of *Prophet Margins: The Medieval Vatic Impulse and Social Stability* (Peter Lang, 2004) and the 2004 volumes of *Studies in Medieval and Renaissance Teaching*.

Russell Rutter is professor of English at Illinois State University, where for thirty years he has taught and published on Renaissance and medieval literature, pedagogy and technical writing.

Mickey Sweeney is associate professor of English at Dominican University in River Forest, Illinois. Her publications include *Magic in Medieval Romance* (Four Courts, 2000) and many articles on *Sir Gawain and the Green Knight* and on various aspects of medieval Romance.

Zacharias P. Thundy is professor emeritus of Northern Michigan University and Visiting Fellow at the University of Notre Dame. He is the author or editor of a dozen books (including *Millennium: Apocalypse and Antichrist and Old English Monsters c. 1000 A.D.*, Cross Cultural Publications, 1998) and numerous articles on topics ranging from medieval literature to anthropology, linguistics, and comparative literature. His forthcoming book is *The Trial and Death of Jesus: Gospel Narratives and Their Sanskrit Sources*.

Index

Achilles 12, 13, 84, 104, 121–33
Ackroyd, Peter 82, 89, 109
Ælfric 4
Aeneas 8–13, 19–21, 30–47, 56–58, 68, 72, 82–111, 112–119, 128, 133, 140, 142, 143, 176, 206, 208
Aeneid 9, 11, 19–22, 27, 30–47, 57, 58, 61,63, 68, 79–81, 83–111, 133–46, 176, 199
Alcibiades 189
Alexander III, Pope 172
Alfonso, Pedro 156
Al-Jurjani 152
al-Khadir 13, 146, 147, 151
alliterative poetry 3–6, 14–15
alliterative revival 4, 14
al-Makkari 156
al-Masudi 156
al-Nadim, Ibn 156, 179
al-Rashid, Harun 154, 164
Ammianus Marcellinus 70
Anchises 19, 34, 35, 44
Ancrene Wisse 52, 62, 63
Anekantavada 144
Annals of Tacitus 190
Antenor 11, 30, 33, 34, 44, 82, 83, 114
Apuleius 13, 188, 189, 194, 196, 199, 205, 206, 207
Arabian Nights 145, 148
Arcana Mundi 184, 188, 189, 205, 209
Arthur, King 6, 7, 9, 10, 11, 14, 21–26, 32, 34, 36–38, 40, 42, 43, 45, 55, 56, 59, 60, 68, 72, 75, 76, 87, 88, 92, 109, 112, 113, 117, 150, 151, 164, 165, 175, 183, 185, 191, 197–99
Arthur, Ross G. 67, 76, 79, 80, 99, 109
Attar, Farid ud-Din 146, 147, 179
Attic Nights 94
Augustine, St. 37, 45, 47, 56, 62, 93, 94, 109, 175, 186, 189, 198, 206, 208
Aulus Gellius 94

Bacon, Roger 189, 191, 206, 208
Barr, Helen 14

Baswell, Christopher 30, 46, 47, 81, 86, 109, 110
Battle of Maldon 37
Bede 20, 21, 190, 198
Belinus 21
Bennett, Michael 72, 80
Benoit de Sainte-Maure 20, 116, 123, 143, 195, 206
Benson, Larry 26, 44, 47, 62, 63, 80, 133, 171, 179, 182, 183, 205, 208
Benton, John F. 196, 208
Beowulf 7, 62
Bertilak, Lady 12, 32, 34, 65, 74, 75, 77, 78, 83, 86, 93, 115, 116, 129, 141, 151
Bertilak, Sir or Lord 34, 37, 39, 41, 43, 67, 68, 73, 74, 77, 86, 97, 102, 116, 119, 129, 130, 133, 136, 140, 150, 151, 166–69, 172, 173, 175, 177
Blanch, Robert J. 44, 47, 109, 206, 208
Bloomfield, Morton 66, 80, 179
Boccaccio, Giovanni 34, 44, 46, 47, 98, 156
Boethius 10, 53, 61, 106, 109, 199
Bolingbroke, Henry 6
Book of Sindibad 156
Book of the Seven Sages of Rome 156
Borroff, Marie 77, 81, 114, 119
Boudica 72, 75, 80
Bradwardine, Thomas 158
Brennius 21
Brewer, Derek 26, 27, 28, 44, 47, 81, 110, 133, 134
Brewer, Elisabeth 18, 26, 192, 193, 208
Briseis 123, 124, 132, 133
Browne, Thomas 46, 47, 118
Browning, Robert 43
Brut (of Layaman) 4
Brutus 8, 10, 11, 21, 22, 25, 26, 28, 31, 55–57, 63, 64, 83, 84, 103, 110, 112, 113, 117, 118, 142, 180
Burrow, J.A. 138, 176, 179

Cadwallader 21–22
Caesar, Julius 10, 28, 69, 80
Calvert, Frank 18, 27
Canterbury Tales 147, 157, 164, 177–79; "The Franklin's Tale" 156, 180, 188, 209; "The Friar's Tale" 147; "The Man of Law's Tale" 156; "The Merchant's Tale" 147–48; "The Miller's Tale" 106; "The Monk's Tale" 106; "The Reeve's Tale" 178; "The Squire's Tale" 97, 132, 147, 177, 179, 180
Capellanus, Andreas 200
Cawley, A.C. 113
Caxton, William 32, 44, 47
Chambers, E.K. 137, 179
Chapman, Otis 83, 84, 108, 109
Charmides 189
Chaucer, Geoffrey 3, 4, 5, 8, 9, 11, 12, 15, 46–48, 83, 97, 102, 106, 121–25, 129–34, 147, 148, 156, 164, 177, 178, 180, 188, 189, 191
Cheshire 5, 6, 72
Le Chevalier à l'Epée 136
Le Chevalier de la Charrette 192
Chrétien de Troyes 188, 191–95, 198–204, 208, 209
The City of God 53, 62, 69, 93
Civil War 188
Clark, Susan L. 86, 109
Cleanness 3, 5, 6, 14, 47, 110
Clement of Alexandria 70, 143
Cligés 185, 194, 208
Confessio Amantis 12, 134
Convivio 158
Coomaraswamy, Ananda K. 70, 81, 145, 146, 179
Crick, Julia 22, 24, 27, 28
Criseyde 121, 122, 124, 130–34
Crompton, Anne Eliot 85, 109
Dante Alighieri 19, 51, 60, 64, 116, 117, 152, 156, 158, 176, 191

Dares (the Phrygian) 8, 9, 20, 24, 27, 30–33, 44, 48, 119, 122, 133, 134, 143, 195
David, Alfred 83, 108, 109, 113, 119, 206, 208
Davis, Norman 15, 26, 28, 44, 48, 108, 110, 120, 134, 136, 137, 140, 176, 178, 203
De bello trojano 20
De consolatione Philosophiae 53, 109
De excidio Troiae historia 20, 27, 124, 143
Delumeau, Jean 186
Dictys 8, 9, 20, 27, 30–33, 48, 119, 122, 133, 143, 195
Dido 19, 39, 40, 41, 45, 46, 84, 91, 92, 95–97, 114–16
Dio Cassius 10, 69
Diodoris Siculus 69, 80
Directorium Humanae Vitae 156
Disciplina Clericalis 156
La Divina Commedia (or *Divine Comedy*) 27, 60, 62, 64, 180
Douglas, Gavin 37, 45, 47
Dove, Mary 88, 109
Duby, Georges 49, 51, 52, 55, 62, 64
Dudo of Saint-Quentin 22, 24, 28

Earl of Stafford 6
Ecclesiastical History of the English People 20, 21
Echard, Siân 200, 207, 208
Eco, Umberto 18
Edward III 6, 44
Eleanor of Aquitaine 20, 21
Eliot, T.S. 90
Elliott, Ralph 72, 80, 81
Eneas 20
Eneydos 37
Ephemeridos belli Troiani libri (or *Ephemeris Belli Troiani*) 20, 27, 143
Erec and Enide 201, 202, 208
Euripides 122, 123, 133
Exchange of Winnings 37, 39–41, 77, 136, 166
Excidium Troie 20, 27
Expositio Vergilianae Continentia 98
Exposition of the Content of Vergil According to Moral Philosophy 31, 48

The Fall of Princes 106
Fall of Troy 30
Fibonacci, Filius Bonacci, or Leonardo of Pisa (and Fibonacci numbers) 157, 160–62, 178, 181
Fihrist 156, 179
Fisher, Sheila 75, 81,183, 208
Fled Bricrend 136
Flint, Valerie 186, 190, 206, 208
Frazer, Sir James 65, 73, 80, 81
Froissart, Jean 156
Frye, Northrop 51, 52, 62
Fulgentius 9, 31, 34, 35, 39–41, 45, 46, 48, 84, 98, 99

Gawain and the Lady Green 85, 109
Geoffrey of Monmouth 8, 9, 15, 17–28, 32, 55, 63, 64, 113, 187, 188, 192, 194–208
Geometria speculativa 158
Gerald of Wales (or Giraldus Cambrensis) 199, 202, 208
Gervaise of Tilbury 202
Gest Hystoriale of the Destruction of Troy 32, 48, 113, 119, 143
Gesta Normannorum 22, 24
Gesta Normannorum ducem 22, 24, 28
Gesta regum Anglorum 198, 210
Gesta Romanorum 156
Gildas 63, 64, 198, 208
girdle (or sash) 10, 11, 12, 25, 32, 34, 65–80, 81, 82, 85, 86, 88, 93, 94, 98, 101–4, 106,

112, 116–19, 130, 133, 136, 137, 140–43, 159, 166–170, 172–78, 196, 205
Gittes, Katherine 164, 178, 179
Golagros and Gawane 5
Gollancz, Israel 113, 120, 176, 179
Gordon, E.V. 15, 26, 28, 108, 110, 113, 114, 1120, 134, 136, 137, 140, 155, 176, 181
Gottfried von Strassburg 200
Gottweiger Trojanerkrieg 20
Gower, John 3, 4, 12, 119, 121, 123–34, 143
Green, Richard Hamilton 63, 64, 160, 177, 179
Green Chapel 23, 32, 35, 38, 39,41, 43, 45, 46, 72, 74, 78, 80, 81, 92–94, 102, 104, 107, 108, 115, 136–38, 165, 166, 169, 179
Guido delle Colonne (or Guido de Columnis) 9, 33, 34, 44, 48, 199, 120, 123, 143, 206

Haines, Victor Yelverton 56, 59, 60, 63, 64
Hanning, Robert 61, 62, 64, 198, 199, 207, 208
Harding, Carol 198, 209
Harley MS 2253 4, 14
Harwood, Britton J. 166, 167, 179
Haskins, C.H. 199
Hazar Afsan 156
Hector 12, 46, 84, 104, 105, 121–23, 132, 133
Hecuba 30, 33, 83, 123, 133
Hecuba 123
Heng, Geraldine 183, 209
Henry I 20
Henry II 200, 208
Henry of Huntingdon 27, 28, 187, 191, 202, 207, 209
Henryson, Robert 106, 211
Herodotus 184, 209
Heroides 20, 27, 102, 123, 134
Hippolytus 70, 134
Historia Brittonum 21, 24, 63
Historia de excidio Troie 24
Historia regum Britanniae 18, 20, 27, 28, 55, 63
History of the Destruction of Troy (or *Historia Destructionis Troiae*) 32, 33, 143, 206
Holcot, Robert 100, 110
Homer 9,11, 12, 18, 19, 27, 30, 33, 34, 84, 104, 105, 116, 122, 133–35, 131, 185, 210
Homo Ludens 37, 48
Hornsby, Roger 92, 104, 110
The House of Fame 124
Huizinga, Johan 37, 45, 48
Hulbert, James R. 4, 14
Humphries, Rolfe 68, 81
Hunbaut 136

Ibn-Said 156
Iliad 18, 20, 27, 84, 104, 110, 123, 133, 134
Imbolc 74, 75

Inferno 27, 51, 116, 176
Isidore of Seville 190, 191, 193
Istorietta Trojana 20

Jerome 13, 190
John of Salisbury 193, 200, 204
Johnson, Lynn Staley 63, 64, 142, 179
Joseph of Exeter 20, 27, 132, 134, 143
Journeys of St. Brendan 156
Juno 19, 91, 96, 142

Kalilah wa Dimnah 156
Kamps, Ivo 183, 209
Kane, George 137, 176, 180
Kaske, R.E. 72, 80, 81
Kelly, Douglas 193, 209
Kelly, Henry 109, 110
Ker, W.P. 137, 180
"The King and the Physician" 145
Kittredge, George Lyman 136, 145, 176, 180
Knights of the Garter (or Order of the Garter) 6, 14, 104, 158
Krappe, A.H. 137, 145, 180

Lancelot 7, 51, 60, 62, 192, 206
Lancelot du Lac 136
Lancelot-Graal 60
Landino, Christoforo 98
Langland, William 3–6, 14, 52
Lanzelet 136
Lasater, Alice 146, 147, 148, 156, 158, 177, 178, 180
Laud Troy Book 32, 44, 48
Layaman 4
le Bon, Jean 157
Legend of Good Women 102
Lewis, C.S. 66, 67, 81
Liber Abace 160, 178, 179
El libre de Alexandre 20
Life of Apollonius of Tyana 188
Liguori, Alphonsus 174
Lindow Man 10, 71–73, 81
Le Livre de Caradoc 136
Loomis, R.S. 158, 176, 178, 180, 183, 192, 209
Lucan 69, 70, 188, 199
Luck, Georg 184, 185, 188, 189, 205, 209
Luengo, Anthony 189, 209
Lydgate, John 32, 44, 48, 106, 110, 114, 116, 117
Lynch, Kathryn L. 156, 180

Macrobius 86, 98, 108, 110
Madden, Frederic 113, 120
Magilton, J.R. 69, 73, 78, 81
Maitland, F.W. 185, 209
Malory, Sir Thomas 62, 63, 109, 114, 116, 117
Map, Walter 200, 204
Markale, Jean 76, 81

Marlowe, Christopher 189
Mary 13, 55, 74, 76, 99, 100, 118, 128, 137, 141, 159, 165, 194–96, 205
Matthews, John 183, 209
McIntosh, Angus 4, 14
Medina, Bartholomew 174
Metamorphoses 20, 27, 70, 123, 134, 135, 137, 140, 190
Moore, Dennis 183, 209
Moore, M.R. 133, 134
Moral Fables 106
Morgan, Gerald 85, 96, 110
Morgan le Fay 13, 38, 67, 68, 70, 75, 78, 79, 85, 86, 89, 96, 114, 119, 138, 142, 150, 155, 183, 191–96, 205, 209
Morse, Ruth 24
Morte Arthure 21, 28
La mule sans frein 136
Mum and the Soth-segger 5, 7

Natural History 189
Nazianzen, Gregory 175
Nennius 8, 21, 22, 24, 28, 63
Nider, Joannes 175, 178
Nitze, William A. 137, 145, 180
Norbury, W.H. 71, 80

Odysseus 9, 11–13, 19, 20, 114–19, 140–43
Odyssey 9, 11–13, 18–20, 114–19, 140–43
O'Mara, Phillip F. 100, 110
Order of the Star (or *Ordre d'Etoile*) 157, 158
Ovid 8, 12, 13, 20, 70, 102, 123, 124, 133–35, 137, 140, 142, 146, 190, 199

Pacioli, Luca 161
Pallas 68, 101–4, 176
Panchatantra 156
Pandarus 121, 122, 130, 132
The Parlement of Thre Ages 5
Parry, A. 84, 110
Partner, Nancy 24, 25
Patience 3, 5, 14, 83
Patrick, Marietta 24
Pearl 3, 5–7, 14, 44, 55, 61, 80, 109, 119, 148, 151, 152, 176, 181
Penelope 20, 115, 132, 141, 143
Pentangle 13, 76, 86, 98, 99, 104, 107, 135, 144, 155, 162, 165, 166, 177, 178, 203, 204
Perceval 55, 62, 185, 202, 205
Perceval 192, 193, 199, 202
Perlesvaus 136, 137
Perrers, Dame Alice 44
Perseus 190
Philip (Count of Flanders) 202
Philip IV 186
Philostratus 188, 205
Pierce the Plowman's Crede 5
Piers Plowman 4, 5, 14, 62, 176
The Pistel of Susan 5

Plato 29, 189
Pliny the Elder 13, 69, 72, 73, 80, 189, 190, 193, 194, 196, 205, 206, 209
Policraticus 200
Pollack, F. 185, 209
Polyxena 83, 113, 114, 123–25, 127, 131, 132
Pomponius Mela 69, 80
Practica Geometriae 160, 178, 180
Priam 19, 30, 32, 82, 91, 92, 113
Prümmer, Dominic 175, 178, 180
Putter, Ad 83, 110

Qur'an 146, 177

Rauf Coilyear 5
Recuyell of the Histories of Troy 32, 47, 143
Richard II 6, 44, 47, 72, 80
Richard the Redeless 14
Richards, Keith 73
Riddy, Felicity 54, 59, 60, 63, 64
Riegel, Alois 163, 178, 180
River Dane 6
Robert, Earl of Gloucester 20
Robert de Beaumont 20
Robertson, D.W. 138, 180, 207
Robins, Don 71, 72, 73, 78, 80, 81
Roman de Brut 21, 209
Roman de la Rose 152
Roman de Troie 20, 27, 119, 143, 195, 206
Ross, Anne 71, 72, 73, 78, 80, 81
Round Table 6, 7, 23, 52, 76, 117, 120, 131, 183, 192
Russell, Jeffrey Burton 186, 209

St. Basil 142
St. Erkenwald 5
Salter, Elizabeth 4, 15
Samhain 74, 75
Sanderlin, George 84, 110
Sash *see* Girdle
Savage, Henry 157, 180
Schliemann, Heinrich 18, 27
Scot, Michael 191, 193
Scottish Troy Fragments 113
The Seege or Batayle of Troie 143
Seneca 123, 134, 199, 205
Servius 9, 31, 84, 98, 133
Seznec, Jean 22
Shahrazad 12, 149, 151, 155, 156
Shepherd, Geoffrey 7, 15, 62, 63
Shoaf, R.A. 78, 81, 86, 110, 177, 179
Silverstein, Theodore 28, 56, 58, 63, 64, 108, 110, 142, 180
Silvestris, Bernardus 9, 31, 35, 47, 84, 86, 98
Smithers, G.V. 54, 60, 63, 64
Song of the Husbandman 14
Soucy, Arnold 23, 28
Speirs, John 66, 137, 145, 146, 180, 183, 209

Index

Spenser, Edmund 46, 98
Stafford 6, 72
Stanford, W.B. 116, 120, 143, 180
Statius 123, 134
"Statute of Treason" 185, 186, 209
Strabo 10, 69, 80

Tacitus 10, 13, 69, 80, 190
Tavenner, Eugene 187, 188, 190, 209
"Telaphus and Teucer" 126, 133
The Testament of Cresseid 106
Thiébaux, Marcelle 95, 96, 111
Thomas, Keith 187, 204, 209
Thomas Aquinas 174, 189
Thompson, Rodney 198, 210
Thorndike, Lynn 190, 193, 206, 209
Togail Troi 20, 27
Tolkien, J.R.R. 15, 108, 113, 114, 115, 136, 137, 140, 155, 167, 181
Tristan 164
Tristan 185
Tristram, Phillipa 88, 111
Troades 123, 134
Troilus 12, 46, 121, 122, 124, 125, 130–34
Troilus and Criseyde 7, 9, 11, 12, 48, 106, 109, 121, 122, 124, 125, 130–34
Trojan War 11, 18, 19, 32, 33, 48, 82, 122, 123, 126, 133
Troy 8–13, 17–28, 30, 32–36, 42, 44–48, 55–59, 62, 68, 74, 83–85, 90, 93, 97, 105, 108, 109, 112–20, 121–30, 142, 143, 164, 192, 204, 206
Troy Book 32, 44, 48, 106, 113, 119
Trújumanna Saga 20
Turner, R.C. 67, 71, 73, 81
Turnus 21, 68, 80, 84, 96, 101–7, 176

Vantuono, William 82, 86, 99, 109, 110, 114, 120
Venus 19, 35, 46, 84, 91, 95, 98, 128, 176
Vergil 9, 11, 12, 19, 20–22, 27, 30–48, 57–64, 68, 73, 79, 80, 81, 83–87, 89, 92, 94, 95, 98, 99, 102, 105, 108–11, 113, 115, 133–35, 137–40, 142, 143, 146, 195, 199
Vita Merlini 202
Vulgate 190

Wace 21, 187, 192, 194, 197, 200, 201, 202, 204, 209
Waleran, Count of Mellant 20, 27
Walsh, P.G. 27, 200, 210
Wanderer 61
Wasserman, Julian N. 47, 86, 109, 206, 208
Weiss, Victoria L. 86, 11, 197, 209
Wendell, Barrett 199, 209
Weston, Jessie 137, 145, 176, 181
Wetherbee, Winthrop 199, 210
White, Robert B., Jr. 140, 181
William of Jumieges 22, 28
William of Malmesbury 191, 198, 199, 201, 207, 209
William of Newburgh 20, 200
William of Palerne 5
Williams, Margaret 158, 181
Williams, R.D. 98, 99, 111
Wilson, Anne 183, 210
Wimberly, L.C. 138, 181
Windeatt, Barry 122
Winner and Waster 5, 7, 8, 10, 14
Wordsworth, William 60, 61, 63, 64
Wulfstan 4
Wycliffe, John 5

Zimmer, Heinrich 145, 181

www.ingramcontent.com/pod-product-compliance
Ingram Content Group UK Ltd.
Pitfield, Milton Keynes, MK11 3LW, UK
UKHW041957140426
5217IPUK00015B/844